Celebrating Poetry

East – Spring 2006

Creative Communication, Inc.

Celebrating Poetry
East – Spring 2006

An anthology compiled by Creative Communication, Inc.

Published by:
CREATIVE COMMUNICATION, INC.
1488 NORTH 200 WEST
LOGAN, UT 84341

ISBN 10: 1-60050-034-X
ISBN 13: 978-1-60050-034-3

Foreword

Welcome! Thank you for letting us share these poems with you.

This last school year we surveyed thousands of teachers asking what we could do better. We constantly strive to be the best at what we do and to listen to our teachers and poets. We strongly believe that this is your contest. Several changes were made to this anthology as we adapt to what was requested.

In this and future editions of the anthology, the Top Ten winners will be featured on their own page in the book. Each poet that is included in this book is to be congratulated, however, the Top Ten Poets should receive special recognition for having been chosen as writing one of the best poems. The Top Ten Poems were selected through an online voting system that includes thousands of teachers and students. In a day and age where television programs use viewer voting to determine which contestant is the winner, it is appropriate that our poetry winners are chosen by their peers.

Over the years we have had many parents contact us concerning the privacy of their children. The comments focus on the fact that publishing a poet's name, grade, school name, city and state with each poem is too much information. We want to address these concerns. In the Fall 2005 edition of the anthology, we made the decision to only list the poet's name and grade after each poem. Whereas we received many calls and letters concerning the issue that we were publishing too much information, we received thousands of calls and letters requesting that we again publish more information to include a student's school name and state with each poem. Therefore, for this and future editions we will publish each student's name, grade, school name and state unless specifically instructed not to include this information. Just as this information is included in a school yearbook, we provide this information in this literary yearbook of poetry. This decision hopefully makes it easier to find classmates in the book and brings appropriate recognition to the schools.

We are proud to provide this anthology. In speaking to the poets in our anthologies we have found that our anthologies are not stuffy old books that are forgotten on a shelf. The poems in our books are read, loved and cherished. We hope you enjoy reading the thoughts and feelings of our youth.

Sincerely,
Gaylen Worthen, President
Creative Communication

Enter Our Next Poetry Contest!

Why should I enter?
Win prizes and get published! Each year thousands of dollars in prizes are awarded in each region and tens of thousands of dollars in prizes are awarded throughout North America. The top writers in each division receive a monetary award and a free book that includes their published work. Poems of merit are also selected to be published in our anthology.

Who may enter?
There are five poetry contest divisions that include almost everyone. Poets in grades K-3, 4-6, 7-9, 10-12, and adults may enter the contest.

What is needed to enter the contest?
You can enter any original poem 21 lines or less. Each entry must include the poet's name, address, city, state and zip code. Student entries need to include the poet's grade, school name and school address. Students who include their teacher's name may help the teacher qualify for a free copy of the anthology.

How do I enter?

Enter online at:
www.poeticpower.com

Or, *Mail your entry to:*
Poetry Contest
1488 North 200 West
Logan, UT 84341

If you are mailing your entry, please write "Student Contest" at the top of your poem if you are in grades K-12. Please write "Adult Contest" at the top of your poem if you are entering the adult contest.

When is the deadline?
The contest deadlines are December 5th, August 15th, and April 5th. Poets may enter one poem in each contest.

Are there benefits for my school?
Yes. We award $15,000 each year in grants to help with Language Arts programs. Schools qualify to apply for a grant by having a large number of entries of which over fifty percent are accepted for publication. This typically tends to be about 15 accepted entries.

Are there benefits for my teacher?
Yes. Teachers with five or more students accepted to be published receive a free anthology that includes their students' poems.

For more information please go to our website at
www.poeticpower.com,
email us at editor@poeticpower.com or call 435-713-4411.

Table of Contents

Spring 2006 Poetic Achievement Honor Schools

* Teachers who had fifteen or more poets accepted to be published

The following schools are recognized as receiving a "Poetic Achievement Award." This award is given to schools who have a large number of entries of which over fifty percent are accepted for publication. With hundreds of schools entering our contest, only a small percent of these schools are honored with this award. The purpose of this award is to recognize schools with excellent Language Arts programs. This award qualifies these schools to receive a complimentary copy of this anthology. In addition, these schools are eligible to apply for a Creative Communication Language Arts Grant. Grants of two hundred and fifty dollars each are awarded to further develop writing in our schools.

Acushnet Elementary School
Acushnet, MA
Joan Akin*

Afton Elementary School
Afton, NY
Nicki Andrews
Amy Kehoe
Diana Torta

Al-Rahmah School
Baltimore, MD
Taihisa Abdul-Aziz*
Selena Al-Qadi
Sr. Deborah Cason*
Sr. Halimah*
Aesha Walee

Bensley Elementary School
Richmond, VA
Carolyn Booth
Maria T. MacLaughlin

Berry Elementary School
Waldorf, MD
Mrs. Darby
Judy Downing
Meg Hoffman
Robert Sondheimer

Bradford Township Elementary School
Clearfield, PA
Pamela L. Gabel
Mary Jo Seprish

Brecknock Elementary School
Denver, PA
Karen Huber
Kerry Kuipers
Beverly Libell

Bridle Path Elementary School
Lansdale, PA
Anita Walker
Ruth Anne Wells

Cabot Elementary School
Newton, MA
Gwen Day-Fuller
Marcie Mann
Mary Emma Robertson
Naomi E. Singer

Christ the King School
Yonkers, NY
Sr. Alice Alter RSHM*

Christ the Teacher Catholic School
Newark, DE
Joan Smitheman*
Ann Voloshin*

Cornerstone Academy
Northborough, MA
Catherine Janiga
Kim More

Daniel J Flood Elementary School
Wilkes Barre, PA
Marie Lishnak*
Carol McNulty
Sheryl Sealock
Kathleen Segar
Suzanne Swithers

Dr Samuel C Eveleth School
Marblehead, MA
Carol Arnould*
Sue Fligor*

Grace Miller Elementary School
Bealeton, VA
Jennifer Armstrong
Susan Aylor*
Amy Costanzo
D. Ginter

Hamilton Elementary School
Lancaster, PA
Mrs. Aulisio
Mrs. Barbusca*

Hebbville Elementary School
Baltimore, MD
Tunia Jackson
Darnell Peaker

Holy Rosary School
Staten Island, NY
Richard Kuberski*

Immaculate Conception School
Levittown, PA
Mrs. Benoit
Sr. Rita Charles*
Mary Katz

Integrated Day Charter School
Norwich, CT
Janine Guillet
Mrs. Ingle

Islamic Academy of New England
Mansfield, MA
Nur'Izzah Binte Khalil*

James M Curley Elementary
School
Jamaica Plain, MA
Quen G. Law*

Jamestown Elementary School
Arlington, VA
Holly Bass
Christine Hess
Ms. Hubusch
Mrs. Kauffunger
Darcy McDonald
Mrs. Ready
Ellen Schaab

Jenkintown Elementary School
Jenkintown, PA
Mrs. Abdollahi
Doris Heise*

John Ward Elementary School
Newton, MA
Robin Andrews
Denise Costello
Brad Hammer
Kathy Lasky
Cari MacKenzie
Hannah Ritchie
Naomi Singer
Kenneth Waldman
Monika Wellenstein

Killingly Memorial School
Danielson, CT
Gloria Morrison*

Klein Elementary School
Erie, PA
Mrs. Brown*
Mrs. Heiter

Little Flower Day Care Center
and Prep School
Brooklyn, NY
Mr. Burgher
Ms. Fenton
Ms. McCarthy
P. Mendez
Ms. Smith
Ms. Somerset

Long Meadow Elementary School
Middlebury, CT
Dawn G. Dinallo*
Noel Siebern*

Mary Matula Elementary School
La Plata, MD
Jacqueline Barrows*
Miss Datcher
Mr. Grimsley
Kathy Guntow*
Mrs. Norton
Carolyn Wentworth

Meeting House Hill School
New Fairfield, CT
Mr. Green
Pam Quist*

Memorial-Spaulding Elementary
School
Newton, MA
Ms. Bortolotti
David Cavanaugh
Cait Florshutz
Marcela Herrera
Norma Sokolowsky

Mount Jewett Elementary School
Mount Jewett, PA
Patricia Driscoll
Linda Hearst
Robynn Kowatch

New Lane Memorial Elementary
School
Selden, NY
Debra Saparito*

Newberry Elementary School
Etters, PA
Jill Boreman
Mrs. Marshall

Northeast Elementary School
Brentwood, NY
  Ms. Betzold
  Mrs. Bloom
  Ms. Chu
  Mrs. Correa
  Ms. Giancaspro
  Mrs. Igneri
  Ms. Kleinhesselink
  Susan Leonard
  Margaret Leonard
  Mrs. McEwen
  Mr. Moraitis
  Mrs. Nolan
  Mrs. Opacke
  Ms. Romano
  Ms. Smith
  Ms. Tapen

Oakdale Elementary School
Ijamsville, MD
  Mrs. Clawson
  Mrs. Codichini
  Lynne Harris
  Mr. Newhouse

Our Lady of Hope School
Middle Village, NY
  Martha Madri*
  Lauren Spiteri*

Our Lady of Lourdes School
Queens Village, NY
  Patricia Reznick*

Our Mother of Perpetual Help
School
Ephrata, PA
  Veida Wissler*

Penn-Kidder Campus
Albrightsville, PA
  Howard Gregory*
  Mrs. A. O'Rourke*
  Diane Reese

Plainview-Old Bethpage
Kindergarten Center
Plainview, NY
  Dawn Castagne*

Public School 122 Mamie Fay
Astoria, NY
  Ms. Antzoulis
  Mrs. Marketos
  Dora Politidis
  Rebecca Victoros*

Public School 131
Brooklyn, NY
  Anita Betances
  Maria Caso
  Catherine Ventiera

Public School 148 Ruby Allen
East Elmhurst, NY
  Ms. Clark
  Lois Ricupero*

Public School 152 School of
Science & Technology
Brooklyn, NY
  Johane Louissaint
  Nicole Marano
  Anna Randisi-Kilkeary

Public School 2 Alfred Zimberg
Jackson Heights, NY
  Lisa Castellano*
  Maria Pilato
  Angela Proios

Public School 23 Carter G Woodson
School
Brooklyn, NY
  Ms. Berken
  Ms. Bouchard
  Ms Estrella
  Ms. Gabriel
  Mr. Holleran
  Ms. Levin

**Public School 23 Carter G Woodson
School
Brooklyn, NY (cont.)**
Ms. Poulos
Mrs. Veney
Ms. Whichard

**Public School 5
Staten Island, NY**
Phyllis Brown
Angela Gianino

**Public School 65 Mother Hale
Academy
Bronx, NY**
Ms. Alvarez
Ms. Fairley
Ms. Hernandez
Mr. Jordan
Ms. Josephs
Mr. Lewis
Ms. Ray

**Sacred Heart School
North Quincy, MA**
Mary Bodkin*
Margaret Hanna
Fran McGillicuddy
Patricia McGowan*
Karen M. Mulvey*
Mrs. O'Connell
Patricia Peck

**Shelter Rock Elementary School
Manhasset, NY**
Mr. Collyer
Mrs. Lawrence
Mrs. Mitchell
Joyce Rappaport
Mr. Sirof
Mrs. Watts

**South Side Elementary School
Hookstown, PA**
Tracy Gessford*

**St Catherine Laboure School
Harrisburg, PA**
Mary Albers*

**St Christopher's School
Richmond, VA**
Mrs. Brown
Ms. DiLucente
Mr. Echols
Mrs. Epes
Ms. Frischkorn
Ms. Gehring
Ms. Grinnan
Ms. Halladay
Paula Jones
G. Jones
Ms. Kirk
Ms. McDonnell
Ms. Parrish
Mrs. Prince
Christie Wilson
Ann Wilson
Nancy Young

**St Clement Mary Hofbauer School
Baltimore, MD**
Christine Godlewski
Linda House
Janice McIntosh
Deborah Neidhardt
Wendy Parker*

**St Joseph School
Garden City, NY**
Barbara Vaupel*

**St Mary School
East Islip, NY**
Michele Picardi*
Maria Scotto-Lavino
Christine White*

St Mary's Elementary School
Worcester, MA
Mrs. Belanger
Mrs. McKeon
Mrs. Moseley
Debra Palumbo
Ms. Paquette
Ms. Rickard

St Rosalia Academy School
Pittsburgh, PA
Gloria Sciulli*

St Rose Elementary School
Newtown, CT
Mrs. Ferri*
Mrs. L. Spina*

St Stephen's School
Grand Island, NY
Jennifer O'Laughlin*
Lynn Ortiz*

St Teresa of Avila School
Albany, NY
Frances Miller*

Susquehanna Community
Elementary School
Susquehanna, PA
Nancee Heath
Mrs. Soden
Mrs. Steele*

The Jefferson School
Georgetown, DE
Brad Barndt
John Gause
Kristina Gundersen

Ulysses Byas Elementary School
Roosevelt, NY
Ms. El Chami
Kirsten Roberts
Shawnée Warfield

Urban League of Pittsburgh
Charter School
Pittsburgh, PA
Ella Macklin*

Wasena Elementary School
Roanoke, VA
Linda J. Bailey*

Watsontown Elementary School
Watsontown, PA
Becky Geiger
Jenn Harer
Don Hodge
Alison Newman
Dana Pick
Marcia Saam
Jan Schreck

Weston Intermediate School
Weston, CT
Mrs. Allegretti
Gregory Cannito
C. Coulter
Lisbeth Dizney
Adrienne Dunn
Ms. Farrell
Mrs. Huynh
Miss Jones
Joan Likely-Cosenza*
K. Mann
Mrs. Nardella
Mary Obermayer
Mrs. Pando
Mrs. Roszman
Shelby Schlotter
Mrs. Strang
Amanda Tiberio
Kendra Verdi

Language Arts Grant Recipients 2005-2006

After receiving a "Poetic Achievement Award" schools are encouraged to apply for a Creative Communication Language Arts Grant. The following is a list of schools who received a two hundred and fifty dollar grant for the 2005-2006 school year.

Acushnet Elementary School – Acushnet, MA
Admiral Thomas H. Moorer Middle School – Eufaula, AL
Alta High School – Sandy, UT
Alton R-IV Elementary School – Alton, MO
Archbishop McNicholas High School – Cincinnati, OH
Barbara Bush Elementary School – Mesa, AZ
Bellmar Middle School – Belle Vernon, PA
Bonham High School – Bonham, TX
Cool Spring Elementary School – Cleveland, NC
Douglas Elementary School – Liberty, KY
Dumbarton Middle School – Baltimore, MD
Edward Bleeker Jr High School – Flushing, NY
Emmanuel/St. Michael Lutheran School – Fort Wayne, IN
Floyds Knobs Elementary School – Floyds Knobs, IN
Fox Creek High School – North Augusta, SC
Friendship Jr High School – Des Plaines, IL
Gibson City-Melvin-Sibley High School – Gibson City, IL
Hamilton Jr High School – Hamilton, TX
John F. Kennedy Middle School – Cupertino, CA
John Ross Elementary School – Edmond, OK
MacLeod Public School – Sudbury, ON
McKinley Elementary School – Livonia, MI
Monte Cassino School – Tulsa, OK

Language Arts Grant Winners cont.

New Germany Elementary School – New Germany, NS
North Beach Elementary School – Miami Beach, FL
Paradise Valley High School – Phoenix, AZ
Parkview Christian School – Lincoln, NE
Picayune Jr High School – Picayune, MS
Red Bank Charter School – Red Bank, NJ
Sebastian River Middle School – Sebastian, FL
Siegrist Elementary School – Platte City, MO
Southwest Academy – Baltimore, MD
St. Anthony School – Winsted, CT
St. John Vianney Catholic School – Flint, MI
St. Paul the Apostle School – Davenport, IA
St. Rose School – Roseville, CA
St. Sebastian School – Pittsburgh, PA
Sundance Elementary School – Sundance, WY
Thorp Middle School – Thorp, WI
Townsend Harris High School – Flushing, NY
Warren Elementary School – Warren, OR
Washington High School – Washington Court House, OH
Wasilla Lake Christian School – Wasilla, AK
Woodland Elementary School – Radcliff, KY
Worthington High School – Worthington, MN

Young Poets
Grades K-3

Note: The Top Ten poems were finalized through an online voting system. Creative Communication's judges first picked out the top poems. These poems were then posted online. The final step involved thousands of students and teachers who registered as online judges and voted for the Top Ten poems. We hope you enjoy these selections.

Top Poem Grades K-3

Night of the Appaloosas

Neighing hoofbeats echo through the sky.
Spotted horses gallop by.
Black with white spots. White with brown.
Dance so freely without a gown.
It's almost dawn, they stop their dance,
And disappear into the mist.
Morning comes, all of them gone.
All that's left are hoofprints in the sand.

Meghan Dougherty, Grade 3
Booth Hill School, CT

Top Poem Grades K-3

Courage

When I have courage, I feel like a lion.
Suddenly I burst into action,
Conquering my fears.
My eyes are like red-hot coal,
Blazing in the wind.
The taste is like victory
And victory is sweet.
I love the bursts of fireworks in my stomach.
When it's over,
I'm normal.
My courage…is gone.

Lilianna Espanola, Grade 3
James M Curley Elementary School, MA

Top Poem Grades K-3

Spring

Smell the flowers,
Fresh and sweet.
Birds chirp and cheep,
Singing spring songs.
Colorful flowers,
Yellow, pink, purple and red.
Beautiful green leaves wave at me.
Warm breezes tickle my hair.
I close my eyes.
It is spring!

Hannah Jones, Kindergarten
Apple Pie Ridge Elementary School, VA

Top Poem Grades K-3

'Tis Cold

'Tis cold right now
on a winter's night.
The windows are fogging
the candles are bright.
Rain may sprinkle
snowflakes may fall
The wind might blow harder
voices may call.
But all I am sure of
because of this weather,
is that during these times
we should all be together.

Madelaine Maloney, Grade 3
Franklin Township Elementary School, PA

Top Poem Grades K-3

A Web of a Dream

In a silk castle,
A wave of silver.
Nothing can harm me,
I am safe.
Spiders spinning the satin gate.
Love whistling all around me,
Then darting off
Into the night.

Antonia Meade, Grade 1
The Spence School, NY

Top Poem Grades K-3

Gold

If gold had a sound,
It would sound like...
Splashing fish in my fish tank,
Buzzing bumblebees around some flowers.
Have you tasted the color gold?
Gold would taste like...
Soft, buttered bread for breakfast,
Breaded flounder for any meal!
The feel of gold is...
Rusty, rough metal in a welding shop,
Hot sunshine shining on me in the spring.
Gold looks like...
A Tiger Swallowtail Butterfly fluttering around,
A shining crown on a king's head.
Do you know the smell of gold?
Gold smells like...
Sticky syrup drizzled on blueberry pancakes,
Melted butter spread on corn on the cob.
If you saw a color that's very old,
Wouldn't that be the color gold?

Matthew Potts, Grade 3
Watsontown Elementary School, PA

Top Poem Grades K-3

Secret Wishes

I wish I could capture
The shine of the moon,
And hide it in my pocket,
And take it out on a dark night.
I wish I could capture
The falling of rain,
And take it out in a drought.
I wish I could capture
The sound of the ocean,
To calm me down.

Jess Reynolds, Grade 2
St Christopher's School, VA

Top Poem Grades K-3

Seashell Fan

A fan from the ocean
a seashell fan
opening and closing
in the sand
slipping and sliding
under water beneath
set down on a vanity
of a coral reef

I bet it belongs
to a mermaid down there
one that gets hot
with her very long hair.

Sarah Scherbak, Grade 2
Harry Lee Cole School, MA

Top Poem Grades K-3

The Old Oak Tree

Some say the old oak tree is a treasure
Some say it's a mystery
But I know the truth
The old oak tree is my best friend

In the summer when it's hot, it gives me shelter
And when I fly my kite and let go
It's always there to catch it

And now that I have it, I'm not letting go
And at night when it sings its gentle lullaby
And rocks its young to sleep
I know I am making no mistake

Larissa Ives Shaughnessy, Grade 2
George Washington School, NY

Top Poem Grades K-3

The Willow Bird

While walking through the willow trees
Above me I did see
A bird with a silver bodice
Staring back at me.
A silver bird, a lovely bird,
A bird beyond compare.
A bird whose every movement
Left a shimmer in the air.
And then as night settled in
The bird began to fly.
From far away I heard him coo
An echoing silver cry.

Lexi Traverse, Grade 2
Pompositticut Primary School, MA

Toys
Toys are fun and great
Toys are always fun for kids
Toys are great for me!

Matthew Rigor, Grade 2
Christ the Teacher Catholic School, DE

My Honey Bunny
I have a little bunny,
her name is Honey.
Brown, white, black and gray,
she's always there to make my day.
She is happiest in the spring,
when she can hear the birds sing.

Candace Casale, Grade 2
St Clement Mary Hofbauer School, MD

My Endless Dream
My endless dream
is sitting on the beach
and daydreaming in the sun.
I smell coconut suntan lotion.
I hear seagulls yelping for food.
I see gray dolphins splashing in the waves.
I taste salt in the water when I fall.
I feel wet sand that is squishy and cold
I hope I will go again.

Gillian Barrie, Grade 1
Skippack Elementary School, PA

Spring
I like spring because it's warm,
You might see a lot of worms!
Flowers blossom in the dawn of spring,
That is one of the very best things!

Animals come out a lot this time of year,
But they're all pretty tiny,
So there's nothing to fear!
The one who created it,
This I know,
God's the one,
He made it so!

Andrew Henry, Grade 3
Elvaton Christian Academy, MD

Springtime
Birds chirp in the spring
We plant flowers in the spring
We see butterflies
Shelbea Makela, Grade 1
St Mary's Elementary School, MA

When Cardinals Fly
When cardinals fly
They make a sound.
They hop like sparrows.
Sometimes cardinals live
in special places.
I know one place.
I saw one outside the CIRCUS!
Tommy Zervos, Grade 1
Public School 122 Mamie Fay, NY

The Big Cat
Brown with black dots,
Running fast and furious,
Scary with sharp nails and biting teeth,
Playing out in the wild,
For miles and miles,
Oh, what can it be?
A leopard is he!
Colin Huvane, Grade 3
Christ the King School, NY

Mother's Day
My mom I am grateful for,
she tucks me in bed,
and gives me a kiss.
I feel so much better,
when she hugs me at night.
I yell out mom,
I hear her sound.
She's always there,
when I need her love.
My mom is the spirit of my life.
I love my mom more than
I love myself.
God, bless my mom and keep her safe.
Pierre Mourad, Grade 2
St Mary's Elementary School, MA

Swirly Wind
Swirl me like
balloons
to go to
space

Swirl me
to the shore
and give
me a tour

swirl me
to the
sky,
and teach me how
to fly

swirl me to
the hill
so I can feel a chill

Swirl me
all around and
start all over again!
Linda Boukersi, Grade 3
Northeast Elementary School, NY

Snow
Cold as an ice age,
White as Santa's beard,
Shiny as a crystal,
Possibly fluff,
As if it were a blanket,
Over my yard.
Danny McCarthy, Grade 2
St Rose Elementary School, CT

Kaleb Deyarmin
Kaleb
Kind boy
Runs very fast
Always does his work
Deyarmin
Kourteney Chilson, Grade 1
Mount Jewett Elementary School, PA

Nature

Trees of teachings
Buds of brilliance
Leaves of lavender
Birds of beauty
Grass of green
Words of wisdom
Flowers of fortune
New cultures of curiosity
Your world is like a puzzle God and the pieces fit together

We love your world God like the way you love us too
The animals circle in form of life.

When our world is white, snowy
In silence, you spin our sun into the golden sky, autumn in the wink of an eye.
When the radiant head of the earth gets drenched in warmth our leaves turn green
Our world splotched with all the colors of the wind until finally
You turn life into a mix of browns when the leaves crunch beneath my feet
You address the world into a silent, cold lively fall.

Micah Zirn, Grade 3
Weston Intermediate School, CT

A Walk in the Wind

I went for a walk in the wind one day.
I wanted to play, but my teacher said, "No way!"
I went next to the fence and my leaf blew away.
I ran and my teacher said, "Stop, no way!"

Junius Rogers, Grade 2
Northeast Elementary School, NY

Halloween

I love Halloween
I dress up as a queen.

Kris and I get a lot of candy.
Bless dresses up as Sandy.

We say trick or treat.
We have a lot of candy to eat.

Don't be late.
We have a room to decorate.

Joy Carter, Grade 3
Little Flower Day Care Center and Prep School, NY

In My Dreams
In my dreams, I found a dino.
Then, it transformed into a rhino.

The rhino turned blue,
with big black shoes.
Next, the shoes turned into big, green, bats

The bats ate really big cats.
When I woke up, I had a fright!

It was still 12:00 a.m., at midnight!
Uzair Alam, Grade 3
Al-Rahmah School, MD

My Favorite Wishes
I wish I had a computer.
I wish I could be a Ninja.
Most of all I wish people could be kind.
Freddy Hernandez, Grade 1
Northeast Elementary School, NY

Dog Park
I took a walk through a park,
man could those dogs bark.
Some dogs were brown
some had a frown,
some were dressed as a clown.
Most were smelly,
more were clean…
this was the best dog park I've ever seen!
Brenna Kelly, Grade 3
Middle Gate Elementary School, CT

Boys
There was a boy named Sammy.
He called his mom, Mammy.
And his friends called him Hammy
He called his friends Kammy.

There was a boy named Jack
He had a sack
He went to town and then came back.
Jazmin Rodriguez, Grade 2
Cornwall Terrace Elementary School, PA

Dolphins
Gray dolphins
Swimming through the sea
They bring joy to you and me!
Hunter Platzman, Grade 1
Cornerstone Academy, MA

You're the Best
Roses are red,
violets are blue,
I think you're the best Mom
and I love you.

Violets are blue,
roses are red,
fall has passed now
we have a winter.

Roses are red,
violets are blue,
you're my mother,
I mean you're the best.
Allan Lau, Grade 2
Children's Village, PA

Sports
S weaty
P lay
O utdoors
R un
T eam
S portsmanship
Sam Anderson, Grade 2
Davis Elementary School, VA

Candy
Candy
Sweet, good
Lick, chew, suck
I like Almond Joy
Buy, get, give
Chocolatey, nutty
Scrumptious
Kimberly Neal, Grade 3
St Joseph School, NY

Winter

Winter smells like warm hot cocoa and marshmallows.
Winter is the soft sound of snow flakes falling from the sky.
Winter is making snowmen in your backyard.
I love the winter.
Winter is fun!

Kyla Helzer, Grade 1
St Teresa of Avila School, NY

The March's Wind

March winds are blowing.
Blowing wind chimes all around.
Wind chimes sing.
Spring colors kites flying high.
Now you blow winter away.
Blue jays whistling and singing around the neighborhood.
Now you spill petals everywhere.
Now in the dark you are blowing me away
Your wind is so powerful that it blows down rain.
when it's June you will be gone.
When it is September I will see your powerful wind again.

Yasin Perez, Grade 3
Northeast Elementary School, NY

Multiplying

My mom said to multiply 1 x 1
I did it, I got one, now I'm done
Now multiply the total to itself she said
I multiplied and I multiplied, this problem is a dread.

Alyssa Almeida, Grade 3
Bridle Path Elementary School, PA

TV

Every time I turn on the TV
I turn to my favorite channel and watch a movie.
When I'm really bored and have nothing to do,
I flip on the TV and watch Scooby Doo.
And on wintry cold days
I hop on the couch and get some Lays!
But when it starts to pour,
It is really a bore,
The power goes out
And I have to do without!

Jay Ullrich, Grade 3
Oakdale Elementary School, MD

Baseball

Baseball
I'm up.
I watch the pitcher wind up
and throw!
Home
      Run!
            Home
                  Run!
The crowd cheers as I jog
the bases, I shout
      we
            win!
      we
            win!
And I scream
      good
            game
                  good
                        game!
Craig Nolan, Grade 2
Dr Samuel C Eveleth School, MA

All About Dolphins

Dolphins are cool and so nice.
Dolphins are mammals too.
But most of all, dolphins are cute too.
Dolphins live in the ocean
and splash in the ocean.
Dolphins also make cute sounds.
Aasiya Tori, Grade 2
Al-Rahmah School, MD

Asparagus Never!

I'd never eat asparagus
Because I can never stand the taste,
I'd rather nibble on some bacon
That would surely not go to waste.

I'd eat chips or dip, or even a live fish,
I might even eat a ball.
But asparagus, that yucky stuff I hate.
No, no, never. Not at all!
Amanda Spitko, Grade 3
Rydal East School, PA

Paper

Paper is skinny for writing on.
Paper is for coloring.
Paper is for work.
Paper is for homework.
Paper is for poems.
Paper is for music.
Paper is really great!
Tyler Burdick, Grade 1
Glover Elementary School, MA

Spring

Budding from the trees
Raindrops make the flowers bloom
Spring makes me happy!
Joseph Santese, Grade 2
Killingly Memorial School, CT

Horses Are Amazing

H orses are wild
O thers are tame
R unning horses are lightning
S ome horses nip
E aster eggs have toy horses
S potted horses are Appaloosas
Hannah Citsay, Kindergarten
Montessori Academy of Lancaster, PA

King of Kings

The heavens shine to the glory of God.
As the King of Night comes out
In the starry light.
He is the King of Kings.
Isaac Schorr, Grade 2
Calvary Chapel Christian School, NY

Spring

Spring is the time
when bears, deer and birds
come out to play.
Flowers bloom
and butterflies
flutter in the air.
Sabrina Phillips, Grade 2
Grace Miller Elementary School, VA

Basketball

Basketball is cool
Fun and teamwork with my friends
It's fun win or lose!

Thomas Oliveros, Grade 3
Christ the Teacher Catholic School, DE

What Is Silver?

A diamond is silver
on a nice spring day.
It makes rainbows appear
in the month of May.

Silver tastes like
water and snow.
Put in a little white
tied with a bow.

Silver is a very beautiful thing!

Matthew Wall, Grade 2
A.G. Richardson Elementary School, VA

Good Friends

A good friend is a treat.
That treat is very neat!

If you ask him or her to play,
I bet he or she would say, "Yes, you may."

I hope your friends are nice,
I bet you they like ice!

I wonder when they do like to play,
I hope they do it in the day.

Lots of my friends like to lend.
They like to lend their friends!

Oh yeah, my good friend Patricie
She is a peachie!

What is my friend Taylor?
She is a mailer!

Angeline Mays, Grade 3
St Catherine Laboure School, PA

Leaves
Leaves sound like
rattlesnakes' tails
shaking in the tree branches.

Leaves move like
an eagle's feather
falling from the sky.
Tyler Grimsley, Grade 3
Mary Matula Elementary School, MD

Fairy Foods
Apples munchy
Cake soft

Juice squizzing out

Crumbs on the floor
Sweet taste of juice

Superb savoring rich taste
It's like munchy Cinderella Applella

And soft Thumbelina Cakealina

Crumbly pillow
Bumpy hill

Spongy like

The munchy apple and the soft cake
So enchanting
Jordan Cohen, Grade 3
Fulton Avenue School #8, NY

Planets
P ouring through space
L ooping rings
A steroids all around them
N ever go too close to Venus
E very day the earth spins around.
T erribly cold Pluto
S cience detects them.
Kyle Alexander Brenn, Grade 2
Marvin Elementary School, CT

Winter
Snowflakes all around.
Snowflakes falling to the ground.
Nothing makes a sound.
Tilon Dixon, Grade 2
Parkside Christian Academy, MA

Snowflakes
Snowflakes are everywhere.
Falling down in the air.
They are so cold and white.
When they fall down
They're so clear and bright!
Claudia Irizarry, Grade 3
Sunquam Elementary School, NY

I Wish I Could
I wish I could
ride a dolphin over the waves
I wish I could
fly like a bird
I wish I could
Cole Shevory, Grade 2
Dr Samuel C Eveleth School, MA

Voices
There are two voices
Inside of you.
That want to tell you
What to do.
One is bad.
One is good.
Which one will you listen to?
I hope you listen to the good.
And never to the bad.
Celine Halt, Grade 2
Elizabeth Elementary School, PA

Snow
Snowflakes are so white.
Snowflakes are so light.
Snowmen left and right.
Snowmen play all night.
Lauren VanEssendelft, Grade 3
Penn-Kidder Campus, PA

Spring

Spring is cool
Spring is great
I go outside and celebrate
I ride my bike,
So can you come along and ride with me.

Juliana Chiodi, Grade 3
Our Lady of Hope School, NY

Bugs!!

Bugs are fun to watch
    A praying mantis looks like he is praying

Bugs are fun to touch
    A worm slithers in your hand

Bugs eat yucky food
    A fly eats dead animals

Bugs move in different ways
    An inchworm moves an inch at a time

Bugs live in strange places
    A bee lives in a hive

BUGS!!

Kyle Elliott, Grade 2
Mount Jewett Elementary School, PA

Jennifer's Mom

M om
O thers come first
T he best
H amburgers are great
E at all your dinner,
R ainbows and rain forests are beautiful.

Jennifer W., Grade 2
Kanner Learning Center, PA

Sun and Rain

The sun is shining.
It is a hot summer day.
I wish for some rain.

Simon Will, Grade 2
Fonda-Fultonville Elementary School, NY

A Hole
I have a hole in me
I have a pain
I have a headache
That hurts my brain
I have a story
I have a soul
I have God's heart
And a big hole

HURTING

Feyisola Soetan, Grade 3
Public School 152 School of Science & Technology, NY

Mall
The mall is so dull.
I hate it all.
I go there all the time.
I come home and whine,
"Mom, please take me to Chuck E. Cheese next time."

Jesse Johnson, Grade 3
Klein Elementary School, PA

The Circle of Friendship
Friendship is lots of fun.
There are good times and bad times.
But in the end, you should make up and be friends again.
Friendship goes around and around.
There might be places that it can't be found.
But around and around, it goes again.
No one in the world knows where the circle of friendship will end.
When we get into fights we should say.
"I forgive you, can you forgive me too?"
The circle of friendship goes around and around.
Who knows where it will be found?

Emma Lammon, Grade 3
Sacred Heart School, NY

Spring
Violets are purple and jelly beans are too
Chocolate bunnies are new
Daisies are yellow and starting to grow
Turtles are slow

Nyjah Cephas, Grade 2
Urban League of Pittsburgh Charter School, PA

All About God

God I love you in every way.
I always think of you when I pray.
I read a scripture about Mary today.
And Jesus her son who is perfect in every way.
He's everywhere I go.
But when I'm asleep he's everywhere I know.
So think of all the things you do
Around the world when God's with you!

Shalese Briana Pasley Royal, Grade 3
Parkside Christian Academy, MA

Fishy

I had a BIG FAT goldfish
As gold as the sun
His name was Bob
He wasn't very much fun.
I actually didn't like him at all
Because he was boring
So when he died I didn't care
I was asleep and snoring.
When I woke up and found him gone
I was thrilled you bet
To find out what my mom had done
She flushed him down the toilet!

His gravestone says R.I.P.
Here lays the dead soul of Bob the dead fish.
Bob HATES toilets!

Natalie Bondra, Grade 3
Ridge Park Elementary School, PA

I Love Softball

Spring is here, it's time for softball,
So grab your hat, glove, and ball.
There are twelve players on the team,
We each have our own hopes and dreams.

Softball is a lot of fun
It gets you out in the sun
It also gives you a chance to play,
And leave our studying for another day.
I love softball!

Alexandra Schlapp, Grade 3
Our Lady of Hope School, NY

Cars

Cars
Fast, red
Driving, stopping, racing
Taking me home from school
Cool
Brandon Mosley, Grade 1
Daniel J Flood Elementary School, PA

My Koala

My koala
Cute, big
Climbing, eating, sleeping
Play, tight
My koala
Olivia Rose Coffman, Grade 1
Seneca Academy, MD

Snow

Snowstorms are noisy
There are gray clouds in winter
You build an igloo.
Jennifer Mazeika, Grade 2
Long Meadow Elementary School, CT

Snow

Snow is as white as a pillow
It is also as fluffy as my blanket.
Snow, snow oh how you blow
By my window
As I make a snowman.
Jennifer Greiner, Grade 1
John F Kennedy School, MA

Bananas

Bananas are yummy.
They are yummy for your tummy.
I will feed a fig to a pig,
The pig is big.
The toys can fit in the box.
I saw a fox.
I am in the house.
I saw a mouse.
Kaylyn Cai, Grade 1
Children's Village, PA

The Sailboat in the Rain

I have a sailboat
And when I was in the rain
I went down by the pond
I sailed my sailboat
And it went away
I did not know where it went
Emily Golway, Grade 2
Shelter Rock Elementary School, NY

Snow

S now every day
N ight and day there is snow
O ver our houses more snow is falling.
W inter is the best time for snow!
Tressa Soucie, Grade 3
Central Avenue School, CT

Do Butterflies Fly?

Yes!
Yes!
A butterfly flies —
You see them at ponds;
They follow you wherever you go!
And they whisper in your ear...
How —
Do —
You —
Do?
Emerson Litvak, Grade 2
Hurlbutt Elementary School, CT

Colors

The color red,
Makes me think of bed.
The color blue,
Makes me think of YOU!
The color green,
Makes me think of someone mean.
The color yellow,
Makes me think of a young fellow.
Red, blue, green, yellow
These are some of my favorite colors.
Sarah LaVelle, Grade 3
Mount Vernon Elementary School, PA

Red

Red is a strawberry ripe and red,
Red is the sunset when I'm going to bed,
Red is the fire that is bright and strong,
Red is a cardinal ripe in song,
Red is the shyness of the neighbor next door,
Red is the valentine I see in the store,
Red is the blood of the knee I hurt,
Red is the clay hidden down in the dirt,
Red is the poppies in the garden down the street,
Red is my blushing with new people I meet,
Red is my nose on a winter white day,
Red is the sun at noon today,
Red is the three pepperonis I ate,
Red is the red paint on the garden gate,
Red is a phoenix making a beautiful sound,
Red is most everything all around,
Red.

Amanda Hayes, Grade 3
Jamestown Elementary School, VA

The Unicorn with That Strange-Looking Horn

Once, there was a unicorn
who possessed a very, very strange horn;
bumpy, dirty, feathery, curvy, glittery,
striped, polka-dotted, squared, glimmery and shimmery.
The unicorn with that strange-looking horn
was laughed at evening and morn.
She despaired of ever being the norm and asked a lizard,
who knew everything, for help, in a storm.
The lizard sang the solution to her;
which brought tears to her eyes and made them blur.
The way to straighten out your horn is to drink upon a magic lake,
in a magic forest, which can't be fake.
Thereupon, the unicorn, guided by the lizard,
searched the known world for this unique lake, sometimes in a blizzard,
snagging her horn on unmagic trees, wallowing in self-pity lakes until finally,
after much time, she waded into a lustrous, cool pool guarded by a wizard.
Splashing and tossing her horn, her bumpy, dirty, feathery, curvy, striped,
glittery, polka-dotted, squared, glimmery, shimmery horn with glistening water drops
began to writh, straighten, shine, untwist, defeather, uncurve,
unpolka-dot and round-out with a glittery, glimmery, shimmery swerve.
The reflection that smiled out of the water at the world was beautiful!

Rachel Chambers, Grade 2
Mary Matula Elementary School, MD

Guinea Pig
Furry, fluffy
Squeak, peep
Cute, hungry
Fluffy friend
Alexa Robinson, Grade 3
Christ the Teacher Catholic School, DE

Spring
Spring is great, spring is fun,
It's good to feel the warm sun.

In springtime you can watch flowers grow.
If you try to smell one it might tickle your nose.

In spring you can go out and play,
If it's not a rainy day!
Mikayla Hebert, Grade 2
St Mary's Elementary School, MA

Flowers
Flowers
Growing, strong
Beautiful, colorful, soft
My favorite is the rose
Flowers
Christina Polsinelli, Grade 2
St Clement Mary Hofbauer School, MD

Books
Books can take you anywhere,
places here or places there.

They can take you up in the sky,
and make you feel like you can fly.

Books can tickle your stomach and your nose,
books can make you numb down to your toes.

Books can make you scared, sad, or worried,
books can make you hip hop and flurried.

Books can do anything!
Sarah Hazel, Grade 3
Bradford Township Elementary School, PA

B-ball
Basketball
Hard, exciting
Dunk, run, catch
What a great shot
Pass, dribble, shoot
Tiring, intense
B-ball
Tommy Harte, Grade 3
St Joseph School, NY

Flowers
Flowers
Red, pink
Blooming, shining, growing
Whispering to other flowers
Roses
Taryn McDonough, Grade 2
St Rosalia Academy, PA

Frog and Dog
I once found a dog
Who was chasing a frog
The frog was so smug
He just ate a bug
Now he is hiding in a log!
Hannah Lamarco, Grade 2
Home School, NY

Alexandra
Alexandra, kid
Active, friendly, gymnastics
Cool, smart, fun, kind, nice
Alexandra Krohn, Grade 3
St Mary's Institute, NY

Summer
S ummer
U mmer
M mer
M er
E r
R
Lucas Golbourne, Grade 3
Public School 164, NY

The Dangerous Snake
The snake is ready to eat rats and worms.
It is going to hiss like this: Sss Sss
Everybody hide from the big snake!
It is going to eat you!
Everybody, the snake is gone!

Keiner Urdaneta, Grade 1
Northeast Elementary School, NY

Spring
Summer will soon be here
Playing outdoors is better than playing indoors.
Riding horses in Long Island.
Nothing is better than going
To my godmother's cousins Gina's house
To see my friends.

Victoria Adams, Grade 3
Our Lady of Hope School, NY

Bumblebees
Bumblebees
Zooming, spinning
Noisy, scary, fast
Chasing me around the yard
Bumblebees

Nicholas Sommella, Grade 2
St Clement Mary Hofbauer School, MD

Titanic
It hit an iceberg and sunk.
It split in half and rose up in the water.
The smokestacks came off.
There are three people alive right now.
They found the sister ship near the stern.
The people got on the Carpathia
From the lifeboats.

Chase Fortunato, Kindergarten
South Side Elementary School, PA

Hats
Hats and hats are everywhere.
You and you are wearing hats.
Hats and hats are all around the planet.

Sam David, Grade 2
Bucks County Country Day School, PA

Grasshoppers
In tall green grass
looking for food to eat
one hot summer day.
Roman Arrieta, Grade 1
Public School 122 Mamie Fay, NY

On the Moon
Moon, moon
I see you in my room.
Boom, boom
I can clean you up with my broom!

Groom, groom
You just like to loom
Zoom, zoom
You're making me bloom!
Hayel Abdulghani, Grade 3
Islamic Academy of New England, MA

I Remember…
I remember when I saw a snake.
I remember when I started to bake.
I remember when I fell.
I remember when I rang the bell.
I remember when I was small.
I remember my dad big and tall.
I remember an ape big and hairy.
I remember his face big and scary.
Omar Shalabi, Grade 3
Al-Rahmah School, MD

Who Am I?
I lay in the sky
There's thousands of me.
I sparkle with joy
You always see me!
I hold all your wishes
They're deep inside me.

I lay in the sky
There's thousands of me!
I am a star.
Sara Prchlik, Grade 3
Meeting House Hill School, CT

Dimitri
Dimitri
Play video games watches TV
Caring special kind
Interesting trustworthy
Dimitri
Nicholas Mennis, Grade 3
William Spyropoulos School, NY

Spring
Spring is here at long last!
Boys and girls are playing…
grass and flowers swaying
The rain leads to rainbows
I just saw the first rose!
It's not too hot it's not too cold
Spring means to me as much as gold!
Regan C. Harvey, Grade 3
Integrated Day Charter School, CT

Spring
S pring flowers growing,
P lants are growing and growing.
R oots growing from flowers.
I nsects sucking nectar from flowers.
N ests getting built by birds.
G rass is getting greener.
Brea Sasser, Grade 2
Hebbville Elementary School, MD

A Truck
A truck has shiny paint,
As shiny as glass,
As heavy as an elephant,
With a torque as strong
As a class.
Jesse Cabral, Grade 2
St Rose Elementary School, CT

Frolicking Horses
Frolicking horses
Dance in the new green meadows
They look beautiful
Taylor Berthelson, Grade 2
Long Meadow Elementary School, CT

Springtime Is

Springtime is playing outside with my family.
Springtime is going to the park for a family picnic.
Springtime is flying kites with my family.
Springtime is family time.

Kevin Velez, Grade 2
Northeast Elementary School, NY

Valentine's Day

chocolate
candy
pink and red
cards
white
circles
and
friends around
you

Valentine's Day

Samantha Hilber, Kindergarten
Plainview-Old Bethpage Kindergarten Center, NY

Autumn

Autumn tastes like sweet pumpkins
Autumn smells like hot apple cider
Autumn looks like leaves changing colors
Autumn feels like family coming together at harvest
Autumn sounds like leaves shaking

John Henry, Grade 2
Ulysses Byas Elementary School, NY

Bacon

Bacon, oh bacon, I love you so much.
You're munchy, you're crunchy, I can't stop to touch.
I'd rather nibble on bacon than a Juicy Couture clutch.
Bacon, oh bacon, I love you so much.
You're gooey, you are greasy.
Sometimes you get piecey.
Bacon, oh bacon, I love you so much.
You're bubbly, and hot.
You leave a big grease spot.
Bacon, oh bacon, I love you so much.

Hannah Abel, Grade 3
Rydal East School, PA

In My Dreams
In my dreams, I walk downhill.
In my dreams, I fall as well!
In my dreams I yell help, help!
In my dreams, it sounds like a yelp!
In my dreams, I see a cloud.
In my dreams, there is a thundercloud.
In my dreams, I fall asleep.
In my dreams, I must seek.
The pleasure of Allah.
The mercy of Allah.
The refuge of Allah.
My parents on my side so:

In my dreams, they love me.
Raadia Khan, Grade 3
Al-Rahmah School, MD

Mrs. Beauregard
Smart and funny
Teaching, laughing
Scaring
Sweet and kind
My teacher
Katelyn Gilroy, Grade 3
Mary Matula Elementary School, MD

The Construction Workers
They build a hole.
The back hoe came.
They all start up their machines.
It sounds like a big rumble.
Then the crane came
With this big driller.
It drilled and drilled and drilled
Until it hit something.
Jared Tellish, Kindergarten
South Side Elementary School, PA

Tiger
Big, sharp, pointy teeth
The tiger has big black paws.
Tigers are not mean.
Isabella Anglero, Grade 2
Public School 148 Ruby Allen, NY

What I Like in the Summer
My favorite season is the summer
Because my birthday is in July.
There are many things to do
Like watching fireworks in the sky.
Hannah Kleimenhagen, Grade 1
St Joan of Arc Elementary School, PA

Lexi Walton
Lexi
Good, cool
Happy smart girl
Helps, colors, runs, walks.
Walton
Kaleb Deyarmin, Grade 1
Mount Jewett Elementary School, PA

Life
So much depends upon,
The legendary miracle of life,
Crafted by Darwinism,
Beside every element.
Henry Tracey, Grade 3
Weston Intermediate School, CT

Puppy
Cute little and nice
She likes to run around me
She licks my face too!
Samantha Vanegas, Grade 2
Public School 148 Ruby Allen, NY

Spring
The flowers will bloom,
In the spring so soon.
The pool won't be sealed,
And colds will be healed.
I will see butterflies in the sky.
They will be flying very high.
We will have barbecues all day long.
And we will song a merry song.
The sun will shine in the sky.
It might only last 'till the Fourth of July.
Nicholas Spiel, Grade 3
Immaculate Conception School, PA

What Is Blue?

The sky is blue
The sun shines all day
In the morning
I could fly away.

Blue smells like
A hot blue blueberry pie
Blue acts like wild waves
Blue sounds like it cries
Blue is a beautiful thing.

Megan Clubb, Grade 2
A.G. Richardson Elementary School, VA

My Cat

I have a cat at home
I let my cats play and I like my cats
I give my cats food and I play with my cats too
And I have 2 cats
1 cat named Angela
And the second cat is named Angel.

Bonnie Zheng, Grade 2
Children's Village, PA

What Is a Bully?

A bully is someone who is very mean.
Who is the meanest person I've ever seen.
He also takes people's lunch money.
This is not a joke and it's never funny.
I would stand up and say,
"Stop bullying or go away!"

Jhanai Lee, Grade 3
James M Curley Elementary School, MA

NASCAR

NASCAR is racing,
to see who comes in first.
Whenever there is the green flag,
they come out with a burst.
NASCAR is on TV
Jeff Gordon is my favorite.
Who is your favorite driver?
You're the one who chooses it.

Anthony Grenus, Grade 3
Bradford Township Elementary School, PA

The Secrets of Black
Black is regret and despair,
And the feeling of the night,
Black is the taste of an espresso.
Burnt wood and fudge smell black.
Loneliness feels black.
Black is the sound of a crack and a train stopping,
Ink and shadows and licorice are black.
Black is a mystery.

Leila Khalil, Grade 3
Lycée Rochambeau (French International School), MD

Spring
Flowers bloom
So birds can fly
So people can be happy.

Kyle Lawrence, Grade 3
Public School 23 Carter G Woodson School, NY

No One Knows
Some day life will stop.
And at the end of life we will all drop.
It is a short time that stays on my mind.
I wonder if it will still go
but I don't think that no one knows.
I wonder if I can go,
go somewhere else and go somewhere far
all by myself.

Tahrel Thompson, Grade 3
Public School 23 Carter G Woodson School, NY

My Orange World
Orange is the color of a tiger and the dust of the desert,
It is the smell of tulips and an autumn fire,
It is the feather of a parrot and the taste of a carrot.

Orange is a mango and the music of the tango,
It is the taste of oranges and apricots,
It is the brightest color of many, including Fantastic Mr. Fox.

Orange is a happy day, but also sad leaves in the fall.
It is a brave color and also the sound of the oriole's song.
It is so great that there is the color orange!

Deniz Dutz, Grade 3
Lycée Rochambeau (French International School), MD

Ice Cream

Ice cream, ice cream,
If I don't get some ice cream
I think I'm gonna die.
Give away my car, give away my house
But don't give away my ice cream.

Chocolate ice cream, chocolate ice cream,
If I don't get chocolate ice cream
I think I'm going to move.
Give away my books, give away my computer.
But don't give away my chocolate ice cream.

Banana split, banana split,
If I don't get a banana split
I think I'm going to run away.
Give away my fish, give away my cat.
But don't give away my banana split.

Carl Burke, Grade 3
Bradford Township Elementary School, PA

The Cat and the Dog and a Frog

A frog chased after a cat, Meow!
And a cat chased after a dog. Wooof!
The cat sat on the dog. Ooof!

ZZZZZZ,
Then the dog awoke.
Wroof! Howl! Screech! Meow!
The cat ran after the frog.
Crash! Bam! Ting, tong! Ribbet!
The dog found the cat.
There was a big spat!
Crash! Bang! Ribbet! Splat!
The dog came out on top.
He could not be stopped.
Their owner came back. Crack!
She was furious, but they didn't even notice.
Slap! Crack! And a creak!
The frog and the cat are still in a spat.
Stop that spat! Just like that!
Pat, pat, pat
Scratch on the back

Vanessa Richardson, Grade 1
The Jefferson School, DE

Summer

Summer
Running outside
Playing with friends
Swimming in my pool
Warm

Maria Schnettler, Kindergarten
St Stephen's School, NY

Robins

Robins
Sing
To
Us
Very
Well

Owen Jimenez, Grade 1
Calvary Chapel Christian School, NY

Winter

Winter is the best time of the year.
Slide on your sled,
Full speed ahead!

It is also fun after you
Warm up with hot cocoa,
And when you are done,
Go outside to make ice cream cones.

It is cold in winter,
But not for the penguins.

James Barry, Grade 2
St Rose Elementary School, CT

Summer Fun

In the summer
I go to the beach,
and then I sit in my seat.
Sometimes I go in the ocean,
then after, I put on suntan lotion.
Then I go home,
and then, I take a seat,
to eat.

Damian Caggiano, Grade 3
Holy Rosary School, NY

Danelle

D irector when we play my little ponies
A lways caring
N ot mean
E ats lots of stuff
L ots of animals
L oves her baby brother
E veryone likes her

Olivia Kumher, Grade 3
Mount Jewett Elementary School, PA

A Beautiful World

The grass is warm
The sun is hot
I am playing outside
With my dad
And we are having
So much fun
We'll rise again
And we'll have another
Beautiful day.

Tyler Perry, Grade 3
Acushnet Elementary School, MA

Volcanoes

Volcanoes are big
Volcanoes aren't small
They can be more than 300 feet tall!
When they erupt
Lava pours out
There's a hole at the top
Like a big, big, spout

Ana Flooks, Grade 3
Weston Intermediate School, CT

Anger

Anger is green.
It sounds like rustling leaves.
It smells like vegetables.
It tastes like broccoli.
It looks like grass.
Anger feels like a sharp point.

Thomas Koo, Grade 3
Christ the King Elementary School, NY

It's Raining

Rain falls down!
Splish splash
On my head.
With a dash,
Down it flows.
Right on me
It tumbles down,
On my knee.
I look up
At the sky,
And ask the question
Why God Why?
And he whispers to me
I'm going to faint.
I can't believe
Just what's happening to me.

Samantha Lewis, Grade 2
Public School 397 Foster Laurie Elementary School, NY

Springtime

In springtime it rains a lot.
And in springtime
new leaves grow on trees.

Jordan Achampong, Kindergarten
Little Flower Day Care Center and Prep School, NY

Green

Green reminds me of the taste of a sour lime floating in a cool glass of ice tea
Green looks like a frog by a pond on a summer day
Green is the sound of fresh cold wind blowing on a fall day
Green feels like moss underneath my bare feet when I walk in the woods
Green smells like a nice mint dissolving in your mouth

Chelsea Miller, Grade 3
Watsontown Elementary School, PA

Spring

S is for the singing birds
P is for the pink lilies in the garden
R is for the red roses that are so beautiful
I is for ice cream that melts away in our mouths
N is for the nice weather it brings
G is for its glorious green grass and weather conditions

Dequan Tuesday, Grade 1
Little Flower Day Care Center and Prep School, NY

My Dad

My dad is funny and I am too
I love my dad and he loves me too.
He drives me to school and goes to work.
He drives me to school in his big blue truck.
He drives me every day and works every day.
My dad is really cool.
He swims in our pool.

Jordan Marino, Grade 3
Holy Rosary School, NY

Blizzard

B rrr it's cold outside
L ots of fun
I n the snow
Z ippers up
Z oom down the hills
A s cold as ever
R ead a good book
D raw a winter picture

Sarah Heagy, Grade 2
St Clement Mary Hofbauer School, MD

Happiness

Happiness is part of life in the world.
Happiness is a great way to feel.
If someone does not care about me
deep inside I feel my mother is counting on me
to feel happy and free.

Amber Delph, Grade 2
Grace Miller Elementary School, VA

Love

Hugs and kisses from my family.
Good and wonderful,
Warm and soft,
Bright and shiny,
Like the star of David glowing.
True and whole,
Peace of God.
Everything is quiet,
Lovely and pure.
Continuing love.

Zach Jones, Grade 2
Apple Pie Ridge Elementary School, VA

Rainy Afternoon

Rainy afternoon,
Everybody is gloomy.
Drip drop drip drop.
Gaze at the sky.
Feels like I can fly.
I fall asleep.
I have a dream.
I wake up.
Oh, what luck,
It stopped raining.
No more saying,
Drip drop drip drop.

Reanna Sherman, Grade 3
The Jefferson School, DE

Leaving Friends

Leaving friends is no fun.
Soon I cry.
Happy thoughts do no good.
No one can see me
behind a dark shadow.
We laughed, we cried,
we played together
like no other person.
But the good is
you always make new friends.

Caroline Sanicola, Grade 2
Pomperaug School, CT

Beach

Beach
Sunny, sandy
Playing, swimming, having fun
Building sand castles
Vacation

Gwyneth Loughran, Grade 2
St Rosalia Academy, PA

Pineapples

Pineapples are good
Pineapples can sting a lot
They are healthy fruits

Tyler Powers, Grade 3
Enfield Station School, ME

My Fish

My fish's name is Hank
My fish, Hank, jumps out of the fish tank!
He's a boy.
He likes fish food.

Shane Robbins, Grade 1
Daniel J Flood Elementary School, PA

My ABC's

A is for ant
B is for band
C is for candy
These are the basic ABC's
Now do you know the 123's?
There is 1 little doggy
2 little cats
And 3 little baseball bats!

Renee King, Grade 2
Media Childrens House Montessori, PA

Sun

The sun is bright.
It gives us light.
Without the light.
It would look like night.

Eric Tarentino, Grade 2
Washington Park Elementary School, PA

Fairies

Fairies, fairies, making wishes...
Fairies, fairies, turning into fishes...
Fairies, fairies, flying high...
Fairies, fairies, in the sky...

Daniel P. Carr, Grade 2
Our Mother of Perpetual Help School, PA

Winter

F rost bite
R iver is ice-covered
O h no! my face is cold
Z ero degree ice temperature
E xtreme snowball making
N ice warm hot chocolate

Brogan Peters, Grade 3
Bradford Township Elementary School, PA

Mr. Paccione
He is our pal
He is a great man and nice
He's the school king
Gina Leon, Grade 3
Public School 148 Ruby Allen, NY

Pig
fat curly tail ears
fat pink very big body
The pig rolls in mud
Danny Herrera, Grade 2
Public School 148 Ruby Allen, NY

Spring
Beautiful sweet smelling flowers,
rain showers rainbows.
Wind whistling by your ears.
Sun shining
it makes
your
heart
fill
with joy.
Birds
making nests.
Apple trees
start
to bloom
peppermint
smelling
green grass
magnificent
beautiful.

Spring.
Julie Rosenthal, Grade 2
Dr Samuel C Eveleth School, MA

Trains Can Take You Very Far
Trains all the way to Maine
Trains in the rain
Trains all the way to fame
Ryan Stewart, Kindergarten
Bowers School, CT

Secret Wishes
I wish I could capture
A snowflake flying through the air,
And put it under my pillow.
I wish I could capture evilness,
And throw it away.
I wish I could capture the sun,
And put it in the sky
On a rainy day.
Coleman Andrews, Grade 2
St Christopher's School, VA

Red
Red is fire blazing at night
Red is an apple, nice an juicy
Red is chili, hot and spicy
Red is the stripes on our flag.
Sudarshan Thirumalai, Grade 2
Cornerstone Academy, MA

paint me a poem
paint me a poem of splashes
    of red

paint me a poem of zashis
    of green

paint me a poem of zigzags
    of yellow and blue

paint me a poem of winter day
paint me a poem of lovely spring day

paint me a poem
please paint me a poem
Jenna Carlton, Grade 3
Thoreau Elementary School, MA

Will the Rain Ever Go?
Rain, Rain, Rain. All I see is rain.
    It bubbles. It struggles. It puddles.
It is spring I know,
    But will the rain ever go?
Christiana Raymond, Grade 3
Afton Elementary School, NY

The Cuisenaires

I can make a
house

I can make a
gate

I can make a
staircase

I can make
rain

Cuisenaires

Thanos Boulukos, Kindergarten
Plainview-Old Bethpage Kindergarten Center, NY

Nice

Nice's face is as pretty as a princess.
Nice's hobby is karate and to keep her safe.
Nice has hearts all over her room.
Nice is very, very, very nice.
Before nice leaves her home, she makes sure everything is very clean.
Nice is nice to everyone!

Saundrea Fenasci, Grade 2
Maryvale Elementary School, MD

Spring

S un shining all around
P laying in its warm rays.
R ainbows forming,
I ce-cream melting,
N ature blooming,
G reen, green, green

Samaha Hossain, Grade 2
Public School 152 School of Science & Technology, NY

White

White tastes like yummy, vanilla ice cream in a dish.
White looks like Yankee fans cheering their team on.
White sounds like a dove chirping on a branch.
White feels like cold ice in your drink on a hot, summer day.
White smells like crispy marshmallows over a bonfire.

Dylan Buck, Grade 3
Watsontown Elementary School, PA

Summer
Summer breeze is hot
Sways gently through tall grasses
Winds shade the field mouse
Cody Wallace, Grade 2
Killingly Memorial School, CT

Pool
Pool is fun.
You can play.
Learn how to swim.
Learn how to listen to the coach.
Anthony Campos, Grade 2
Ulysses Byas Elementary School, NY

Puppy
A puppy is cute.
A puppy is so playful.
A puppy is born.
Karina Galabay, Grade 2
Public School 148 Ruby Allen, NY

Spring
Spring is fun.
Spring is nice.
Spring will give you a geyser splash.
Spring can be a blast.
Christian Steckiewicz, Grade 3
Our Lady of Hope School, NY

Flowers
Petals stand around
Orange flowers look like fire
Flowers smell good, too!
Michael Lloyd, Grade 2
Long Meadow Elementary School, CT

Chocolate
Chocolate
Brown, hard
Melting, chewing, eating
Good to eat at Easter
Cold
Nyeheem Kenzakoski, Grade 1
Daniel J Flood Elementary School, PA

Spring
S unflowers
P inecones growing,
R oses growing,
I nsects flying,
N est for birds,
G rowing plants.
Jewels Keyser, Grade 2
Hebbville Elementary School, MD

Disobedient Icarus!
Icarus was a 14 year old boy,
Who did not listen to Dad,
He fell to a horrible death,
All because he was bad!

His father said, "Oh, dear!
I am awfully sad."
But down deep inside,
He was pretty mad!
Emma Grosskopf, Grade 3
Spotswood Elementary School, VA

Stormy Day
Splash! Splash! Splash!
Darkened raindrops
falling
from the sky.
They are splashing
with the feel of sadness.
Raindrops
black and icky
coming
from the sky.
Moving toward us
is a shower
dark and sad.
Darker darker darker
gets the sky.
The rain and the darkness
are forming another night.
Today is not a happy day.
Today is sad.
Evan Klos, Grade 3
Blue Bell Elementary School, PA

Ice Cream
Sweet, creamy
Melty, dreamy
Cold, sticky
Frozen treat

Katya Monarski, Grade 2
Christ the Teacher Catholic School, DE

My Walk
I walked in the wind one day,
I felt wind going through my sleeve.
I looked and saw a bird.
Then I felt warm.
I just saw a butterfly!
And I walked back in. I felt warm again.

Ryan Calderon, Grade 2
Northeast Elementary School, NY

Pink
Pink is a pig, rolling in the mud.
Pink is a lemonade, which is very sweet.
Pink is an eraser, erasing on paper.
Pink is lips that are kissing

Isabella Houley and Apoorva Rege, Grade 1
Cornerstone Academy, MA

Fall Colors*
I see orange I see red.
I see leaves upon my head.
I see yellow I see green.
I see fall colors I lighted up with beam.

Kaitlyn Matthews, Grade 3
Milford Elementary School - Heron Pond, NH
*Dedicated to Dad.

The Holiday Spirit
I see the snow so white and cold.
I smell the cookies,
Warm and crunchy.
I feel the warmth of the fire,
And taste the yummy hot cocoa.
I hear the Christmas bells ringing,
And I feel the Christmas spirit.

Kaya Bos, Grade 2
James M Curley Elementary School, MA

The Spring
The spring
Is fun
'Cause the sun
Is shining!
Ryan McLaughlin, Kindergarten
John Ward Elementary School, MA

My New Bear
I went to the store to get a new bear.
My bear had a lot of furry hair.
I called him Mr. Furry Blair.
He wanted to go to the city fair
He sure did have a blast there!
Soon he became city mayor.
So then his name became Mr. Blair Mayor.
Aliyah Sharif, Grade 3
Al-Rahmah School, MD

Football
Football can be fun
If your favorite team has won
In the Super Bowl!
Cullen Robinson, Grade 2
Christ the Teacher Catholic School, DE

Kites
Kites, kites, kites,
I try with all my might.
It is hard to make,
I think I'll eat a snake.
It's too hard to make a kite,
I just don't think it's right.
Nina Tang, Grade 2
Thomas Fitzwater Elementary School, PA

Winter
W hite blanket
I gloos are frozen
N o school
T oo cold
E armuffs
R ough winds
Katelin Holleran, Grade 2
St Clement Mary Hofbauer School, MD

Baseball
Baseball
Dirty, exciting
Run, hit, pitch
Good for the muscles
Fun, interesting
Grand slam
Liam O'Connor, Grade 3
St Joseph School, NY

Stars in the Night
Stars in the night
Flickering in the distance
Clear ones on the outside
Stars in the middle
Half moon
Half beautiful view
A little room
Painted with stars
A moon on the bottom
Nick Messina, Grade 1
Harry Lee Cole School, MA

Fall
In fall
the leaves
are no longer green
instead
all yellow and brown
then
the leaves
will turn to the ground
next spring
new leaves
will
sprout out
Hannah Kehoe, Grade 2
Roger Sherman School, CT

Pot of Gold
A black pot of gold
You make me happy and rich
Shining with brightness
Kaya Cooper, Grade 2
Killingly Memorial School, CT

Nature and Me

Nature has lots and lots of trees
and water
some waters are ice.

John Johnson, Grade 3
Public School 23 Carter G Woodson School, NY

Summer

Summer! Summer!
It's so bright.
And it's so hot.
I can't wait until it's summertime.
Summer! Summer!
It's nice and hot.
I can't wait until I get out.
To be free and shout out loud
Summer! Summer!
You're absolutely glorious
I am feeling very happy
Summer you're so cool.

Rasheon Nicholas, Grade 3
Public School 397 Foster Laurie Elementary School, NY

Spring

Spring is here
Spring is here
Spring is here
Birds are chirping everywhere showing spring is in the air
Dragonflies dancing in the sky the bright sunshine kissing the cold good bye
Spring is here
Spring is here
Spring is here
Going to the beach or going in your pool
Staying under your umbrella to keep yourself cool
Tulips bursting open sending a great scent
Standing straight and tall instead of squished and bent
Bears awaken from their long sleep chicks hatch and start to peep
Caterpillars start their wrinkled cocoons that can hang from a maple tree
Waiting and waiting inside so it can grow into a Monarch butterfly
And drift off happily water flows and leaf buds grow
Spring is here
Spring is here
Spring is here

Meg McGuinness, Grade 3
Jeffrey Elementary School, CT

Spring

S unny,
P lants are growing,
R obins are flying.
I nsects are living in the grass.
N o more hibernating.
G reen grass is growing.
Charli Holland, Grade 2
Hebbville Elementary School, MD

Winter Fun

Winter
Snowman, snowballs
Skiing, snowboarding, sledding
Snow forts, winter
Snowy
Ryan Briggs, Grade 1
Seneca Academy, MD

Care Bears

Care Bears do nice things.
They help people from different lands.
They have stuff on their tummies.
Their noses are shaped like hearts.
They are all different colors.
I think they're very nice and beautiful.
Jordyn Floyd, Kindergarten
South Side Elementary School, PA

The Scary Snakes

Dangerous.
Can eat eggs and worms.
Some are fat and some are skinny.
Different colors.
Don't be scared.
Some are nice.
Manuel Romero, Grade 1
Northeast Elementary School, NY

Sun

The sun is burning!
It has a lot of heat rings.
The sun makes you hot.
Josie Caton, Grade 2
Long Meadow Elementary School, CT

My Friend, David

David has a train,
That's on street main.
We each have a Tonka game.
That is the very same.
February is his birthday,
His brother's is in May.
He has a truck
That looks like a duck.
He has a pen
That looks like a den.
We once slept in a tent
Using a pole with a dent.
He's my best friend to me
He is also very funny.
Victoria Rossi, Grade 3
St Catherine Laboure School, PA

Four Leaf Clovers

Green clover
Two leaf clover
Three leaf clover
Four leaf clover
Some are hard to find
But the hardest one to find

Is the four leaf clover.
MaKenzie Wright, Grade 1
Central Elementary School, PA

Sapphire Scales

One fish
But millions of scales.
Such flexible pieces of your body!
So flexible
You could join the circus.
(The underwater circus, of course!)
Maybe flexible enough
To spell out
All the words on this page.
Wow!
I wonder how your scales
Shift into shapes so quickly.
Gates Dupont, Grade 3
Thoreau Elementary School, MA

The Storm

Bang! Crash! The clouds were battling.
The doors and windows were loudly rattling.
There was a flood from the pond outside.
My brother got scared and had to hide.

Stephanie Shanahan, Grade 2
JF Kennedy School, CT

Spring

Flowers bloom,
Grass so green,
Sun is bright and warm.
Playing at the park,
Riding my bike,
Time to have a picnic.
Springtime brings lots of fun.
I love spring!

Madison Rush, Grade 2
Washington Park Elementary School, PA

Mountain Dew

M y favorite drink
O verloaded with sugar
U nderrated soft drink
N ow I can relax and drink my favorite drink
T oo tasty
A n amazing mixture of sugar and lime
I rresistible
N othing like it

D o the dew
E xceptional
W ow! Mountain Dew is good

John Fergusson, Grade 3
St Christopher's School, VA

Alison's Favorite Sport

S ocks up to your knees
O ffense blocks
C orner kick
C enter forward
E verybody cheers
R un and boot the ball

Alison Di Paola, Grade 3
New Lane Memorial Elementary School, NY

Having Fun in Snow!

Snowball fights making snow forts
S
  l
    e
      d
        d
          i
            n
              g

                 D
               o
                w
                 n
                  h
                  i
                   l
                    l

Ice skating playing in fluffy snow with your pet rest   from a l   day.
                              i   o
                              n   n
                              g   g

Michael Blaney, Grade 2
Dr Samuel C Eveleth School, MA

Orange

Orange tastes like a crunchy carrot on my plate.
Orange looks like a warm bonfire at night.
Orange sounds like a growling tiger when it is hungry.
Orange smells like sweet oranges when you peel them.
Orange feels like a basketball when you shoot and score.

Lance Pealer, Grade 3
Watsontown Elementary School, PA

Reading

Reading is fun —
in the sun,
in the night,
with a light.
By the lake,
by the cave.
Everywhere.

Gillian Patrick, Grade 2
Public School 152 School of Science & Technology, NY

White

White tastes like sweet vanilla ice cream
melting in my mouth.

White sounds like a fat polar bear
snoring in the Arctic.

White feels like smooth white chalk
rubbing into my hands.

White looks like tiny cold snowflakes
landing on my nose.

White smells like cool minty peppermint
in a Peppermint Patty.

Saniah Carson, Grade 3
Watsontown Elementary School, PA

Yellow Is...

Yellow tastes like juicy ripe lemons
Yellow feels like a wet sponge in the afternoon
Yellow smells like buttery corn at a picnic
Yellow sounds like a duckling quacking happily
Yellow looks like a candle's flame at midnight

Shawn Weaver, Grade 3
Watsontown Elementary School, PA

People and Animals

People
Clothes, cars
Reading, driving, drawing
Knit, games, play, nap
Defending, making, finding
Fur, forest
Animals

Bryce Hession, Grade 3
Our Mother of Perpetual Help School, PA

About Me

I like to play with my baby brother.
I like to paint.
I like to go in the swimming pool.
But, I don't like to play with my grandma's cat.

Tracey Leroy, Grade 1
Northeast Elementary School, NY

Spring

S now melts
P onds come to life
R ain comes down
I see blossoms
N ests are made by birds
G reen grass to play on
Dakotah Jackson, Grade 1
Mount Jewett Elementary School, PA

Tootsie Pop

Inside it has a Tootsie Roll
That I put in a bowl.
The lollipop is round
And on the wrapper there is a clown.
It is lolly,
And it is jolly.
The lollipop is yummy,
And is up my tummy.
Anthony Phillips, Grade 3
St Catherine Laboure School, PA

Trees

Trees have lots of leaves.
Coconut trees have long leaves.
Trees give oxygen.
James Tuller, Grade 2
Long Meadow Elementary School, CT

Sun

The sun is orange
It is bright in the day sky
Warming the cool Earth
David Desmarais, Grade 2
Long Meadow Elementary School, CT

My Puppies

My puppies are nice,
Sometimes they slide on ice.
If one tries to fight,
The other one is in fright.
One likes to sleep in my bed at night,
So I have to keep on the light.
Amanda Gonzalez, Grade 3
Holy Rosary School, NY

The Ancient Cup

The monsters guard the ancient cup
under the whipping splashing sea
the others go and catch some fish
to eat for the day.
Danny Cosgrove, Grade 2
Harry Lee Cole School, MA

Stage Fright

I don't like to go on stage,
It makes me really afraid,
I feel like I'm in a cage.
When I don't react,
The crowd is in a strange rage.
Evan Mancini, Grade 3
Our Lady of Hope School, NY

Ice Cream

I ce
C ream is good for me when I eat it
E very day.

C ream is
R eally yummy
E ach time I eat it.
A nd I like it when I
M ake ice cream.
Devon Yu, Grade 3
Sacred Heart School, MA

Sunset

Sunset beautiful sunset
red orange yellow
painted with a flaring sun
Sunset beautiful sunset
David Gage, Grade 3
Buckley Country Day School, NY

Grass

Grass is very green.
There are so many blades of grass,
Out there in the world.
Jake Pirri, Grade 3
Hereford Elementary School, PA

The Sun Will Always Win

When the moon comes out to play
the sun goes to sleep and ends the day.
When the stars twinkle up above
they will show who you really love.
When the morning cracks and the moon goes down
some will smile and some will frown.
The dark will never win
and the day will begin.
That's why the sun will always win!

Sophia Zahner, Grade 3
St Clare School, MD

Spring

J aybirds come out
U mbrellas go up when it rains
S pring
T ents go up in spring
I n the spring Easter comes
N ests are made

Justin Stanford, Grade 3
Susquehanna Community Elementary School, PA

The Sun

The Sun is like…
An orange with fur
A pumpkin with quills
A yellow football with spikes
A golden delicious apple with worms sticking out
A big ball on a ball-point pen
Jupiter in the night sky
The Sun

Ben Davis, Grade 3
Houghton Elementary School, MA

A Walk in the Wind

I went for a walk in the wind one day,
And all I wanted to do is play (on the swings).
I wanted to play, but my teacher said, "No way!"
The golf course looked empty.
I felt the wind tickle my face.
And as I walked back in,
I looked back to look at the wind one last time.

Kiara Rodriguez, Grade 2
Northeast Elementary School, NY

Sky

I am sky
Wrapping up the Earth
From the ground
To the clouds
I am blue when you see me
Sun shining through me
Moon reflecting on me
Stars you see from space
My neighbor
I am what you see
Anywhere you'll be

Michelle Bohin, Grade 3
Meeting House Hill School, CT

The Storm

A thunder storm was on its way.
"Tornado," I heard people say.
The funnel twirls,
it whips and whirls.
Tomorrow will be a better day.

Amber Grass, Grade 2
JF Kennedy School, CT

My Favorite Time of Year!

Spring is my favorite time of year.
Old stale crisp leaves,
Crunching in the fresh breeze.
New leaves sprouting,
Will be twirling soon.
Spinning green.
Now I can feel spring.
Excited.
No boundaries.
Running around!

Dylan Couch, Grade 2
Susan Odell Taylor School, NY

Halloween

Halloween is scary
Costumes and frightening lightning
Ghosts and zombies, ahh

Jake Saxon, Grade 3
Penn-Kidder Campus, PA

Computer

C ustom backgrounds
O n and off
M any viruses infect
P asswords make security
U p to date welcome screen
T echnical
E -mail
R isky websites

Edward (Buck) Shockley, Grade 2
The Jefferson School, DE

Snow

White snow falling down.
Children happily play yay!
Warm fire waits for them.

Rachel Kriebel, Grade 2
Marlborough Elementary School, PA

My Brother

My brother and I
Come from the same mother.
Even though we might fight,
We are really tight.
He might be a pest.
I think he is the best.
I love him will all my heart
and nothing will never bring us apart.

Michelle Gangone, Grade 3
Our Lady of Hope School, NY

My Little Tadpoles

Green little tadpoles
Floating in the clear blue creek
They turn into frogs

Riley Currie, Kindergarten
Valley School of Ligonier, PA

The Friends

At school Emily plays with me,
Haley likes to play soccer with Kaley,
Katerina likes to play with Haley,
And Emma likes to play with Gemma.

Marina Renzi, Grade 2
St Rose Elementary School, CT

Toys

I
play with toys
in East Meadow house
in the middle of the day
because my mother lets me play with them.

David Gravely, Grade 3
Montessori Childrens School, NY

Books

Books are like a world waiting to be seen
And every word is like a fairy queen
Everything in its rightful place
The words in books have such grace
I read through the night, I read through the day
Reading sometimes swings and sways
It's usually quiet when I read
Yet sometimes there's that noisy seed
Books are something I admire
The best was about a girl named Sapphire.

Julia de la Parra, Grade 3
Eisenhower Elementary School, PA

My Family

M y loving caring mom.
Y ou love me. I love you.

F orever you'll be my family.
A nd you'll always be there for me.
M y family.
I n my heart.
L aughing all the time. Laying down to rest.
Y es I love them.

My family.

Casey Smith, Grade 2
Hyman Fine Elementary School, MA

Black

Black is a chess piece, winning the game.
Black is tar, paving the road.
Black is a hole, deep and dark.
Black is my pet kitty, Rusty!

Kyle Beck, Grade 2
Cornerstone Academy, MA

Christmastime

I can't wait until Christmas comes.
It is the time of year when I have the most fun.
We always decorate the Christmas tree
With beautiful ornaments as you can see.
I also count my blessings for everything
And am thankful for Jesus Christ the King.
I am off to sleep until tomorrow,
Then it might snow enough to sled.

Nicholas Andricola, Grade 3
St Anastasia School, PA

Sharks and Dragons

Sharks
Fins, gills
Swimming, attacking, diving
Water, fast, claws, fire
Flying, sleeping, walking
Wings, scales
Dragons

Liz Hauck, Grade 3
Our Mother of Perpetual Help School, PA

Monkeys

Cute, friendly
Furry, soft
Noisy, giggly
Chimpanzees

Ashley Hutchinson, Grade 2
Christ the Teacher Catholic School, DE

What Is Black?

The sky is black
in the middle of the night
I pull my blanket over my back
and wake up from a big fright.

Black acts like a running horse
playing in the field all day
in the evening he hurries
back to the stable for hay.

Black is a beautiful thing!

Jennifer Bosserman, Grade 2
A.G. Richardson Elementary School, VA

I Fly

I'm flying I'm flying
Way up high in the sky
Way up high
But my brother can't fly
My sister can't fly
So how can I?
So how can I fly that high
Very very high in the sky?

Asjah Brown, Grade 2
Children's Village, PA

Shar-Pei

Dog
Nice, furry
Walk, run, fetch
Dogs are nice pets
Catch, play, sleep
Exciting, friendly
Shar-Pei

Adelaide Cooke, Grade 3
St Joseph School, NY

Spring

S pring is fun!
P laces are warm!
R oses smell nice!
I like spring.
N othing is boring!
G reat things happen!

Daniel Stekol, Grade 1
Adelphi Academy, NY

The Silver Dollar Fish

flat little fish
with very big eyes
swimming around the tank
plants floating
through the water
big rocks
in the corner
it is like a jungle
under water

Declan Noonan, Grade 2
Harry Lee Cole School, MA

White

If white had a sound it would sound like an Arctic Owl
flying through the Arctic Tundra.
White looks like a dove flying through the sky.
If white had a smell it would smell like a rose blooming in the spring.
White tastes like an ice cream that I like to eat every day.
White feels like a cold ice cube floating in my cold water.

Katressa Baker, Grade 3
Watsontown Elementary School, PA

Blizzard

He is
black and white

He has
blue eyes

He has
black stripes

He has a
pillow

He is a
tiger

Gillian Zimmerman, Kindergarten
Plainview-Old Bethpage Kindergarten Center, NY

Pink

Pink sounds like two quiet friends whispering in the dark night
Pink looks like ice-cold raspberry lemonade being slurped down on a hot day
Pink feels like a bunny quickly hopping through my hand
Pink smells like fragrant roses growing in a garden

Mackenzie Gardner, Grade 3
Watsontown Elementary School, PA

Annoyance

Annoyance is like orange.
It sounds like a roaring lion.
It smells like burnt popcorn.
It tastes like hot salt water.
It looks like a place where a tornado hit.
Annoyance feels like you don't know what to do with yourself.

Emily Steffke, Grade 3
Christ the King Elementary School, NY

Disney World

exciting,
scary,
    fast,
    bright,
staying up late to watch the fireworks,
    fun
hugging characters,
    spinning,
going on roller coasters,
getting autographs,
    getting wet,
seeing 3-D movies,
DISNEY WORLD

Ana Curtin, Grade 2
Dr Samuel C Eveleth School, MA

Spring

Trees start growing leaves.
Flowers start to grow in spring.
I see birds in spring.

Emily Kamyck, Grade 1
St Mary's Elementary School, MA

A Visit to the Zoo

I want to go to the zoo!
Don't you?
We could see cuddly bears
And lions that give us a scary stare!
We could see many mammals,
And ride on a camel!
I want to go now to the zoo!
Don't you?

Brian Muscatella, Grade 2
Christ the King School, NY

Spring

S pring flowers are blooming
P eriwinkles are here
R obins are singing
I nsects are crawling
N ests are full of eggs
G reen grass growing

Destini Johnson, Grade 2
Hebbville Elementary School, MD

My Grandma

Grandma makes good apple pies.
She makes good cookies.
We go shopping.
She baby-sits us.
I love Grandma.

Maddy Knight, Kindergarten
South Side Elementary School, PA

The Rain Forest

R ains every day
A ll species of birds
I nsects are everywhere
N ewborn animal babies

F lowers bloom in every space
O rangutans fly through the trees
R eally beautiful place
E choes travel tree to tree
S ome medicines come from plants
T ime to save the animals

Brian Regan, Grade 3
Sacred Heart School, MA

Joe

There once was a turtle named Joe
He was always slow
He wanted to play
Along every day
But then he hurt his big toe…

Chyna Ford, Grade 2
Ulysses Byas Elementary School, NY

I Am Stars

Fluttering above Earth
Twinkling in the sky
Disappear in light
Appear at night
Knowing what is happening on Earth
Earth is beautiful from where I shine
I know what I am doing, I must do
Space is my home!

Kevin Jenkins, Grade 3
Meeting House Hill School, CT

Snowballs

S nowball fights
N o school
O utside it's cold
W inter vacation
B oots protect your feet
A ll are happy
L ovely picture
L ike hot chocolate
S nowy day

Kristina Button, Grade 2
St Clement Mary Hofbauer School, MD

A Frog's Life

Hip hop a frog goes.
It does this all night and day.
This is a frog's life.

Jack Derby, Grade 2
Fonda-Fultonville Elementary School, NY

Winter Is...

Winter is the sound of bells jingling.
Winter feels cold like my frozen face and hands.
Winter is bears hibernating.
Winter is children sledding.
Winter is making snowmen.
Winter is fun!

Joshua Flores, Grade 1
St Teresa of Avila School, NY

Trees

I hear the trees
their language is wind
I feel their song swaying in my heart
they sing their song swaying in my heart
they sing such beautiful words
that you cannot describe them
in English
I know which trees are kind
and who will protect me
for as long as love flows
through our hearts forever
and ever

Cady Sanderson, Grade 3
Thoreau Elementary School, MA

If the Earth Could Speak

If the Earth could speak, she would say many things like:
Be thankful for the seasons the sun brings.
Keep bullies away from children who are small.
But the most important thing she would say to us all is:
Love one another from winter to fall.

Anisa Eshraghi, Grade 3
Montgomery Elementary School, PA

All About Rain

Rain comes from water
Rain comes from the sky
Rain comes from clouds
Rain comes once in a while
Rain comes in drops
Rain comes like teardrops.

Arifa Rahim, Grade 3
Public School 152 School of Science & Technology, NY

Moon

What is that?
The moon
It looks like a ball
That was cut in half
Soon you will see
A whole moon

The moon looks so little
It looks like it can go on a spoon

My lovely moon
It is gone so soon
Where is my moon
That left me so soon?

Keston Williams, Grade 3
Public School 152 School of Science & Technology, NY

Christmas

Christmas is coming, Christmas is coming.
I like Christmas so we could have some presents.
Christmas is the day we could throw snowballs at each other
and make snowmen with clothes.
Christmas is the day that you give Santa some chocolate chip cookies.

Johnson Zhao, Grade 2
Children's Village, PA

Page 67

The Rainbow Parrot
The Rainbow Parrot came to town
With his feathers like a crown
His colors shone so brightly
As he flew across from me
His head was blue like the ocean sea
His body was green as the top of a tree
The orange of his plume was a grand sight
I'm sure it even glows in the night
He's a beauty as everyone knows
He's the king as a bird goes

Courtney J. Sullivan, Grade 3
St Casimir School, MA

Whisper
Whisper to the winds above you.
Whisper to the sun at dawn.
Whisper to the moon at night.
Whisper to the stars that shine so bright.
And whisper to the wind.

Jessica MacLean, Grade 2
Hartland Elementary School, CT

The Adventure of Books
I'm in a far off jungle across the south sea
I'm riding a clear blue wave
I wash on the sand filled with stony shells
I'm in a bear's cave

And then the cave disappeared
I was in the misty sky
And how beautiful it looked
Though frightened was I

I landed on the silver moon
And touched the golden stars
and further in
I landed on the red Mars

Then I flew to Earth
the story closed, it was at an end
and I could tell another one
was just around the bend

Sahara Bebo, Grade 3
Plymouth Elementary School, VT

Football Game

One day we played a football game
It was not lame.
We had the ball
But not in the hall.
Our guy got a touchdown
And he started saying pronouns.
Then we got a first down
But next it turned all around.
There was a referee
Whose name was Jeffrey.
Our receiver
Had a fever.
We won by eight
So we went to celebrate.
It was fun
But it is done.

Joseph Kepp, Grade 3
St Catherine Laboure School, PA

Basketball Fun

Shooting through hoops,
Bouncing the ball,
Rooting and cheering,
By saying, "GO TEAM!"

Stealing the ball,
Fouling and scoring until it's over.
Someone will win,
It might be this team,
Or maybe that team.
And all of this,
Is very, very fun!

Liam Palilla, Grade 2
St Rose Elementary School, CT

A Man with a Shoe

There once was a man with a shoe.
He slept all alone in a zoo.
His shoe got taken
Then he smelled bacon.
Now awake, he saw a barbecue!

Christopher Koogle, Grade 2
Oakdale Elementary School, MD

Dreams/Imagination

Dreams
heart's desire
waiting in anticipation
feeling happy and free
Imagination

Sophia Karamatzanis, Grade 3
William Spyropoulos School, NY

Cats and Family

My cat is fat
she likes to sit
on Daddy's lap
One is fat
two are slim
There are no hims,
only hers
They all purr
when we watch TV

Amber Mindy, Grade 1
St Joan of Arc Elementary School, PA

Brown

Tall dog
Small dog
Bird
Sand
Dirt
Monkey
Brown
Is a monkey that is funky.

Jessica Terry, Grade 3
Weston Intermediate School, CT

I Am a Tree

I am a tree
I sway in the wind
I am tall and skinny
I am weak
My branches are small twigs
I hear strong gusts of wind
And see big snowflakes
I hope winter ends soon

Robbie Gallacher, Grade 3
Meeting House Hill School, CT

Hot Cocoa

Hot cocoa as brown as a Hershey Chocolate bar,
Hot cocoa as hot as a flame-lit stove,
With tiny white marshmallows
Floating at the top of the cup,
Until they start melting, melting, melting away
It tastes so chocolatey that I could drink it in
One sip, two sips, three sips!
MMMMMMMMMMM! All gone!

Olivia Mailey, Grade 3
Ridge Park Elementary School, PA

Our Feather Friends

The eagle flies, so high, in the sky.
The other birds say, "Hi," as they fly by!
From far away, we see them soar,
Let's take care of them forevermore!
The American eagle all covered with feathers,
Will join with all the other birds to fly forever together!
It's amazing to see them spread their wings so wide,
And you know that this bold eagle is a symbol of our freedom and pride!

Patrick Bernacchia, Grade 3
Christ the King School, NY

Winter Is...

Winter is the sound of deer sleeping.
Winter smells like hot cocoa and marshmallows.
Winter feels like cold snow
coming down on your head.
Winter looks like people
skating on the ice.
Winter is fun!

Claire Mroczkowski, Grade 1
St Teresa of Avila School, NY

Blue Dove

Your blue feathers glitter like the sea.
Your green eyes like the grass.
Your beak is like sunrise and sunset.
But deep down inside the red color of your heart
Is just like a blooming rose.
Nothing can go wrong when you sing a peaceful song,
Oh take me where the tender angels belong!

Krista Laforest, Grade 3
Sacred Heart School, MA

Christmas Morning

On Christmas morning in our house.
We wake up as quiet as a mouse.
Our family comes from far and near
And brings lots of holiday cheer.
We stuff our bellies with lots of food
And don't play until we are in the mood.
When Christmas evening is all done,
We look back and see all the fun.

Vincent Armideo, Grade 3
St Anastasia School, PA

Baby Sea Turtles

Baby sea turtles, so cute, so small,
I love them all!
I love them all!
Baby sea turtles so grown up,
Now they're the size of my pup.
Adult sea turtles,
Oh, the eggs they lay,
I watched the eggs all night and day.
Then they hatched and went away.
Baby sea turtles on their own adventure,
Goodbye, goodbye, goodbye forever.

Jaclyn Creaturo, Grade 2
McQuistion Elementary School, PA

To Hatch a Heart

It takes some time to hatch a heart
Love must be there right from the start.

Happy together…to have some fun
Playing and caring for everyone.

You can be just like me
And love each other gracefully.

Serena Ruggiero, Grade 3
New Lane Memorial Elementary School, NY

Sick Sun!

Sick sun, don't get sick.
Unfun is when the sun gets sick.
Now make my popsicle melt so I can't lick.

Keaton Santella, Grade 3
Afton Elementary School, NY

The Puppy

Puppy
Cute, small
Eating, sleeping, playing
White, girl
Puppy

Brittney Shin, Grade 1
Seneca Academy, MD

Places

Some places are good
Some places are bad
Some places are fine
But the best place is mine

Sabreenah Khan, Grade 2
Al-Rahmah School, MD

Dragon

Dragon
Scary, ugly
Flying, swimming
Breathing fire
Snake

Luke Rizzo, Grade 2
St Rosalia Academy, PA

Family

Family
Cool, fun
Play, run, jog
They're a great family
Color, dance, sing
Friendly, nice
Biscardi's

Sarah Biscardi, Grade 3
St Joseph School, NY

Freedom

Freedom is like…
Watching a cloud go by.
Relaxing on a bed.
Playing on a beach.
Hugging a big cloud.

Matthew Fernandez, Grade 2
St Christopher's School, VA

Everlasting

Time,
Space,
Eternity,
Are all things
That never come round.
They keep on going,
Their end is never found.
They keep on going
Round and round,
Trapped on an everlasting
Carousel.
There is no beginning,
Nor an end.

Daniel Morgenstern, Grade 3
John Ward Elementary School, MA

Summer

Summer
Indoor soccer
Kick the ball
I will play goalie
Save

Nicholas Lenz, Kindergarten
St Stephen's School, NY

Lollipops

I had a lollipop
that was as red as
a cherry and
as sticky as
a candy cane
and as delicious
as a strawberry
and it got…
smaller
smaller
smalle
small
smal
sma
sm
s

Collin Wood, Grade 3
Ridge Park Elementary School, PA

Easter

E aster eggs
A round and around I look for eggs
S hiny colored days
T he tastes of chocolate bunnies
E aster eggs with round candies
R ound candies inside eggs

Ashley Mongillo, Grade 3
Central Avenue School, CT

Spring

S pring
P ink
R oses
I nsect
N ight
G arden

Michaela Oddy, Grade 1
Christ the King Elementary School, NY

Red

Red is the best.
Like a sun sets in the sky.
Red is my favorite.

Carl Krolikowski, Grade 2
Fonda-Fultonville Elementary School, NY

Christmas

It is midnight now.
Santa is coming to town.
It's Christmas day now!

Brett Taylor, Grade 2
Fonda-Fultonville Elementary School, NY

Change the World

Build homes for the homeless.
Share food with the hungry.
Give medicine to the sick.
Make money for the poor.
Wish happiness for the sad.
Hope for peace for the world.

Amanda Vasquez, Grade 2
Northeast Elementary School, NY

School

School is very fun,
Especially at recess when we run.
My favorite subject is writing,
Because it gives your brain a little lighting.
The coldest thing that you can do in school,
Is to go sledding when it's cool.
The greatest special is gym,
Even in basketball when I hit the rim.
School is very fun,
Especially at recess when we run.

Matthew Bell, Grade 3
Wood Road Intermediate School, NY

My Nanny

I love my nanny.
My nanny loves me.
She watches TV with my brother and me.
She gives me presents.
I like to hug her.

Michael Goss, Grade 2
James M Curley Elementary School, MA

What Is Blue?

The sea is blue
in the middle of the day
when I sink in the sea
and I float away.

A blue boat passes
and sails away
I watch it sail by
in the beginning of May.

Camryn Clore, Grade 2
A.G. Richardson Elementary School, VA

Olympics

You can win the gold if you don't that is okay
All that matters is if you play
In the summer you can jump high
Maybe to the sky
When you're snowboarding in the air
Maybe you could fly somewhere

Jake Russell, Grade 3
Eisenhower Elementary School, PA

Red

Red is the color of a rose blooming in the spring.
Red sounds like an apple when you bite into it.
Red smells like a juicy tomato grown from a garden.
Red feels like a burning fire at night.
Red tastes like ketchup on chicken for dinner.

Jesse Paul Poligardo, Grade 3
Elkridge Elementary School, MD

In the Cafeteria

In the cafeteria, I see busy kids rushing as fast as cars.
In the cafeteria, I hear the keypad beeping loudly.
In the cafeteria, I feel the smooth texture of the lunch trays.
In the cafeteria, I smell the glazed teriyaki dippers ready to eat.
In the cafeteria, I taste the smooth saucy cheese on the pizza.

Caughey Zachery, Grade 3
Broadneck Elementary School, MD

Fall

Looks like paint splatters on a wall
Smells like pancakes and syrup
Sounds like wind blowing through the trees
Tastes like sour apples when I pick them off the tree
Feels like dead leaves crumbling in my hand

Joshua Howard, Grade 3
Hardwick Elementary School, VT

In Springtime

In spring the flowers grow and then they fly away
All the way up in the sky
In springtime I ride my bike

The wind is cool the birds are going to stay
They come back in spring
From where they went to in winter

They fly all over the place.
The sing. They go, "Chirp! Chirp!"
In their nests in the trees.

The green grass goes to the flowers
And to the playground
And all the leaves grow back on the trees.

Kimani Douglas-Williams, Grade 1
Children Studio School Public, DC

Leaves

The leaves are
falling all around.
Lightly they land
on the ground.
C. Blair Marine, Grade 1
New Canaan Country School, CT

Cats

Cats are very cute
We like to play with yarn balls
We love to meow.
Molly Richardson, Grade 2
Long Meadow Elementary School, CT

Harry Potter

H as a scar on his forehead
A wizard
R eally brave
R on and Hermione are his friends
Y oung

P lays Quidditch
O nly one to survive Afada Kedavra
T ough
T ackles Uncle Vernon
E very year he goes to Hogwarts
R ides a Firebolt
Danelle Troutman, Grade 3
Mount Jewett Elementary School, PA

Hockey! Hockey! Hockey!

I love hockey.
The sound of the buzzer going
ehh-ehh-ehh!
The sound of the skates going
s-s-s-s-s.
I love hockey.
The sound of the crowd going
Yah! Yah! Yah!

I LOVE HOCKEY!
Josh Tassinari, Grade 2
Dr Samuel C Eveleth School, MA

Hamburger

H amburgers are delicious
A dults all like hamburgers
M y mom loves hamburgers
B aby Westley loves hamburgers more
U nable to resist a hamburger
R ound hamburger
G od even likes hamburgers
E veryone likes hamburgers
R eally hamburgers are good.
Stephen Cook, Grade 3
Sacred Heart School, MA

Tornadoes...

Twisting,
Going in circles,
Looks like a nail,
Draining water,
Twirling,
Whirlpools,
Watery,
Sparkling,
Sounds like airplanes,
Tornadoes.
Danny Szottfried, Grade 2
Dr Samuel C Eveleth School, MA

The Ocean

I love the ocean
It is like a pretty potion

The wind the water and the breeze
I love it when it hits my knees

When I'm in the sun
I like to run

I feel the sand with my hand
I feel the sand that makes up the land

I see the waves come one two three
I love it when we go to the sea
Danielle Pius, Grade 3
Klein Elementary School, PA

Bubblegum, Bubblegum
Bubblegum, bubblegum, you're so sweet
You're a very tasty treat.
Bubblegum, bubblegum, I will blow
And then POP! You will explode.

Bubblegum, bubblegum, I will buy
Lots of you all the time.
Bubblegum, bubblegum, you're the best
Better than all the rest.

Bubblegum, bubblegum, in every flavor
In my mouth it's you I savor
Bubblegum, bubblegum, chew, chew, chew
Bubblegum, bubblegum, I love you!

Rebecca Amendola, Grade 3
Klein Elementary School, PA

Angels
Angels are everywhere
Even if you do not see them
Once you go to sleep
You know they are all around
You know they are watching
And if you get to behave
You can go to heaven.

Thalia Tirado, Grade 3
Public School 65 Mother Hale Academy, NY

Winter
Winter is so cold
Sledding, snowman, snowballs, too!
I love wintertime!

Nicholas Mahler, Grade 3
Christ the Teacher Catholic School, DE

Rainbows
Rainbows are in the air,
At its end a leprechaun would be there.
Rainbows are pretty,
Not like a city.
Rainbows probably lead to a pot of gold,
And if you find it you've reached the goal!

Joey Duero, Grade 2
St Rose Elementary School, CT

The Luge

When some people get into the luge
They think they are better than others.
When they go out and see all the eyes on them,
They're going to wish not to go down again.

Speed and knowledge is all you need,
If not, you'll end up on your face, indeed.

The faster the better,
But control is what you need
Because if I lose that now,
No finish line for me.

Shanyce DeJesus, Grade 3
Hamilton Elementary School, PA

Clothes

Fun to wear and show
Cool clothes count as an A plus
Clothes are comfortable

Emily Marron, Grade 3
Christ the Teacher Catholic School, DE

Blue

Blue is the morning sound of the ocean,
Blue is the taste of water on a hot summer day,
Blue is the smell of the flowers in the spring,
Blue looks like the sky every day,
Blue feels like blue water in the spring.

Monica Baker, Grade 3
Watsontown Elementary School, PA

Spring

Daffodils dance in the garden
Roses blossom to see the sunshine
Robins chirp a beautiful song
Hawks soar in the endless aqua blue sky
The sky gets brighter
The temperature rises, getting warmer
Enjoying the sunlight
Trees sprout leaves
And get happy once again
Spring is a time of life!

Christopher Parker, Grade 3
Jeffrey Elementary School, CT

Jordan

Jordan Graser, cool
Basketball, football, baseball
Michael Graser, cool

Jordan Graser, Grade 3
St Mary's Institute, NY

The Sunshine State

Florida
Warm, sunny
Play, run, kick
It is warm there
Skip, jump, hide
Exciting, fun
The Sunshine State

Michala Palmer, Grade 3
St Joseph School, NY

Garbage

Stinky, rotten
Bug's favorite paradise
Disgusting

Philip Cross, Grade 3
St Christopher's School, VA

When I Was Sick

Coughing, sneezing.
I feel wheezy.
I eat my pills…yuk!
It's so icky!!
Sitting on the couch
with some water near me.
I'm sick.
I want to feel like a winner.

Mason Lee, Grade 2
Pomperaug School, CT

The Tiger Thingy

Tiger
skinny, red eyes
eating, sleeping, smelling
weird, big
Tiger

Alex Post, Grade 1
Seneca Academy, MD

Myself

I am kind of smart,
I love my sweet tarts.

I am fast,
I never get last.

I am very small,
I love basketball.

I am strong,
I am never wrong.

I am lazy,
When I get candy I get crazy.

Austin Felter, Grade 3
Susquehanna Community Elementary School, PA

All That I've Missed

I've missed knowing them.
I've missed growing up with them.
I never got to see their smiles or hear them laugh.
We never shared a room or clothes or stories about our day.
I've missed the chance to play games with them
I wonder if they would have won.
Taking walks together was never a possibility.
Sharing secrets with them was only a dreamy wish.
Often I wished I could have hugged them.
I'll never know how much I could have loved them.
My mom tells me about them but it's just not the same as me knowing them.
Sometimes it feels weird that I never met them.
This is all that I've missed
Because my sisters died before I was born.

Nyasha Sprow, Grade 3
Enterprise Elementary School, VA

Black

Black looks like a bunny running speedily on his wheel.
Black sounds like my mom and dad snoring at night together.
Black feels like squishy mud at the beach when I step in it.
Black tastes like cookies out of the oven.
Black smells like licorice at the candy store.
Black makes me feel happy!

Tyler Reynolds, Grade 2
Orleans Elementary School, MA

Good Sport
A good sport passes to people.
A good sport doesn't fuss at you
When you make a mistake.
A good sport helps you get up
When you fall down
I hope my friends think
I'm a good sport!
David Weatherford, Grade 2
St Christopher's School, VA

White
White is a snowflake
That flies through the air
Lands ever so gracefully
On the palm of my hand.
White is a dove
That sings us to life
Without a stammer
It sings through the night.
White is a cloud
White is a pencil
White is a fish
Swimming in the sea.
White is a promise
That winter is here.
White is a headband
As white as the snow
That glitters on your head
Every wonderful day.
White is a swan
A sailing ship in the lake
So that is white my very good friend.
Sarah Wicks, Grade 3
Eli Terry School, CT

Spring
S pring, it's wonderful!
P erfect time to play ball.
R ule: have fun, fun, fun!
I n the cool breeze we lay.
N ow is the time to play.
G ardening starts now!
Zoë McLean, Grade 3
Susan Odell Taylor School, NY

Winter Summer
Winter is white
You do not fly a kite.
It is not as light
As summer bright.

Winter is cold.
I think I am very bold.

I like summer because it's cool.
I like summer because of pools.

Summer is bright
You have lots of light.
Winter is cold
It's colder at night.
Raven Blakeney, Grade 3
The Jefferson School, DE

Bunny
Bunnies are white now
Hopping over the very white yard
Back to their warm hole
Rebecca Haynes, Grade 3
Afton Elementary School, NY

Junk Food
Sometimes it's hot
Sometimes it's cold
Junk food is sweet
Junk food is sour
Junk food always hits me with power
Joshua McCormack, Grade 3
Eisenhower Elementary School, PA

Spring
S oft chicken peeping.
P uppies barking.
R ains in April.
I ncredible.
N est full of eggs.
G ive cheers for Spring!
Kelsey Clark, Grade 3
Immaculate Conception School, PA

Come Out to Play

You can't, you can't stay away all day,
You have to come out to play!
Out to the garden, out to the pool,
Come out to the warm summer day!

Julie Grace, Grade 3
Vergennes Union Elementary School, VT

Wendy

There once was a woman named Wendy
Who was very nice and very friendly.
She wanted to be cool,
so she hanged out by the pool,
and dressed very trendy.

Cynthia Marini, Grade 2
Northeast Elementary School, NY

Summer

Summer is very, very hot
And I like it a whole lot

You can ride your shiny bike
You can go on a nice long hike

The warm summer breeze
Fills your heart with happy glee

You could play in the pool
But you just can't go to school

You could have picnics on the warm beach
Or walk your dog on his leash

When it ends it is such a bummer
That is my poem about summer

Paige Mackenzie Brigham, Grade 3
Klein Elementary School, PA

Jellyfish

Jellyfish jellyfish, just if I were you
Then I would be something totally brand new
Because I would like to swim
In the deep ocean blue

Rory Dunne, Grade 3
Meeting House Hill School, CT

The Moon

In the sky the moon is white
As it shines so big and bright

You may try to find its power
But only your mind can do that

High, high, high, the moon is
In the morning you must say bye
To the moon in the sky
Goss Ferneyhough, Grade 2
The Jefferson School, DE

Cloud

I am a cloud
So fluffy and white
Sometimes I am full of rain
The rain goes down and evaporates
I block the sun
So it won't shine
I turn into other shapes
Like a cow or a car
That's what I do
Danny Amorando, Grade 3
Meeting House Hill School, CT

Snow

White and bright
Filling the night with sparkling light
The temperature has dropped.
Time has stopped.
It's soft like a blanket,
Rough like a rock.
"It's actually snowing!"
Tasmina Khair, Grade 3
Public School 131, NY

Sun

I love the feeling of the sun
It just makes me want to run
I love the warmth it feels so good
I would share it with all I could
Joey Buczynski, Grade 3
Klein Elementary School, PA

My Friends

My friends are fun
Especially my
Three best ones.

My friends are fun
We are always the first ones
To be done.

My friends are fun
We fool around and then run.

My friends and me
Love the fun in the sun.
Waseem Khan, Grade 3
Islamic Academy of New England, MA

My Dog Pal

My dog Pal, he is nice
And he runs fast.
I love him.
If my dog Pal ran away
I will be sad but if he came back
Then I will be happy
And I will love him again
And he will love me.
Courtney Furlong, Grade 1
John F Kennedy School, MA

Animal Step

The toad can jump as far as a bunny.
A bunny can run as fast as a horse.
A parrot can fly as high as an eagle.
Veronique E. Pugh, Grade 1
Bainbridge Elementary School, MD

Red

Hot fire
Caught fire
Coke can
Heart
Cherry red
Is the color of a strawberry.
Jordan Schaffer, Grade 3
Weston Intermediate School, CT

By My Window
In the night I look out my window,
The stars shine like crystal diamonds in the sky,
The moon shines like a clear pool of water.
Later on I climb into my warm covers,
And will go dreaming in my own mystical world.

Latishia Reid, Grade 2
The International School at Rogers Magnet, CT

Diseases, Ice Cream and the Fair
"I'm sick, I have a cold, a cough
Chicken pox, cow pox too,
Please believe me, I'd never lie to you
Check my throat, is it red?"
"I do believe I'm almost dead."
Dad looks in, nods his head and then with a smile said
"I see, it's true, you'll miss the Woodstock Fair
and the chocolate kiss I promised you."
"Hey wait!" says the kid, "I'm really not sick, I just meant to play a trick
There's medicine for my disease
Such as germy blood streams
It's a huge bowl of Moose Tracks ice cream."
"I see," said Dad, "It's a rare disease you have,
So if it will stop swelling your calves
I'll give you your cure plus some things for sure
Cabbage, carrots, beet roots, some greens,
Lettuce, raw onions, red, white and black beans."
"Hey wait, I'm really not sick, my calves aren't swelling,
it's my mush muscles yelling
Please let me go to the Woodstock Fair
If you don't let me, I DON'T CARE!!! — I'll go myself."

Korey Caron, Grade 3
Pierce School, MA

On My Birthday
On my birthday I see my fun friends dancing to the loud music. After the party I
sadly see my friends leave!
On my birthday I listen to the loud party music like roaring waves in my ear. I
also hear my friends loudly yell "HAPPY BIRTHDAY!"
On my birthday I touch my presents that are exciting and special because they're
from my best friends!
On my birthday I smell the cheesy hot pizza that is so good I cannot wait to eat it!
On my birthday I taste the cold, chocolate ice cream melting in my mouth!

Shannon Stevenson, Grade 3
Broadneck Elementary School, MD

Transportation
Airplane
High, windy
Flying, soaring, landing
Jet, helicopter, carriage, covered wagon
Riding, eating, trotting
Bumpy, lumpy
Horse

Patrick Walsh, Grade 3
Our Mother of Perpetual Help School, PA

The Tornado
I saw you in the gray, gray sky,
And passing me by and by.
And all around I heard you twirl,
like mixing a vanilla swirl.
Oh Tornado twirling all day,
I fear it much when you sway!
I saw the horrible things you did,
but always your sweetness you hid.
You tortured me, you made me fall,
but all you really did was call.
Oh Tornado twirling all day,
I fear it much when you sway!
Oh you that are so fearful and strong,
you probably never sing a sweet song.
Are you the nightmare of all living things,
or just that you have very strong wings?
Oh Tornado twirling all day,
I fear it much when you sway!

Erika Koury, Grade 3
Booth Hill School, CT

Trees
Trees
Trees can give you shade.
Trees can give you shelter
to eat and play.
It can give you apples and oranges
for all the animals.
Monkeys can eat bananas from the tree.
You can get anything
from the tree.

Keenan Turner, Grade 3
Baltimore White Marsh Adventist School, MD

A Walk in the Wind

I went for a walk in the wind.
It felt cold.
I felt air on my face.
The swings had no people,
But they moved anyway.
I heard the wind.
It was sunny and cold.
I walked on the blacktop,
And as I walked back in, the wind pushed me in.

Charly Ben, Grade 2
Northeast Elementary School, NY

Valentine's Day

Candy
Red
Pink
Balloons
Valentine's Day

Evan Dimoulas, Kindergarten
Plainview-Old Bethpage Kindergarten Center, NY

Broadway

I'm walking down the street,
It's eight o'clock at night.
I think I'm on Broadway!
Look at all the light!
I was four when I opened the Broadway door.
I saw *The Lion King*. It was the greatest thing!
I saw *Beauty and the Beast*. That was such a treat!
When I got older, my mind became bolder.
I saw *Wicked*, a great show.
It's awesome, don't you know?
My favorite show is *Spelling Bee*,
The funniest show you'll ever see!
I love waiting at the stage door.
You see all the stars galore!
See a Broadway show. It rocks!
Get ready! Put on your shoes and socks.
I'm walking down the street,
It's eight o'clock at night.
I think I'm on Broadway!
Look at all the light!

Peter Diamond, Grade 3
John Ward Elementary School, MA

Butterflies
I watch butterflies
Oh butterfly, butterfly
Butterflies are cool
Hannah Cormier, Grade 1
St Mary's Elementary School, MA

Flowers
Flowers, flowers
you are so sweet
and smell so good
you need a lot of water
and you need to sleep.
Yarisbel Hermita, Grade 3
Public School 2 Alfred Zimberg, NY

Devil/God
Devil
Mad, weird
Hating, fierce, maker, peace
Loving, forgiving, blessing
Lord, king
God
E.J. Jones, Grade 3
Wasena Elementary School, VA

Puppy
cute, loving, little
a poor dog out in the cold
took him in my home.
Joshua Diaz, Grade 2
Public School 148 Ruby Allen, NY

In My Family
In my family
My dad is very tall.
My mom is a little small.
My brother likes to dig.
My sister likes to wear her wig.
My dog likes to play.
My cat likes to run away.
In my family
We are all very special to each other!
Devon Pierce, Grade 3
Sacred Heart School, MA

Homework
I like to do homework.
We get table tally at FACTS.
I like to read books
I like to play with my friends.
I like my teacher at FACTS.
I like to play computer.
I like my teacher at Children's Village.
Nancy Yang, Grade 1
Children's Village, PA

Red
Small rose
Tall rose
Fire
Apple
Bird
Red
Little foxes
Can be heard.
Rachel Roberts, Grade 3
Weston Intermediate School, CT

Goldfish
I swim
I frolic
in the salty vat
of water.
How I wish
I could dance
a jig
in the real ocean
instead
of being
locked up
in my watery home
I find it worse
than an aquarium
there you have
much larger space to roam
I hate my tank!
Goldfish
Amber Born, Grade 1

What Is Blue?
The sky is blue
on a cold winter day.
I play in the pool
and Jacuzzi all day.

Blue acts like a good
little angel.
She helps out her friend
just like she should.
This makes blue feel good.

Amberly Harlow, Grade 2
A.G. Richardson Elementary School, VA

All About Dolphins
Dolphins are nice.
They are so beautiful that I can't blink twice.
Do dolphins eat rice?
Dolphins are amazing.
I love them.
They feel like silk.
I like their smooth and silky skin.
They live in saltwater.
We ride on their back.
We play with dolphins in summer.
They swim like mermaids.

Amirah Arafat, Grade 2
Al-Rahmah School, MD

Plants and Flowers
P lants can be green, plants can be pink
L ovely flowers are pretty plants.
A t nighttime, some flowers close their petals
N ectar comes from plants.
T ime passes by, and plants grow
S hy, blowy plants grow big

Jenna Wallace, Kindergarten
Montessori Academy of Lancaster, PA

Basketball
I think it's awesome
You get exercise with friends
Shooting baskets rocks!

Audrey Ostroski, Grade 2
Christ the Teacher Catholic School, DE

Spring

Spring is fun.
Spring is cool.
I have fun in the sun.
And I'll be happy to get out of school soon.
Allyson Layton, Grade 3
Our Lady of Hope School, NY

Fun Comes In

When the moon goes away
And the sun comes out,
That is when the fun comes out.

When the fun comes out,
I play and play and have fun all day.

And when I play and play all day,
I play on the monkey bars.
The monkey bars are from a galaxy far away.

Also I play on a swing
To take me to a soccer game
And hit it to a galaxy far, far away.

When I'm upside down,
I feel a hundred feet away from the ground.

When it comes late at night,
The fun is not over.
The night is the most fun of all.
Jeffrey Renner, Grade 3
Trinity Christian School, VA

A Piece of My Heart…

A piece of my heart is falling apart
I may put a dart in my heart
The part that I want is to play outside the park
I really want to go, but I can't
Oh I can't…
I will survive yeah
Go! Go!
WOW!
I went to the park!
Daniel Stewart, Grade 2
Public School 65 Mother Hale Academy, NY

Parrot

Animal
Interesting, exciting
Runs, bites, yawns
We have so much fun
Eats, talks, flies
Small, winged
Parrot
Chris Larkin, Grade 3
St Joseph School, NY

Lunch Box

Lunch box
Hard, plastic
Opening, closing, carrying
Holding my lunch
Yummy
Jessica Denzer, Grade 3
St Rosalia Academy, PA

Mermaid Song

Under a silvery,
magical moon,
in the place
where mermaids
frolic and play,
the mermaids
dive and sing
their song
until night
turns into
day
Megan Sawicki, Grade 3
Mast Landing School, ME

Tennis

Tennis
Fun, hard
Hit, swing, serve
Have to work hard
Run, move, jump
Hot, crowded
Racquet
Nora Proce, Grade 3
St Joseph School, NY

School Is Fun!
School is fun
You learn at school

There are big kids
There are small kids

Some kids learn
And some do not

There are a lot of boys and girls.

The students learn
While teachers teach

You learn Math, Reading, Science, Social Studies
We go to Art, Music, Gym, Library

We paint in art
We play instruments in music
We run in gym
We read in the library
And we have fun.

School is fun!!

David Garcia, Grade 3
Bensley Elementary School, VA

What Is Yellow?
Have you ever smelled yellow?
Yellow smells like sweet banana cream pie that is so terrific!

Yellow looks like
A big yellow school bus going to school.

Yellow feels like soft ducklings
Swimming in my pool.

Yellow tastes like corn
With butter in the summer.

Yellow sounds like a lion
Roaring in the jungle.

Alicia Vognet, Grade 3
Watsontown Elementary School, PA

A Husky

Husky
Happy, playful, cheerful
Barking, stopping, licking
Pulling a sled makes them tired
Snow dog
Zachary Foley-Cox, Grade 3
Houghton Elementary School, MA

Halloween Night

On Halloween night,
In the spooky light,
A fierce pumpkin stands.

As the bats fly,
And the kids skip by,
They ask for a delicious treat.

During the harvest moon,
While the autumn leaves fall,
Baskets are filled,
With candy and fruit for all.
Grayson Batsche, Grade 3
Spotswood Elementary School, VA

Flowers

F resh sprouts
c L imb
O ut of the
W et soil
E xploding into bloom
R eady for
S ummer
Haley Magoon, Grade 3
Hardwick Elementary School, VT

Rock Boa

Quick tongue
Camouflage
Beneath rocks
Very fierce hunter
Very long body
Miller Farley, Kindergarten
St Christopher's School, VA

A Pair of Pants

There once was a pair of pants,
That knew how to do a cool dance.
It broke its leg,
Then sucked on an egg.
But it was really ants in his pants.
Nicholas Mayo, Grade 2
Oakdale Elementary School, MD

Cake

C ake is very tasty.
A cake is very big.
K iwi is a good fruit on cake.
E ating cake is very delicious.
Sunny Chan, Grade 3
Sacred Heart School, MA

Spring Cheer

It is the last night of winter,
My dream has come true,
All the flowers are blooming,
It is almost midnight,
Right now it is 11:59,
We have one minute to go.
I can stay up to midnight,
And still be awake,
I want to be the first one to see
The clock turn to 12:00 AM.
But I know that won't happen,
When it is finally spring.
Spring is my favorite time of year,
All the flowers have that special cheer!
Nothing feels better than spring cheer.
Winter, fall, and summer are also fun,
But when spring has arrived,
All the fun has begun!
Rebecca Lamore, Grade 3
Home School, CT

Butterflies

Butterflies are pretty,
You can see their colorful wings,
As they flutter about.
Vanessa Wheeler, Grade 3
Marlborough Elementary School, PA

I Took My Cat on a Play Date

I took my cat on a play date
to meet my grandma's cat.
I thought it would be fun for them,
but I was wrong about that.

First they sniffed each other,
and then they started to hiss.
When they made awful meows,
I knew they wouldn't make up and kiss.

I quickly took my cat back home,
and she was happy as could be.
From now on I'll just make play dates
for my human friends and me.

Molly De Prospo, Grade 1
Penn-Mont Academy, PA

Christmas Is Here

Christmas is here.
I love Santa.
He says, "Ho, ho, ho!"
When he is bringing me presents,
I am dreaming and sleeping.
What I dream about is Santa
Bringing me toys.
I wake up and I say,
"See you!"

Gabriela Martinez, Grade 2
James M Curley Elementary School, MA

Wonder

Every day I see a flower grow
And I wonder how do they know?

Every day I see a rose to become as tall as me
And I wonder what do they see?

Every night I see the stars grow bright
And I wonder are they just light?

Every night I see the moon
And it just looks like a big balloon.

Mariam Abdelgany, Grade 3
Islamic Academy of New England, MA

Butterfly

Butterfly
Pretty, peaceful
Searching, flying, eating
Fluttering from flower to flower
Angel
Jordan Bon, Grade 3
St Rosalia Academy, PA

Ryan

R yan likes to read.
Y oyos are fun to me.
A nything is fun.
N ever lies.
Ryan Sanchez, Grade 2
George L Cooke Elementary School, NY

Cats

Soft, cute, cuddly,
The cat is black and white.
The cat loves running.
Cristina Peralta, Grade 2
Public School 148 Ruby Allen, NY

About Me

Alec is a fun guy.
He knows just what to do.
He never likes to say goodbye.
When the day is through!
Alec Downey, Grade 1
St Joan of Arc Elementary School, PA

Leaves

The colorful leaves
Falling off branches on me.
Squirrels climbing branches.
Dean Mandelos, Grade 3
William Spyropoulos School, NY

Mud

Slopping on my shoes.
Playing in the mud with trucks.
Your shoe can get stuck.
Logan Abraham, Grade 2
Wells Central School, NY

Baseball Homeless Guy

I met a homeless guy in Cleveland
After an Indians' game.
He was holding a cup with money
He was acting kind of funny.

He was dark and he was tall
He was asking people for their money
Because he wanted to go to the mall
Probably to buy some honey.

But then I started to look at his jersey
I bet it cost a lot
Maybe he wasn't homeless at all
But a crook who hasn't been caught
Chris Deuel, Grade 3
Klein Elementary School, PA

Snow

I love when it snows
because it glows.
I love the cold
because it snows.
I love when the snow blows
because it goes on my nose.
Even though it may come and go,
now you know why I love snow.
Nicholas Jezina, Grade 3
Public School 5, NY

Spring Is Beautiful

Spring is beautiful
Angels are sweet
Butterflies fly
And so do you!
Mia Kussman, Kindergarten
John Ward Elementary School, MA

Beauty

One canary sun
Two electric pink flowers
One shocking red rose
Hailey Oliveira, Grade 3
Acushnet Elementary School, MA

Ice Cream

I love ice cream it is sweet and good.
C ream on top tasted even better.
E ven ice cream can cheer you up!

C ats maybe like ice cream.
R ed cherries are the best for ice cream.
E very day ice cream is great.
A cherry on top will be even better.
M y friends and I eat ice cream on summer days.

Jenny Kung, Grade 3
Sacred Heart School, MA

Valentine's Day

Hearts
Tarts
Valentine's
Hugs
Kisses
And
Poetry

Valentine's Day

Anthony Merolla, Kindergarten
Plainview-Old Bethpage Kindergarten Center, NY

Spring

S unny
H elp plant flowers
E aster is fun
L eaves are colorful
B ees buzz
Y ards are green

Shelby Brinton, Grade 3
Susquehanna Community Elementary School, PA

Cupid

Love is in the air if cupid hits you
You can't escape
Cupid has arrows of magic if one of his arrows hits
You'll be in love with the first person you see
You send her a gift
She send you a kiss.

Jair Farciert, Grade 3
Public School 131, NY

A Lamb Named Bracket

There once was a lamb named Bracket.
And he owned a painted wool jacket.
But the jacket got ripped,
So he had a big fit.
Then he yelled and made a racket!

Riley Gill, Grade 2
Oakdale Elementary School, MD

What Is Blue?

The sea is blue
in the middle of the day.
I get in my boat
and then I play.

Play Dough is blue
Kool-aid is too
I drink it for dinner
what about you?

Cara Fisher, Grade 2
A.G. Richardson Elementary School, VA

Summer

I like summer!
Winter is a bummer!
I like summer
It's
    funner
        than spring.
    Swim in the summer
        it's kind of cold in spring.
I like summer
    more
        than fall.
Swim in the summer
    It's kind of cold in fall.

Dustin Maines, Grade 3
Bradford Township Elementary School, PA

God Is Awesome

G od is big and strong
O ur God is tough, caring, and loving
D ad is in heaven waiting for me and you.

Dominick Villacarlos, Grade 3
Growing Life Christian Academy, NY

An Enchanted Feeling

Writing,

Has a,
Superb feeling,

Contemplating,
Beautiful things,
To write!

Facing
The page,

I feel that I don't want
To.

Too scary,
People could look in

At my private
Feelings,

And make
Fun of me!

Alexa Hoovis, Grade 3
Fulton Avenue School #8, NY

Is That a Bat or a Cat?

Is that a bat or a cat?
Do you know?
Wow, just watch that thing go.
Do you think it will show.
It went fast then slow.
Is that a bat or a cat?

Bijan Chaudhuri, Grade 3
Adelphi Academy, NY

Friends

Ice cream is good,
But friends are better
I would not like a porcupine
To be my best friend
Would you?

Owen Dwyer, Grade 2
Cabot Elementary School, MA

Summer

Shall I compare you to summer?
You are full of warmth and laughter.
Your joy lasts forever.
You have no thorn bushes to prick the unwary.
Only good is in you.
You have no cold in you.
Your wit gives light.
Your heart is warmed by your own happiness.
Others look to you for advice.
You mingle with the best feelings I've seen.
Your warmth comforts those in need.
Rays of sunshine adorn your heart.
My heart feels full because of you.
You are my world.

Chloe Mandell, Grade 3
Weston Intermediate School, CT

Seven Silly Snowmen

Seven silly snowmen sang a song
The song was not super strange
They started throwing super big snowballs
They made strange, silly snow puppy
They made more super silly snowmen
Then the sun came out
All the super silly snowmen melted

Alanna Mergel, Grade 3
St Stephen's School, NY

Red

Red as the sun,
As red as Mars.
Red is the color of Saturn's ring.
Red as the evening day.
So as roses blooming in a breeze
And a red as a toasty fire at night.
So as a shooting star light
And some of the stripes on the flag of the USA.
Red is a strawberry field
And the fire alarm when it rings.
So as cherries in a tree
Red is an apple in a bush.
Red is the color of the sun setting.

Mickey Elliott, Grade 3
Eli Terry School, CT

Remember Me

In 300 years
look in a book
and you will see
a story all about me.
I will be an athlete.
I will run and compete
in many, many track meets
I will study
about penguins
how they live their lives
what they eat and how they fish
this will be my wish.
Remember me
Remember me
Remember me.

Joseph Palazzo, Grade 2
Blessed Sacrament School, RI

Teacher

She has long brown hair
She is nice and beautiful
My teacher is great

Guadalupe Lopez, Grade 2
Public School 148 Ruby Allen, NY

E Is a Cool Letter

E is a very cool letter,
because it starts my
name.
I like
E so
very
much,
because it starts
many names. It
starts
Elana,
Emily,
Erica,
Emma, Electra, and
many more names.

Elana Schwartz, Grade 3
Montessori Childrens School, NY

Animals

I saw a moth
on a cloth.

I saw a duck
in much.

In the fog
there was a frog.

And a dog
on a log.

There was a crow
and a cow on a bow.

I think I saw a flea
on a tree.

There is a mammal
called a camel.

Sarah Dermes, Grade 3
St Catherine Laboure School, PA

Snow

On a snowy day,
A snowflake fell on my nose.
Cold, white, shiny, bright

Laura Hasselstrom, Grade 2
Calvary Chapel Christian School, NY

Chick's Walk

When they're born, they're little.
And cute. And fluffy.
They grow up and run around a lot.
Peep! Peep! Peep!

Makenna Vogan, Kindergarten
South Side Elementary School, PA

Cats

Cats are lovable
I see cats all over the place.
Cats are cuddly.

Gisselle Yepes, Grade 2
Public School 148 Ruby Allen, NY

What Do I See All Around Me

What do I see all around me? I see trees big and small.
The earth and sky up and down.
I see kites flying in air, and people going to a fair.
I see fireworks bursting everywhere.
I see people walking 'round without care,
and dancing, singing happily...

...but most of all I see them with family.

Brittany Watson, Grade 3
Middle Gate Elementary School, CT

Orange

Orange tastes like a juicy tangerine in the summer.
Orange sounds like a campfire down by my creek.
Orange looks like a pumpkin that is going to be carved at Halloween.
Orange feels like a bright fall day.
Orange smells like orange slices at soccer break.

Casseday Rice, Grade 3
Watsontown Elementary School, PA

All About Me

My name is Michael. I want to ride a motorcycle.
My favorite color is red and I like to sleep in bed.
I like to ride bikes and some think my nickname is Mike.
I like to go to the pool when it's not cool.
My favorite food is ravioli and my best friend is Michael Lapioli.

Michael Miller, Grade 1
St Joan of Arc Elementary School, PA

Sky Blue

Blue smells like juicy, soft blueberries freshly picked in the summer.
Blue feels like a lonely, icy cold winter.
If you see blue, it looks like misty frost on a lake.
Blue tastes like scrumptious blueberries from a garden at the park.
Blue sounds like a quiet sea when the waves are gone.

Gabrielle Oberdorf, Grade 3
Watsontown Elementary School, PA

My Green Apple

Apples are so sweet
Apples are so colorful
I love apples so

Sarai Monargent, Grade 3
Public School 152 School of Science & Technology, NY

Sunny Days

Sunny days they're so great,
We laugh and play and eat some grapes
In the sunny day
Then we settle down and play some games.
We run and jump as the sun goes down

Connie Chan, Grade 2
Public School 205 Alexander Bell, NY

The Sky

Birds fly in the sky.
The sky is shining brightly.
The sky is bright blue.

Howard Moore, Grade 2
Fonda-Fultonville Elementary School, NY

Waking Up

My eyes slowly open
 and slowly close again
  when I open them for the second time
I stare
at the clock
 7:02
I lie
in bed for a
little longer
but when I
stare
at the clock again
it says it's
 7:20
I creep
out of bed
 it's morning
 get up sleepy head

Meredith Saunders, Grade 3
Mast Landing School, ME

Springtime Is

Springtime is when I have a barbecue.
Springtime is playing with your friends outside.
Springtime is riding my quad.
I love springtime!

Alexander Jennaco, Grade 2
Northeast Elementary School, NY

I Believe

I believe in my family
I believe in my friends
I believe in my history
And God believes in me!

Ashé Mary Nervil, Grade 1
Public School 185 J Mercer Langston School, NY

Allah (swt) Creations

Allah* (swt) is very nice
Way more than twice
Let me give you some advice.

You are a grain of sand
Compared to him
He doesn't need to eat
Not even one beet.
He knows when you cheat
He made us all very neat
Al-hamdu-lillah** if you're complete.

He made trees and bees
He made your knees and sesame seeds
Al-hamdu-lillah I am free
And flying like a bee
Al-hamdu-lillah he let me be.

*Allah is the Arabic word for God (the creator).
**Al-hamdu-lillah means — All praise is due to God.

Fatimah Mahamed, Grade 3
Islamic Academy of New England, MA

Kittens

Kittens are nice pets.
They can be cute and furry.
Would love to have them.

Melissa Pierre, Grade 2
Public School 152 School of Science & Technology, NY

The Spiny Pocket Mouse

The Spiny Pocket Mouse is spiny,
The Spiny Pocket Mouse is tiny.
The Spiny Pocket Mouse has a tiny, spiny pocket.

Nicolette San Clemente, Grade 3
Cornerstone Academy, MA

Water
The sun picks up water from
a pond
a lake
a river
and comes down from the sky
like tears from an angel.
Timo Nicolakis, Grade 1
Public School 122 Mamie Fay, NY

Mom
Mom
Nice, kind
Cooking, cleaning, hugging
Loving and caring for everyone
Forever!
Katelyn Clewell, Grade 1
Daniel J Flood Elementary School, PA

A Bat
A bat
Is like the wind
Slashing through the air

As still
As a stone
While hanging during
Sleep

Its wings
Spread as if it
Were the blanket
Covering the night
Sky

It eats the fruit
Hanging on a tree
As it itself does
While
Asleep

That's the world's
Bat
Sophia Dettling, Grade 3
Jamestown Elementary School, VA

Invitation to My Heart
Come in. Come into my heart
The things I love.

I love my heart.
Come in. Come in.

I want my friends in my heart.
I feel rainbows in my heart
When I think of my friends.

I love rainbows and so do my friends.
Come in. Come in.

Come in my family.
My family is important.

Come in. Come in.
The people I love.
Come into my heart.
Ira Lindsay, Kindergarten
Children Studio School Public, DC

Feelings
Feelings are like mail,
You receive every day.

You might get an angry letter,
Because your brother got a toy,
But you didn't.

A happy letter,
Puts a smile on your face.

A hurt your feelings letter,
Makes you sad.

A new friend letter,
Makes you glad.

I wonder what mail,
I'll get today?
Ethan En-ching Chou Smith, Grade 2
John Ward Elementary School, MA

Dogs

Cute, furry
Loud, noisy
Fluffy, smooth
Stinky, smelling of shampoo

Kelly Muschiatti, Grade 2
Christ the Teacher Catholic School, DE

Candy Is Very Sweet

Candy is very sweet
Candy is fun to eat.
Candy is fun to eat when it's hot.
Sometimes I feel like I'm boiling up in a pot,
Like a hot dog.
I can explain what candy is like.

C anadian candy
A rithmetic candy
N utty candy
D ancing candy
Y ummy candy

Candy
Candy is sweet.
Do you like candy?

Shamiah Cheeks, Grade 3
Parkside Christian Academy, MA

Pink

The smell of pink is the sticky sweetness
of cotton candy at the fair.

Pink tastes like juicy raspberries
that were picked off a bush in the summer.

The feel of pink is a soft furry bunny
hopping in a meadow.

The sound of pink sounds like someone
whispering in a friend's ear.

The look of pink is ribbons
blowing around in a young girl's hair.

Kaylynn Hart, Grade 3
Watsontown Elementary School, PA

What I Like to Do

Here are things I like to do,
Let me tell you about a few.
I really like cuddly kittens,
Muttie has one named Mittens.
Playing soccer is a lot of fun,
My favorite part is when I run.
At the beach I go on rafts,
When I'm sick I like to make crafts.
Last week I tried something new,
Ice skating is fun to do.

Madison Koepfer, Grade 1
St Joan of Arc Elementary School, PA

A Snake

Reptile.
Doesn't like the snow.
Different kinds.
Bad.
No legs.
Poisonous.
Be careful!

Benjamin Ramos, Grade 1
Northeast Elementary School, NY

The Poem

My assignment was to write a poem
And now I'm sitting at my home
Thinking about what to write…

My topic can be anything
So I could write about a king
Who has a lot of might…

Or I could write about a skateboard
Fit for a lord
Who has a trustworthy knight.

But then…
I had a great idea!
The end is almost near
I'll go fly my kite.

John Michael Giannone, Grade 3
Public School 5, NY

Flower

Lazy flowers
swaying in the breeze
hidden in a peaceful spot

Kiana Cruz, Grade 2
Buckley Country Day School, NY

Bald Eagle

Bald Eagle
Swift and light
Flying high
Soaring in the bright blue sky
Cozy nest
Bald white head
Golden eyes
Soft comfortable fur
Loud screeching cries fill the air
Bald Eagle

Parker Widhelm, Grade 3
St Christopher's School, VA

Snow

Frosty in the air
white flakes that form in the sky
a beautiful sight

Christie Kingsley, Grade 3
Acushnet Elementary School, MA

Hockey Is…

Pucks sliding across the ice.
Having hot dogs
and popcorn at the game,
the sound of SH — SH
when you stop.
Hearing college people
scream!
I love hockey
hearing yes when
somebody scores!
I like hearing boooooo
when the other team scores.

I LOVE HOCKEY!

Nick DiGiovanni, Grade 2
Dr Samuel C Eveleth School, MA

Snow

The snow is cold,
It's hard to hold.
The wind blew,
and the snow flew.
The plow plowed the snow,
The driver was Joe.
You can have a snowball fight,
my snow pants were mighty tight.

Shawn Martin, Grade 3
Susquehanna Community Elementary School, PA

Spring

S is for the shining sun
P is for the pretty flowers
R is for the rising grasses
I is for the ice cream that melts
N is for the nice days
G is for the glowing weather

Emani Delk, Grade 1
Little Flower Day Care Center and Prep School, NY

Snowmobile Rocket

I get my gear:
Helmet, goggles, snowsuit, and gloves.

Dad says, "Go take the tarp off of the snowmobile."
I smile.

Dad grips the pull start.
He pushes the throttle.

I lock my fingers together and
Hold him around the waist.

We're off!

We go through obstacles like a rocket.
I lean with my dad.
Then my dad goes down in the woods.
We come up and get good air.

I want to drive it myself!

Robbie Hancock, Grade 3
Meeting House Hill School, CT

Air

I love the air,
so I gave the air a dare.

I said, "I'll glare,
while you sit in a chair."

The air had something rare,
it was his crazy hair!

I can't believe I scared the air,
right out of that hair!

I couldn't stop staring,
but the air was starting to do some sharing.

He gave me a pear
that said, "No dare!"

It was time for the fair,
so I left the air!

Tyler Smith, Grade 3
St Catherine Laboure School, PA

Sun

The sun is the biggest star in the sky.
It fills the sky with a very bright light.
The sun is very round to me.
They say there is a man on the moon
but I just think it's the astronauts.
I think the moon is light blue.
Stars are very small on Earth,
but when you get closer they are very very big!

Jasmine Hitt, Grade 2
Grace Miller Elementary School, VA

The Storm

Boom crackle, something crashed.
As thunder boomed and lightning flashed.
Wild wind made the window break.
My room in the house began to shake.
Bang went the lightning.
My brother thinks it's frightening.

Gabrielle Gluhanich, Grade 2
JF Kennedy School, CT

My Dog Missy

My dog Missy
is the best in the world.
My dog Missy can jump
and loves to play.
My dog Missy is sweet
like Mr. K. from Holy Rosary.
My dog Missy can run away,
my dog Missy can be a pain.
My dog is smart
like a bee.
My dog is funny
just like me.

Steven Doyle, Grade 3
Holy Rosary School, NY

Mad

Checks so black,
Eyes so down.
It feels like night,
Stomping around.

Kristen Taylor, Grade 1
Home School, VA

Chess

Chess
Fun to play
You move the pieces
I feel excited
Chess

Daniel Hennig, Grade 2
Davis Elementary School, VA

Lovely as Can "Bee"

You're lovely as a bee
You're as sweet as honey
You're as pretty as the sea
You're richer than money

You're like a hive
I'm glad you're alive
No need to fear
I am glad that you're here

Hannah Jacobson, Grade 3
Klein Elementary School, PA

Summer

What is summer?
Is it warm?
Sun is shining down on me.
Tiny bunnies,
Hopping so happily.
Watch my feet
Fly up and down.
While I jump on and off the ground.
Name me "Queen of Summer!"
With a daffy gown
And lilied crown.

Madeleine Braksick, Grade 2
Montessori Children's Community School, PA

Puppies

Puppies are very playful.
Sometimes they are not careful.
They bump into things.
I think puppies dreams of having wings.
They dig fast to find a bone.
Puppies bark in a "Woof Woof" tone.
You give them treats when they do a trick.
Then, they lick your hand, lick, lick, lick!
Puppies learn to pounce by chasing a lace.
Puppies run fast when in a race.
I hope you learned more about puppies now!
Bow Wow!

Fiza Shaikh, Grade 2
Davis Elementary School, VA

Friends

Friends are very nice
Friends are extremely caring
Friends can really help

Mikaela Kaess, Grade 3
Christ the Teacher Catholic School, DE

My Favorite Wishes

I wish I had a new Bratz.
I wish I could go to Chuck E. Cheese
Sometimes, I wish that I could fly.
Most of all I wish that my grandma was alive.

Gabriela Menendez, Grade 1
Northeast Elementary School, NY

Snake
Snake
Brown, spotted
Slithering, eating, hunting
Snakes can bite
Dangerous
Soni Ayoung, Grade 1
Daniel J Flood Elementary School, PA

Spring
S ome trees get buds
P retty flowers bloom
R ain falls
I t is warmer
N ew animals are born
G ardens are planted
Anissa Bennett, Grade 1
Mount Jewett Elementary School, PA

Baby Sister
I love my sister.
She is my pumpkin pie.
She is cute in the tub.

I love my sister.
She is a baby.
Her name is Raegan.

She's adorable.
She is such a cutie.
I play with her...like peek a boo.
She flies in the air.
I love my sister!
MacKenzie Johnson, Grade 1
Williamstown Elementary School, NY

Colors
Red is the smell of roses
Brown is the taste of chocolate
Orange is the feeling of the sun
Blue is the sound of water
Black is the nighttime sky
What is your favorite color?
Alexandra Ibach, Grade 2
The Jefferson School, DE

Snow
The sun is outside
It is very cold and white
I play in the snow.
Ambria Capson, Grade 2
Long Meadow Elementary School, CT

Summer
Drinking lemonade
Sitting in the hot sunshine
Diving in the pool
Samantha Jones, Kindergarten
Montessori Academy of Lancaster, PA

The Earth
The Earth is like...
The world's largest bouncy ball
A colorful picture
The biggest grape ever seen
A giant clock
The Earth
Adam Jakubowski, Grade 3
Houghton Elementary School, MA

People
Boys, girls, they're people
Daddies, Mommies, they're people
Grandmas, Grandpas they're people
Cousins, Aunts, Uncles they're people
Families are everyone
Zoe Lach, Kindergarten
Nysmith School for the Gifted, VA

My Dog
My dog is brown,
with brown paws
and a brown tail.
She is a brown dog.
I love to play
with her on Saturday afternoon.
I hug her, she kisses me.
I love my dog.
Ashley Matteo, Grade 3
Holy Rosary School, NY

Nature
What does nature have?

Nature has lots of things
Like people, lots of trees,
Green grass, rivers and oceans.

People live in nature
Nature is so nice.
Nature gives us vegetables that people eat.

Nature is a big house where people live
Nature is the sky, sun and moon
Nature is blue, red and white

Syeda Hillary, Grade 3
Public School 152 School of Science & Technology, NY

Yellow
Yellow smells like daffodils
Blooming in the spring.

Yellow sounds like a school bus
Pulling up on the first day of school.

Yellow tastes like a fresh piece of corn on the cob
With butter dripping off of it.

Yellow feels like a sunny warm day
When I can play outside.

Yellow looks like a lion
Running around in the grass.

Brent Dunkle, Grade 3
Watsontown Elementary School, PA

Camping
Having fun with friends hiking in the woods
Getting firewood for the fire, swallowing down the goods
Telling scary stories about kids in the woods
Screaming their heads off about a flying octopus
Going to bed without a grin because you think the octopus struck again
You're as scared as a petrified tree
Thinking you're the size of a little little bean

Cullen Murin, Grade 3
Eisenhower Elementary School, PA

GameBoy
I like to play GameBoy
but I can't play it too much
then I will wear glasses and I don't like that
so I will play my GameBoy a little bit.

Yong Yu, Grade 2
Public School 205 Alexander Bell, NY

A Day in the Sun I Walk
A day in the sun I walk.
While the flowers bloom and light the room.
A day in the sun I walk.

A bright blue sky the sun sits in.
The boredom comes out, the fun comes in.
A day in the sun I walk.

Claire Nance, Grade 3
Trinity Christian School, VA

Sophie
Sophie is the greatest dog,
She is cute, soft and always licks her paws,
I love to kiss her nose while I scrunch my toes,
I'm glad she is a part of our family.

Emma Horne, Grade 2
Middle Gate Elementary School, CT

Snow and Clouds
The snow is falling.
It is a cold snowy day.
I wish for more snow.

Kim Galusha, Grade 2
Fonda-Fultonville Elementary School, NY

Love
Love is the key to a successful life.
Love is the image of every heart.
Love is the message to your world.
Love is the healer of every wound.
Love is the light of every soul.

How do I know this? I just do.
You will too…when you find the love in you.

Emily MaryAnn Torrey, Grade 3
St Patrick's School, ME

Go Back and Start Over Again

When I got up today everything was out of whack.
The first thing I did was trip over the cat.
The next thing I did was really quite silly.
I tripped over the broom and squished the kitty.
I never know when and I never know how.
I think I'm going to start over again now.

Kylie Jusseaume, Grade 3
Sacred Heart School, MA

Spring

One day I woke up, and my what a beautiful sight I saw,
The red, blue, pink flowers blooming by twos and threes

Rain beating down for what seemed like forever,
Drops glistening on the leaves like crystals,
O' see o' hear the rain drops falling one after another.
Glistening on leaves like crystals

The deer start sneaking and eating flowers from gardens,
Fawns are born with white spots all over,
Sometimes lying still in patches of moss,

Three sports begin soccer "Boom"
Baseball "Whack"
Field hockey "Whoosh"

Pretty birds, cardinals, goldfinches, hawks
All start appearing in yards and feeders,
Appear in threes and fours bringing again life to the outside world

East, rays of sunshine warming up the land
Like lava bubbling out of a volcano
With the sun, the glistening rain drops,
Oh what a beautiful day it is

Hannah Grant, Grade 3
Middle Gate Elementary School, CT

Yellow

If yellow had a taste it would taste like a lemon, really sour in winter.
If yellow had a sight it would look like a little girl playing on a yellow slide.
If yellow had a sound it would be someone laughing in the sunshine.
If yellow had a feel it would be like a soft, juicy lemon on a hot summer day.

Darren Webb, Grade 3
Watsontown Elementary School, PA

Abe Lincoln

A good lawyer
B ecame 16th president
E ven hated slavery

L iked to read
I n 1865 he died when he was shot
N eeded a tall hat for his papers
C abin was where he lived
O nly sometimes went to school
L ived in Kentucky
N ickname was 'Honest Abe'
Katelyn Kimble, Grade 2
Mount Jewett Elementary School, PA

Flowers

Colorful flowers
Visited by hungry bees
Dance in the warm sun
Emily Morrissey, Grade 2
Long Meadow Elementary School, CT

My Bath

I take a bath
In my tub

I rub, rub, rub
I scrub, scrub, scrub

I start with my face
Then my arms
Then to my stomach
And finally my feet

I soak my body
I splash the water

I get out of the tub
And look in the mirror

I am clean!
I am clean!
Eric Coleman, Grade 3
Bensley Elementary School, VA

Dog

Fluffy, cute, playful
Licking
Inside, everywhere, quickly
Isidora Papagiannakis, Grade 3
William Spyropoulos School, NY

After It Rains

Everything dripping,
With water in the air,
And it is so cold out there.
Mara Fulmer, Grade 3
Marlborough Elementary School, PA

Snowflakes

S nowing like it will
N ever
st **O** p
W ith
F lakes
L eaping
A ll around
different **K** inds landing on my cold
nos **E** as I
S lip down the path
Brittany Richardson, Grade 3
Hardwick Elementary School, VT

Fall

Fall looks like a colorful rainbow
Smells like a mug of hot chocolate with
marshmallows floating around
Tastes like warm apple pie
Sounds like honking geese flying south
Feels like it's time for warmer clothes
Devin Fadden, Grade 3
Hardwick Elementary School, VT

Ms. Hearst

Nice, smart
Helps all children
Teaches us to read
Friend
Dylan Keller, Grade 1
Mount Jewett Elementary School, PA

Spring

Spring is like,
A bunch of new growth in a garden.
Spring is like,
A time of year when all the fairies grow.
Spring is like,
New seeds of life giving joy.
Spring is like,
New life emerging from each person.
Spring is about joy and laughter,
New fairies coming into this world.
Spring is like,
New leaves on growing trees.
Spring is like,
Wearing cool new clothes.
Spring is like,
All about having fun!

Cheyenne Finkle-Green, Grade 2
Susan Odell Taylor School, NY

A Girl Named Bloom

There once was a wee girl named Bloom.
Who loved her birthday month, June.
Then she made a deal,
To not eat her meal.
She got sent to her locked up room.

Clio Kerr, Grade 2
Oakdale Elementary School, MD

Basketball

I am a basketball
I love being bounced between legs
Zipped back and forth
In important games

I love swooshes
And hate backboards

I'm spinning through the air like a ballerina
I am soaring over heads like a falcon
I'm resting on fingertips
Ready to be shot through the hoop

Sam LaCour, Grade 3
Meeting House Hill School, CT

Freedom Is Like...
Water running down a smooth rock.
A lion running in the crisp yellow plains.
An eagle soaring through the light blue sky.
A lizard sunning itself on a rock.
Max Dodge, Grade 2
St Christopher's School, VA

Dolphins, Dolphins, Everywhere
I love the dolphins like a teddy bear
they are soft and cute and they're everywhere
they jump in the water in a flash
and when I look at them they make a splash!
I miss dolphins so very much
that before I go I want to give them a kiss.
I love dolphins.
Nadiya Youssuf, Grade 2
Al-Rahmah School, MD

Spring and Flowers
At spring
A sunny day
We know that daisies are cool
They are pretty
They are blue
Blue like the sky
And violets are too!

That is nice
That is cool
And we all know that too!

Sometimes light colored daisies are girls
And dark ones are boys

Sometimes boys are mean
And sometimes they are nice

You never know
You never might

But that's okay
That's all I could ever say.
Saimy Fernandez, Grade 3
Bensley Elementary School, VA

Crystal Clear
As the crystal curves
into the sky
a shining light
comes above
and a happy smile
comes as winter goes
Devin Molloy, Grade 1
Harry Lee Cole School, MA

One Hundred
100 makes me feel old
Triple digits
So many cramps
Can't have any fun
I'm surprised I lived this long
Myles Brown, Grade 3
St Christopher's School, VA

Monkeys Are Wild
Swing, a monkey swings
Ow-ew-ih-ah he chatters
Dark brown arms flaying
Connor Fillmore, Grade 2
Killingly Memorial School, CT

Horseback Riding
I went horseback riding.
It was oh so quite exciting.
I went horseback riding.
I fell off with quite a flying.

I went horseback riding.
I was wearing my lucky ring.
I went horseback riding.
And it felt like I had wings.
Naomi Rose Lewis, Grade 3
Cambridge Day School, MD

Cat Hunter
Claws sharp as a knife
A cat is like a hunter
Chasing mice, meow!
Nicholas Malone, Grade 2
Killingly Memorial School, CT

A Cloud

A cloud is like...
A cotton pillow in the sky
A kite floating in the air
A shape of an animal above me
Cotton candy at the fair
Santa's beard
A cloud
Lesley Simpson, Grade 3
Houghton Elementary School, MA

Floating

Fluttering down,
Floating around.
Happening slowly,
Falling carefully,
And just as slowly.
Fall, fall, fall!
Elena Fandrich, Grade 3
Harrison Road Elementary School, VA

The Dog

The dog. The dog.
With a twinkle in its eye
Ears like silk
Nose so wet
As a river.
He's my dog.
Karina Korsh, Grade 3
Weston Intermediate School, CT

The Lights

The lights
are an angel
from Heaven
and God sent
that angel for
only one reason
and that
reason is...
for the world
to have
light!
Kendyl Harmeling, Grade 3
Middle Gate Elementary School, CT

When I'm Feeling Blue

When I'm feeling blue,
I know what to do.
I might take a walk
With a friend or two.
Whistle a tune,
Look at the moon,
Read a book to my sister
'Bout Winnie the Pooh.

When these things are through,
I know what to do.
Slippers off,
Go to bed,
Then I dream of you.
Kayla Bradley, Grade 3
General Wayne Elementary School, PA

Delicious Coffee

Coffee coffee in a pot
Be careful it's very hot
Kona coffee, chocolate latte
I can't wait until I get my coffee card
Waiting is just so hard
Gimme gimme my coffee card
Michael Sitver, Grade 3
Weston Intermediate School, CT

Why Is Spring Special...

Spring is special because it bring joy
to kids.
And moms.
And dads.
And God.
And it brings joy to everyone.
Rayne Troxell, Grade 2
Warwick River Christian School, VA

My Dad

My dad is the best
My dad is the greatest pal
nice, old, and friendly
Kevin Romero, Grade 3
Public School 148 Ruby Allen, NY

My Dreams
I often dream of me playing basketball!
And wishing for my team to win.
I think of who I should pass it to in different situations.
And, when I dream we always win
I feel great when I do good
I often dream of my playing basketball!

Ryan Shadoan, Grade 3
Oakdale Elementary School, MD

Ode to Cerberus
Cerberus was a three-headed dog,
He wouldn't let anybody into the underworld.
If you tried, you would have to be strong to get by him.
You could only get in if you played music like Orpheus
or overpowered him like Hercules.

Jarred Doody, Grade 3
Harrison Road Elementary School, VA

Lucy
Lucy is 17 and really hates jelly beans.
She has good grades in school, she doesn't play pool.
She picked out a bowling ball and knocked into a wall.
She had a kidney stone and loves the Ramones.
She has funny teachers that have a lot of features.
I think she's a great sister that once in a while gets bad blisters.

Izzy Hanson-Johnston, Grade 2
Public School 116 Mary L Murray School, NY

Secret
I have a little secret that I will never tell,
You might make a fool of me if you knew as well.
This little secret is safe and sound at home,
Tucked inside the garden gnome!

Crosbie Marine, Grade 3
New Canaan Country School, CT

If I Were a Snowflake
If I were a snowflake…
I would glide in the air, drift back and forth.
If I were a snowflake…
I would land on a human's hand and peacefully evaporate,
knowing that I will one day come to life.

Imani-Grace King, Grade 3
Elkridge Elementary School, MD

I'm Sick

I have a big bad cold,
My scarf and mittens are sold.
My bed I am in,
No more medicine.
Then I threw away my apple core,
But then I felt quite sore.
It was an awful day!
But my friend came to play.
I said "where have you been?"
My friend said "let's go play!"
I said "I can't I'm sick."
"Oh! Look who delivered the medicine!"

Sophia Plant, Grade 2
Roger E Wellington School, MA

Spring

Blue sky, you're so bright —
You make me want to fly my kite!
I hear bees,
I see flowers, by my knees;
Green grass on the ground,
Kids on the merry-go-round

Micah Bell, Grade 2
Georgetown East Elementary School, MD

The Seasons

Winter is cold.
Summer is hot.
Fall and spring
Are somewhere in between.
I don't know which one I like better,
Summer, spring, winter, or fall.
I really like them all.
I really don't know what to do.
I have to answer now.
I know what I'll do.
I'll say I like them all.
Without winter there can be no snow.
Without summer there can be no rain to flow.
Without fall or spring what will be?
Oh, I guess they're all a part of me!

Emily Gambardello, Grade 3
Sacred Heart School, MA

Water

Water
blue, heavy, thin
moving, floating
water is good to drink
Water
Chris Godfrey, Grade 2
Hyman Fine Elementary School, MA

School

School is so cool
But it is not for fools
It's such a blast
Even though I've gotten an F in the past

I don't mind the tests
But I do try my best
My teacher rules
She used to go to this school

I love lunch
Because I love to munch
But my desk is a mess
I don't pay attention, I guess
Sydnie Rager, Grade 3
Klein Elementary School, PA

A Rain Drop!

Damp, watery, moist,
"Look out quick get an umbrella
It's going to rain!!!"
Splish splash
Splish splash
Splish splash
Rain
Molly McCoubrey, Grade 2
Hyman Fine Elementary School, MA

Birds

Birds make lots of noise.
They keep on flying around.
A bird makes a nest.
Kaelen Encarnacion, Grade 1
St Mary's Elementary School, MA

Zebras

Z ig zags on the skin
E verywhere
B right brains
R unning from enemies
A frica is where they live
Darius Bopp, Grade 2
McQuistion Elementary School, PA

Cute Little Shapes

Cube can stack,
Cylinder can too,
But sphere can only roll.

Cone can stack if
Cylinder is there,
But sphere can only roll.

All the prisms can flip,
But sphere can only roll.

Pyramid can slide,
But sphere can only roll.
So sphere is left out!
Eddie Godino, Grade 2
St Rose Elementary School, CT

Winter

In winter I skate
In winter I go sledding
In winter it snows.
Alison Reilly, Grade 2
Long Meadow Elementary School, CT

See All You See

A tree is a tree,
And a bee is a bee,
There are many new things to see.

When you walk in the park,
And you see all you see,
You get the feeling,
That you are free.
Alex Samaha, Grade 3
John Ward Elementary School, MA

Spring

I like spring
During spring it is cool.
During spring I play on a swing
I don't have to go to school.
Spring is a fun season
I play in the spring all day.
The sun comes out in the spring
I love to stay outside and play.

Jedaiah Perrier, Grade 3
Little Flower Day Care Center and Prep School, NY

Green Is...

Green is cold watermelon on a hot summer day
Green is peas being boiled on a hot stove
Green is a tasty lime lollipop being sold on a hot summer day
Green is a pond with frogs croaking with peepers singing on a spring night
Green is soft moss sitting in a yard under a sour apple tree
Green is a pine tree covered with snow

Richard Gardner, Grade 3
Watsontown Elementary School, PA

My Family

I have a mother who likes blue
I have a father too
I have a brother who likes to play
And we play all day

My aunt has a dog too
I give their dog a ball that is blue
We all have so much fun
My family is number one!

Megan Yip, Grade 2
Public School 205Q Alexander Graham Bell, NY

My Cat Max

Even if I had six cats.
My favorite one is Max.
He's not too big, he's not too small.
He's not too anything at all.
He's lovable and huggable and has the softest fur.
And that is why I cannot lie.
My favorite cat is Max.

David Voss, Grade 3
George Grant Mason Elementary School, NY

Kitty Adoption

I found a kitty
At the city pound
A tiny creature
My hand wrapped around
I held it up
Against my cheek
And I felt his
Wild heart beat
It touched me
With his icy nose
we liked each other
From our heads to toes.

Krystal Rodriguez, Grade 3
Public School 65 Mother Hale Academy, NY

Games

G alaxy
A pples to apples
M ummies gold
E veryone plays games
S cattergories

Robert Dukat, Grade 2
Bucks County Country Day School, PA

Pudding

P ut whipped cream on your pudding.
U p the aisle is the pudding.
D elicious chocolate in every spoonful.
D elightful pudding once a week.
I love pudding.
N o other dessert tastes as good as pudding.
G ood people deserve a cup of pudding.

Kaleigh Joyce, Grade 3
Sacred Heart School, MA

Spring

Spring
Flowers, sun
Birds, nesting, Halloween, cold
Raking, jumping, Thanksgiving
Leaves, windy
Fall

Madeline Jones, Grade 3
Our Mother of Perpetual Help School, PA

Fall

Leaves fall off the trees
Floating gently to the ground
Early snow in the morn

Michael Warner, Grade 2
Killingly Memorial School, CT

Emeralds

Emeralds
red, cool
shining, poisoning, coloring
black, dark
emeralds

Sean Sullivan, Grade 1
Seneca Academy, MD

Fall Is...

Seeing rain falling,
Hearing leaves crunching,
Smelling turkey cooking,
Tasting apple pie,
Touching flowers.

Mason Glasco, Grade 1
St Christopher's School, VA

Halloween

Halloween
Candy, costume, nighttime
Trick or treat
I am eating candy
Scary night

Rene Polley, Grade 2
St Rosalia Academy, PA

Friends

There are so many friends
For you to meet
If you know that
You're in for a treat
You must say, "Hi," and
"How do you do?"
Here's the problem
I've only got two.

Matthew Rohrbaugh, Grade 3
Berry Elementary School, MD

The World Can Be a Better Place
The world can be more
Beautiful, no matter what they say
The world can be more beautiful
In many different ways.
The world will be more beautiful I say
And I will help in many different ways.
I will help kids learn to speak
I will help kids in many different ways
Different ways
To make the world a better place to live.

Aryana daSilva, Grade 3
Acushnet Elementary School, MA

My Rainbow
Red is the rose in my garden.
Orange is the sunset over the sea.
Yellow is the pencil I am writing with.
Green is the grass in my lawn.
Blue is the water in my pond.
Violet is the flower on my table.

Zoe Menendez, Grade 3
Milford Elementary School - Heron Pond, NH

Power Rangers
Power Rangers are really powerful!
If they were real, they would help save lives.
My favorite is the Black Power Ranger
Because he is the most powerful.

Seth Rettinger, Kindergarten
South Side Elementary School, PA

The Sun
A vast fireball,
Sprouting flames and magma from its core.
A million times larger than Earth,
Maybe more!

Liquid fire escapes madly
From its red-hot face.
I would not like to be there,
What a fiery place!

Frédéric Gagliolo, Grade 3
Jamestown Elementary School, VA

My Room

My room is…
comfortable
to be in,

I get to be
alone when
I am sleeping

and to get away from my
SISTERS!!!

I get my own stuff,
and I get to
read read read!

My room!

Caroline Tripodi, Grade 2
Dr Samuel C Eveleth School, MA

Rain

Play in the puddles.
Rain drizzles down on the ground.
Have fun in the rain.

Mano Sundaresan, Grade 3
Cornerstone Academy, MA

Halloween

We see monsters.
And we smell candy.
We hear screams.
And we taste chocolate candy bars.
We touch the doorbell, and we scream.
That's what you do on Halloween!

Jacob Pitney, Grade 2
St Christopher's School, VA

Dear Grass

Dear Grass,
You are the happy bug's home.
You are the sun's bed.
You are the smiling world's hair.
The end

Ryan Sweeney, Grade 1
Glover Elementary School, MA

Spring

A soft cozy nest.
Her eggs hatch in the big world.
They are very safe.

Jordan Scott, Grade 3
West Branch School, PA

Flowers Are Nice

Roses are red.
Violets are blue.
I am so pretty
And so are you.
You are so nice.
I love to learn.
I love flowers.
You love violets.
We love daisies.
We love you!

Anastasia Perez, Grade 2
Ulysses Byas Elementary School, NY

Valentine's Day

I made a Valentine
For a very special person
With little hearts and big hearts
Tall hearts and small hearts
Outlined with lacy flowers
And paper flowers too
But one thing I forgot is
That I made it for you!!

Brittany Seward, Grade 3
Bensley Elementary School, VA

No Dogs at School

Sarah,
don't bring your dog to school.
Cuz if you do,
I'll tell on you.
So leave him home.
Give him a bone.
And play with him
when you get home.

Vanessa Heidrick, Grade 3
Frenchtown School, RI

Primary Colors

Red, red like a crisp apple in the dawn of the fall.
Red, red like a fox in a tomato patch hiding.

Blue, blue like a bulging patch of blueberries in the twilight of the summer.
Blue, blue like a dolphin in the ocean diving.

Yellow, yellow like a scrumptious banana ripe and ready to eat in the afternoon
    of the spring.
Yellow, yellow like a bee in a daffodil drinking sweet pollen.

Jordan Helfand, Grade 3
Memorial-Spaulding Elementary School, MA

Pink

Pink sounds like a soft whisper coming from two little girls as they share a secret
Pink tastes like sweet cotton candy at the fair
Pink feels like a soft bunny hopping through my yard
Pink smells like the sweet pink blossoms blooming in my garden
Pink looks like a beautiful pink rose growing in the sun room

Gracie Maneval, Grade 3
Watsontown Elementary School, PA

Red

My favorite color is red.
When I think of the color red I think of my heart, fire, hearts, and apples.
Sometimes I wish the world were red.

Keilan Lopez, Grade 2
Ulysses Byas Elementary School, NY

My Shirt

It is
pink

It says
Sweet Princess

It has a
crown

It has a
bow

My Shirt

Annika Khajuria, Kindergarten
Plainview-Old Bethpage Kindergarten Center, NY

The Northern Star
In the night it shines a light
over the hills and down the street.
You see it up there glowing so bright.
It's the Northern Star in the night.

It glows and glows and glows all night.
It shows the way north.
This is the star that helped
Harriet Tubman
go to freedom.
It's a special star.
It's glowing bright
every night.
Leanne Doherty, Grade 2
Dr Samuel C Eveleth School, MA

Snow
When I wake up what did I see
Everything was white to me
I got dressed
Went outside really fast
I like to have snowball fights
I throw with all my might
Thomas Casalino, Grade 3
Public School 5, NY

Pizza
Pizza —
Tasty, yummy
Bubbly, hot, cheesy
I like the hot sauce and cheese.
Tasty
Robert Dawson, Grade 3
Afton Elementary School, NY

Basketball
Basketball
Orange, bouncy
Bouncing, throwing, passing
Goes flying in the hoop
Dribbles
Jaelyn Hollitt, Grade 1
Daniel J Flood Elementary School, PA

Baseball
Baseball
Slide, run
Fielding, hitting, pitching
I pitch fast balls
Baseball
Matthew Furtado, Grade 2
Hyman Fine Elementary School, MA

The Horse
There were horses
From all different sources:
Brown, white, and black.
Oh, there's something he lacks!
I don't know what to do!
I could train him!
I will have a lot of pain
But, I won't give him away.
Carolyn DelRossi, Grade 2
St Rose Elementary School, CT

Snakes
Snakes
  slithery, dry,
hiss,
  getting close, creeping,
                it snatches
  really, really fast
                Killer.
Christian Griffith, Grade 3
Afton Elementary School, NY

Sun
Makes hot fire in sky
The sun is yellow and red
The sun makes hot light.
Douglas Schmiedel, Grade 2
Long Meadow Elementary School, CT

Tigers
In the rain forest
Sleeping in a dark cool cave
In the cold morning.
Jeenera Hossain, Grade 1
Public School 122 Mamie Fay, NY

Mom

Mom I love you
You gave birth to me
You take care of me
You are my soulmate
We play
We laugh
We have fun
You are my mother

Trenis Dantzler, Grade 2
Public School 65 Mother Hale Academy, NY

Love

Love is good.
Love is exciting.
Love is what you have in your body.
Love is what you will have every day.
Love is what you have right here right now.
Love you will always have.

Gustavo Hernandez, Grade 3
Public School 131, NY

What Am I?

I am an insect.
I eat cloth.
What am I?
I am a moth.
There are lots of other things to be,
But today I'm just a moth, you see.

Sasha Edwards, Grade 2
Washington Park Elementary School, PA

A Walk in the Wind

It was windy.
The wind was blowing on our body.
The wind was going east.
My leaves blew away.
The wind sounded like an ocean.
I heard birds singing.
It looked like a tornado was coming.
Outside the school, the swings were blowing
When I walked in the wind.

Rubi Marquez, Grade 2
Northeast Elementary School, NY

Purple
Have you ever tasted purple?
Purple tastes like plums in the summer on a hot day.

Have you ever seen purple?
Purple looks like a violet in the spring.

Have you ever smelled purple?
Purple smells like wet paint in my bedroom.

How does purple sound?
Purple sounds like the blues at a jazz club.

Have you ever felt purple?
Purple feels like gooey blueberry muffin dough in your hand.

Kassandra Bachman, Grade 3
Watsontown Elementary School, PA

Dolphin
Dolphin, dolphin how do you live under water I ask.
Why do you jump so high in the sky?
Why do you eat fish dolphin why?
I live under water because I have a blowhole.
I jump to blow water and suck in air.
I eat fish to survive.
Living under water is quite easy you know.

Duncan Rogers, Grade 3
St Christopher's School, VA

Fall
Leaves are gold, orange, brown, and yellow in the fall
The trees are bare and very tall
I rake a big heap of leaves
They just fly around in the cool breeze
In fall I love to weave every day
I wish fall would never go away.

Deanna Leung, Grade 3
Sacred Heart School, MA

The Sky
The sky is blue
It reflects from the ocean
The sun makes it brighter

Juwan Isidore, Grade 3
Public School 23 Carter G Woodson School, NY

You Never Want a Spanky
There was a boy named Frankie.
He was really, really cranky!
He was cranky
Cause his mommy gave him a spanky.
So that's why he was cranky.
Good thing he had a hanky!

Sara Shomgard, Grade 2
Cornwall Terrace Elementary School, PA

A Bunny Named Goo
There once was a bunny named Goo,
He liked to crawl in a shoe,
A person came along
And saw what was wrong,
There was the bunny named Goo in his shoe.

Gigi Minsky, Grade 2
Cabot Elementary School, MA

Ballet
Just give it a chance!
Pink leotards, tutus and ballet shoes.
You learn a lot of moves.
With ribbons and bows
Don't forget to point your toes!
Pirouettes, grand jetes and arabesques
All put you to the test!

Angela Preziuso, Grade 3
Christ the Teacher Catholic School, DE

Emma, the Kitten
E very place Korin goes, she wants to go
M y sister's kitten
M eows
A shy kitten

Hannah Ross, Grade 3
Mount Jewett Elementary School, PA

The Earth Is Sweet
Candy is sweet. Candy is good
and so are you and my family is too.
And the whole world is too and the sunset too.

Bruce Sapp, Grade 2
Media Childrens House Montessori, PA

Horse

I saw a horse that was white.
It was a stallion
A horse in the sky.

When the horse is sad it gets dark.
When it cries, it is raining
And I have to go inside.

In the morning my horse is gone
But I will see something else
Clouds are like that, you know.

Cassidy Shanhai, Grade 3
Growing Life Christian Academy, NY

Hurry Mousie!

Hurry mousie! Do be quick!
Hope the tabby cat is really sick.
Don't take chances,
Don't get caught!
Pray you will get breaks a lot.
Out of your hole,
Quick, quick quick.
What do you feel on your neck,
A lick?
Tabby cat got you!
Oh no! Oh no!
Hope you'll be fast,
And he'll be slow.
You escaped,
Hooray! Hooray!
Now that you're safe,
Be on your way.
Bye, bye mousie,
When we meet again.
Hope you'll be my best friend.

Alex Hayes, Grade 3
Jamestown Elementary School, VA

Spring

The magic flowers
The frisky squirrels on the bark
The new baby leaves

Carly Ng, Grade 2
Long Meadow Elementary School, CT

Turtles

Lays eggs under sand
They can come out of their shell
Swim in the ocean.

Elijah Hawkins, Grade 2
Killingly Memorial School, CT

Winter

Winter is cold,
And the trees are as bold
As an 80-year-old man.
Snow is falling and
Snowballs are calling…
Silently, waiting patiently to be made
Kids are playing
And snowballs are laying
After flying by my window…
Crash!!!

Carly Abbott, Grade 3
Ridge Park Elementary School, PA

Baseball!

B atting and hitting the ball.
A mazing pitches.
S uper steals.
E xtra innings to play!
B last a homerun.
A wesome hits.
L ast all the way through.
L ose or win just have fun!

Sean Kennedy, Grade 3
Central Avenue School, CT

The Bad Twister

There was a team on the soccer field.
Then a bad twister came.
It felt very windy.
So, we went into the breakhouse
And found a place near no windows.
We crouched down into a little ball.
Cover your heads!
Until the twister stops.

Isaac Martin, Kindergarten
South Side Elementary School, PA

Spring

D aisies come up
A nts come out
L adybugs come out
E arthworms come up

R ain
E xcited for spring to come
I like to build with Legos in the spring
D affodils come up

Dale Reid, Grade 3
Susquehanna Community Elementary School, PA

Black

Black is the color of a stormy day.
Black is a color of the night we say.
And it can also be a boot.
Black can be the color of a marker.
It can be also a dog.
It is the color of the end of a nice little fire,
    when all is left is the pitch black color of the wood.
After the rain comes down, the dirt is black.
Black is the color of colored paper.
Black is also the color of a water bottle case.
Black is the color of a shirt.
Black is the color of sweat pants.
Black is the color of my backpack.
Black is the color of nighttime dresses
    and also the color of people's eye makeup.
It can be the color of a Dell computer.
Black is the color when a banana gets very stale.
Black is the color of pepper that you put on your food.
Black is the color of some paint and some balls.
Black is the color of the big sky.

Billy Masciovecchio, Grade 3
Eli Terry School, CT

What Is Yellow?

Yellow tastes like sour lemons that I drink in lemonade in the hot summer.
Yellow sounds like cute quacking ducks in the spring.
Yellow smells like sweet blooming buttercups in a meadow.
Yellow feels like golden butter melting on a hot potato.
Yellow looks like the hot sun on a warm summer day.

Breanna Herriman, Grade 3
Watsontown Elementary School, PA

Teeth
Teeth should be clean,
Cavities are mean,
Clean them three times a day,
If you may.
Laura Wicker, Grade 2
Washington Park Elementary School, PA

Snowflake, Snowflake
Snowflake, snowflake
In the air,
You travel from here to there.
In the night,
You look like light.
Snowflake, snowflake
Brandon Markiewicz, Grade 2
St Clement Mary Hofbauer School, MD

My Family
My mom is pretty as a rose
Sometimes my mom buys too many clothes.
My dad is really cool
One day I hope my dad can rule.

My sister is very weird
With her clothes as fuzzy as a beard.
My other sister is very funny
She is like a crazy bunny.

One of my sisters has a fish named Betty
She has a little bear named Teddy
Then there's me, C.J. the Great
The only boy, I guess that's fate!
Conner Coppersmith, Grade 3
Klein Elementary School, PA

Spring
S unny days with
s P rinkling showers creating
R ainbows bending across the sky
I nside I play
waiti N g for sunny times
a G ain
Shania Collins, Grade 3
Hardwick Elementary School, VT

Seashell
See the ripples
In the sand
Not many but grand.
Shiny as the amber sky
Turn it and you will see.
A new land of great discovery
You will also see what I see
I see snow that shines.
Maddie Casey, Grade 1
Harry Lee Cole School, MA

Best Friends
B usy bee buzzing.
E asy game.
S o let's play.
T o the park.

F ire in the hole.
R un from the trigger!
I n the house!
E veryone is having fun.
N o don't leave me!
D o you want to play?
S o much fun!
Angel Kennedy, Grade 3
Central Avenue School, CT

My Funny Puppy!
Funny my puppy
Plays fetch dropping slimy ball
Goes in house and eats
Reneé Poirier, Grade 2
Killingly Memorial School, CT

Christmas
Christmas
Fun, exciting
Play, talk, give
I get many presents
Walk, run, sleep
Cold, icy
Santa
Meaghan FitzGerald, Grade 3
St Joseph School, NY

Cats

Cats are nice and cuddly.
They are very good pets.
Their fur is real soft.
They won't scratch you
Unless you are being mean to them.
You can play with them all the time.
They are very cute.

Madison Beardmore, Kindergarten
South Side Elementary School, PA

Friends

Friends come in threes
Friends come in twos
Friends will come from everywhere
Just to be with you!

Gillian Orlando-Milbauer, Grade 3
James M Curley Elementary School, MA

Tacos

Yummy tacos Yummy
Too many in my tummy
You can bake
Then you'll start to ache.

Adelle Pitsas, Grade 3
Milford Elementary School - Heron Pond, NH

It's the Best

The zoo is a fun place to be.
There is much to do and plenty to see!
Lions, tigers and snow leopards are here,
And seals, elephants and hippos too!
So, come to the zoo,
And give all a good cheer!

Leanne McKeown, Grade 3
Christ the King School, NY

Spring

The grass is green
The birds go "tweet"
The flowers are bright
And smell very neat.

Alana Luppino, Grade 2
Washington Park Elementary School, PA

Pizza
Pizza
Red, triangle
Eating, chewing, delivering
My favorite food to eat
Good
Robb McClay, Grade 1
Daniel J Flood Elementary School, PA

Cats and Kittens
Cat
Cuddly, cute
Runs, hides, purrs
They are so furry
Scratch, jump, meow
Small, friendly
Kitten
Francesca Zambrano, Grade 3
St Joseph School, NY

Pride
Cats stroll
With their necks holding
Up the world
Puffed high with pride
Like queens and kings
I think
The animal kingdom
Would be shocked
If they walked with their necks down

It would be a
Depressed
Way to lead.
Ruby Klein, Grade 3
Fulton Avenue School #8, NY

Diving
ocean, goggles
seeing, floating, snorkeling
I see the beautiful gold fish
swimming
Mario Malagisi, Grade 2
Marvin Elementary School, CT

A Snow Day
When you
wake up
look out your window.
What do you see?
Snow!
Snow!
Snow!
It must be a snow day!
No school!
Kids playing in the snow.
Snowmen!
When you get in
get some hot chocolate.
A Snow Day.
Crew Whittier, Grade 2
Dr Samuel C Eveleth School, MA

Snakes
Snakes shed.
Snakes have fangs.
Some snakes have poison.
Some snakes hide under rocks.
I like snakes!
Jason Cajamarca, Grade 1
Northeast Elementary School, NY

Teddy
My daddy bought me a teddy bear,
He has soft brown curly hair.
I take him to bed with me every night,
And I squeeze him very tight.
Aimée Teitelbaum, Grade 3
Our Lady of Hope School, NY

Trains
T rains carry people place to place
R unning on train tracks
A round bends
I n the train station
N ighttime trains go fast
S wishing past trees
Nicholas Kramer, Kindergarten
Montessori Academy of Lancaster, PA

Spring

The flowers start to bloom
Inside my room.
The sun is so fun.
It makes me want to run.
I do not like the shine
It makes me want to whine.

Ashley Fisk, Grade 3
Susquehanna Community Elementary School, PA

Spring

S is for sunflower.
P is for planting seeds.
R is for rain falling.
I is for insects flying.
N is for nests in trees.
G is for gardening flowers.

Diamond Headlam, Grade 2
Little Flower Day Care Center and Prep School, NY

Gum

My gum
has feelings
same as you
when it is chewed
it says ew
when it is
spit out and
stepped on
it is gone

Alexandra Simon, Grade 3
Public School 152 School of Science & Technology, NY

Summer

Summer is the best season of the year.
The weather is hot and humid.
The sun is bright and shiny.
It is time to splash all your energy in the water.
It is time to swim and have fun on the beach or the pool.
It is time to have fun with families and friends.
It is time to enjoy without having to go to school.
Summer is the best season of the year.
I love the summer season.

Christopher Li, Grade 3
Public School 131, NY

Fashion

F ashion is
A
S tyle that I like to
H ave
I like to look hip
O n the runway and hope I
N ever fall.

Aalayh Alston, Grade 2
Ulysses Byas Elementary School, NY

Winter

Winter
Bears hibernate
Birds fly south
Squirrels collect many nuts
Snowy

Liam Carey, Kindergarten
St Stephen's School, NY

Maybe in a Nightmare

Maybe in a nightmare,
But not in a dream.
Maybe in a town,
Where it may seem true.
I'm trusting you.
You're blaming me.
There's no reason,
You will see.
I want a difference.
So do you.
Clouds soaring in your eyes,
When they come
Is a surprise.
Maybe in a nightmare,
But not in a dream.

Emma Roush, Grade 1
John Ward Elementary School, MA

Puppies

small furry and cute
like to go outside and play
they make a big mess.

Jazmin Juarez, Grade 2
Public School 148 Ruby Allen, NY

Panda

Panda
Panda party
Pandas like to play much
Pandas sometimes sleep up in trees
Bamboo

Thomas Ibach, Grade 2
The Jefferson School, DE

The Wind of the World

Once I was by the door
singing by the wind of the world.
Now is the time to say goodbye forever.
Then I thought about you.
You are so sweet to my heart.
Don't come to me
I'll come to you — forever.

Kyra Taylor, Grade 2
Hickory Elementary School, VA

Cats

I love my cats.
My cats play with bats.
They're very sweet.
They can stand on their back feet.
They are white.
They chase my kite.
They are nice.
They don't have lice.
They sleep with me.
They never got stung by a bee.
I love my cats.

Olivia Martin, Grade 3
Weld Elementary School, ME

Freedom Bell

The 4th of July is when fireworks fly
And parties and parades start, too!

We celebrate freedom
Flags wave in the wind
And we wear red, white, and blue!

Madeline Sulich, Grade 3
Meeting House Hill School, CT

Bernie

My dad had a bunny named Bernie,
Who had the middle name Ernie.
He hopped all around,
All over the ground.
Got heat stroke and got put on a gurney.

Christine Meder, Grade 3
Marlborough Elementary School, PA

Strategies

S canning and skimming
T hinking carefully about the best answer
R ereading the passages to look for clues
A lways digging for details
T rying to build stamina
E ncourage everyone to explain
G uessing some of the questions
I s important to scan the questions first
E liminating what doesn't make sense
S earching for evidence to answer questions

Ms. Betances' Class, Grade 3
Public School 131, NY

Santa

Santa's nose is red.
Santa is a jolly guy.
Santa is coming.

Jamie Kasza, Grade 2
Fonda-Fultonville Elementary School, NY

Flowers

I love the flowers that shine in the spring
What beauty they will bring

They bring color to the spring
When the kids love to sing

They are so beautiful in bloom
In the summer it will be here soon

That is why it is so clear
I love them any, any time of year

Ashleigh Nicholl, Grade 3
Klein Elementary School, PA

Pansies

Pansies
Blooming, picking
Pretty, bright, purple
Put them in a vase
Pansies
May Bennett, Grade 2
St Clement Mary Hofbauer School, MD

Sports

Sports are my favorite thing in life.
Sometimes it gets me into some serious fights.

Ice hockey is what I play the most.
We all play it here on the east coast.

Baseball is also really quite fun.
It is great to play in the real hot sun.

Sports fill my life with joy.
And make me a very happy boy.
Robert Hines, Grade 3
Sacred Heart School, MA

The Eagle

Big, black and white eagle,
quiet and still,
on top of a tall, old, brown tree.
Sitting in its nest,
staring at a big, fat squirrel,
scampering across the hot beach.
Olivia Muse, Grade 2
Montessori Children's Community School, PA

Froggy

Froggy Froggy,
On the ground;
Froggy Froggy
Turn around;
Froggy Froggy,
You're so sweet;
Let's go hopping,
On our feet!
Lucy Lupinek, Grade 2
Georgetown East Elementary School, MD

Holiday Heroes

I love the Easter Bunny
Because he is very funny
He is so bright and sunny
He has a lot of money

Santa is such a guy
But he is also very sly
He is always on the fly
I see him in the sky

Mr. Leprechaun is magic
He can cause a bit of tragic
He is very quick
He does funny tricks
Miriam Syed, Grade 3
Klein Elementary School, PA

Neysa

N ice as a kitten
E asy to scare
Y ou can
S ee her
A s a little bear
Ashley Braungard, Grade 3
Afton Elementary School, NY

Dog

Dog
Cute, kind
Eating, loving, chewing
Getting into trouble
Kessie
Victoria Trost, Grade 3
St Rosalia Academy, PA

Spring

S kip and run!
P eople play.
R ick and I ride scooters.
I ride my bike.
N ice flowers grow.
G ive flowers water.
Matthew Frenkel, Grade 1
Adelphi Academy, NY

Apples

A pples are really good protein.
P lease, oh, did you know that apples help your breath?
P eople really like apples.
L ads love apples to make them big and strong.
E at apples and you will grow big and strong.
S o I hope you know all about apples.

Robert Thompson-Hines, Grade 3
Sacred Heart School, MA

Snowy Days

We started our day with a nice warm breakfast.
We watched the snow fall outside.
As my mother walked out of the room
I saw the beautiful snow falling
from the big tree in our backyard.
Then the snow started coming toward our home.
As I sat in the window I watched the squirrels
sitting on the bird feeder.
I looked over and saw my cat Turbo,
he looked so comfortable by the fire.
So this is why I love snowy days so much
because we all get to cuddle up next to the fire...

Amanda Campbell, Kindergarten
Fannie E Proctor School, MA

Snow Dog

My dog was in his bed,
Then suddenly he was on a sled!
Right then he saw an owl,
Next he saw a wolf howl.
He saw a bunch of kittens,
They were all holding mittens.
Right then he dropped his bow,
Lying there, in the snow.
Then he saw a really cool ski,
Right after that he hit a tree.
He had to go tinkle,
But then he saw snow sprinkle.
After he caught a snowflake,
He went inside to bake.
When he finished baking, he went out to go play,
But then he noticed that the day had gone away.

Brian Mays, Grade 3
St Catherine Laboure School, PA

What Friends Are

F eelings to talk about
R ight there when you need them
I nside you when you miss them
E veryone has a friend
N obody like your friends
D ays with friends
S ometimes away from you
"**H** ello," they say to you
I love my friends
P laying with your friends

Isabella Cataldo, Grade 3
Frenchtown School, RI

The Nature Wind Blows

Butterflies are free.
Autumn leaves fall straight down low.
Birds fly all around.

Matt Dresselhouse, Grade 3
Frenchtown School, RI

Sea Shore

Shells on the beach
Birds flapping their wings
Up and down

Sunset the color of peach
Waves beating
Upon rocks, pounding
On the sea shore

Caroline Dinh, Grade 2
Mary Matula Elementary School, MD

Love Is...

A romantic evening
Cupid aiming an arrow
Dancing around at a wedding
Hearts floating around two people
Two people on a special date
A romantic honeymoon
Two people kissing
Laughter in the air

Monica Legere, Grade 3
Enfield Station School, ME

Donuts!

Donuts are round,
Just like balls.
Donuts taste so good,
It feels like heaven in your mouth.
They have sprinkles, and chocolate,
Cream, and jelly too,
Donuts feel good in your belly,
Woo-hoo!

Christine DeRosa, Grade 3
Public School 5, NY

Cherry

Cherry
Red yummy
Rolling growing sparkling
Taste very delicious
Fruit

Veronica Moore, Grade 3
Greenock Elementary School, PA

The New Girl in School

We met a very nice girl.
Who made us a very nice curl.
We play with her every day.
So we can help her play.
Her hair is so nice.
That people would stop and stare.
Ha!!!

Tzipporah Marchette, Grade 2
Shaloh House Hebrew Day School, MA

Rain Forest

If I lived in the forest,
I would have no tourists.
I would live in a hut,
And have a pet mutt.
Bugs I would eat,
Because berries are too sweet.
It's hot, rainy, and wet,
Never cold I would get.
What a life it would be,
As I would be free.

Colby Hill, Grade 3
Graham Intermediate School, VA

About Me
I like to ride my bike.
I like to play video games.
I like to eat ice cream.
But, I don't like to cry in front of people.

Darius Garcia, Grade 1
Northeast Elementary School, NY

Spring
Spring is great, spring is neat.
That, I don't think needs repeat.
Trees grow big, birds fly high,
Clouds make figures in the sky.
Flowers bloom, people play,
That all happens every day.
It's so great, it won't rest,
Don't you know that spring's the best?

Andrea Wang, Grade 3
Memorial-Spaulding Elementary School, MA

Roller Coaster
Roller coasters swirl
And they twirl
They go up
And they go down
They go all around.

Roller coasters are fun
And some are not
But that does not matter to me a lot!

The kids smile
The grown-ups frown
They don't like it when it goes all around.

The teenagers are in the middle
That sounds like fiddle.

I like roller coasters
Some people do not
Why should I care
I think I need to go to the fair!

Celina Wickham, Grade 3
Bensley Elementary School, VA

Springtime
Springtime is a time when flowers pop out of the earth.
In the springtime you can hear the birds sing.
Spring is a time when you can play and have fun.

Rackean Roberts, Kindergarten
Little Flower Day Care Center and Prep School, NY

Good Lady Rose
Rosa Parks bloomed into a rose
Like the soft swirly part she was kind,
She was a nice lady from her head to the top of her toes.

Like the thorn on a rose
Rosa Parks did not move her seat on the bus,
She was brave from her head to the top of her toes.

Like a rose blooming in the spring,
Rosa Parks began the civil rights movement,
She was a good leader from her head to the tops of her toes.

Like the swirly top of a rose
Rosa Parks loved all types of people,
She was loving from her head to the top of her toes.

Lauren Davis, Grade 2
Urban League of Pittsburgh Charter School, PA

Sun
It is yellow,
It is a circle and bright.
It comes in the day,
It is very hot too.
It is nature,
It's like a fire ball.
It's very, very nice,
And it's in the sky.

Nicole Barnes, Grade 3
Susquehanna Community Elementary School, PA

Trees in the Seasons
Fall is the time when the leaves fall.
Winter is the time when the trees are bare.
Spring is the time when the trees grow.
And summer is the time when the trees are there.

Aisha Marfani, Grade 3
Al-Rahmah School, MD

Winter

Winter is fun.
So are you.
I wish winter was now.
We can go sledding.
The winter is when it snows.

Haley King, Grade 1
Media Childrens House Montessori, PA

Washington

W as a good soldier
A merican Revolution
S aid that he lived with his brother
H as many brothers and sisters
I n 1789 George became the 1st president
N ever went to school
G eorge was a farmer
T he Father of Our Country
O n 1759 he married Martha Custis
N ever lived in the White House

Jasmine Beane, Grade 2
Mount Jewett Elementary School, PA

Winter Is...

Winter is the time of year when you see
snowflakes quietly falling to the ground.
Winter is the sound of having fun
and screaming Wheeeee! — on your sled!
Winter feels like ice when the pond freezes.
Winter smells like hot chocolate.
Winter looks like a beautiful cloud.

Cailin Counihan, Grade 1
St Teresa of Avila School, NY

I Wish

Sometimes I wish I was a super hero
Sometimes I wish I had a puppy
Sometimes I wish I can do 15 cartwheels
And I wish I had a car
And I wish I was a teenager
And even if I wasn't a teenager,
I wish I was still big

Melshon Brown, Grade 1
Northeast Elementary School, NY

What's in My Refrigerator

What's in my refrigerator was...
Some moldy cheese
And some black eyed peas,
Some out of date yogurt,
Also some bad go-gurt.
Some Progresso soup,
And something that looks like goop.
A moldy apple,
Some sliced pineapple,
Some dumplings,
Some fruity things.
Some eggs cracked
And some meat, hacked.
That's what's in my refrigerator.

William Ma, Grade 3
Sunquam Elementary School, NY

Brothers

Brothers

Oldest, Lee
college freshman
funny, a leader, helpful
friend, huge
football player
learner

Middle, Jon
high school freshman
love history, baseball player, thin
team player
loves going to games
spends time with friends

Youngest, Alex
generous
2nd grader, dependable, caring
football fan, baseball player
computer whiz
beach person

Brothers

Alex Rosenthal, Grade 2
Dr Samuel C Eveleth School, MA

Hockey

Hockey
icy, goalie
playing, sliding, shooting
hockey is my favorite sport
cold sport

Barry Turner, Grade 2
Marvin Elementary School, CT

Raining

Raining raining it's an inside day
And it's not a good time to play!
Maybe tomorrow it will be a nicer day!
Raining raining it is so bad,
If I cannot play I will play with my dad!
Raining raining it is not good,
I will go outside with my giant hood!
Raining raining I am snoring
If I do that it will be boring!

Diego Escobar, Grade 2
Public School 205 Alexander Bell, NY

Skiing

Fun on snow sounds good to me,
That is why I like to ski.
I get such a big thrill,
When I'm skiing down the hill.
When I ski at a fast pace,
That is when I win the race.

Roy Colter, Grade 3
Our Lady of Hope School, NY

What I Do?

W hat I do?
H ang out with my friends
A nd always staying cool
T oday I might stay up all night!

I fight my brother and never lose...

D o you do the same?
O nto my bed and go to sleep.

Kenan Ghibih, Grade 3
Islamic Academy of New England, MA

Spring

The flowers bloom, in the middle of June.
The breeze feels cool when you sit on a stool.
The trees turn green if you know what I mean.
I caught a fish, to make a nice dish.
The rabbits are hopping and they are not stopping.
We can go to the zoo and the cows moo.

Nicholas Ferreira, Grade 1
Little People's College, MA

Dumb and Dumber

D ance
U nder
M onkeys
B anging drums

A nts
N ever
D rum

D elivering
U nbelievable
M usic
B y
E lephants
R inging bells

Jaymecka Green, Grade 3
Urban League of Pittsburgh Charter School, PA

The Joys of the Ocean

When I swim swimming with the polka dotted fish
and seeing blue dolphins and red coral
tasting the salt and hearing the waves
and feeling the water smacking against me.

Ismael Abdul-Malik, Grade 2
Al-Rahmah School, MD

A Morning at School

Thud.
The ball went whistling through the air.
Splash! Splatter!
The ball splattered mud all over mom.
Time to go in now.

Ryan Gick, Grade 3
Southeastern New Hampshire Christian Academy, NH

A Bit About Me
Alec is my name,
chess is my game.
I have brown hair,
and skin so fair.
Now I must take a look
at my favorite book!
Alecsander Nguyen, Grade 1
St Joan of Arc Elementary School, PA

Just Begun
The roller coaster is super fast
The people are excited to get on
The people now want to get off
Too late to get off now
The ride just begun
Melissa Normoyle, Grade 3
Fulton Avenue School #8, NY

Pink
Pink is Katie's coat
And a new baby goat
Pink is cotton candy at the fair
Where pink balloons fly in the air
Pink is the shells
That sit in the sand
Pink is the nail polish
That's on Melissa's hand
Pink is the sunset
That ends the day
Mikelle Anne Petersen, Grade 3
Jeffrey Elementary School, CT

Snakes
Snakes are
green,
curvy,
squiggly,
long,
scaly,
but not
cuddly.
Wilber Perla, Grade 1
Northeast Elementary School, NY

The Earth
Round
big
green
and
blue
more
sea
than land

the
solar
system
is
where
it
lives,

loves
to
orbit

it
is
my home.
Caroline Tucker, Grade 2
Dr Samuel C Eveleth School, MA

Flowers
Flowers are pretty
My favorite is roses
I love buttercups
Carly Bavone, Grade 2
Long Meadow Elementary School, CT

Night/Day
Night
Dark, mysterious
Sleeping, dreaming, creeping
Moonlight, owls, sunshine, shadows
Awakening, renewing, living
Bright, warm
Day
Amelia Brague Deacon, Grade 3
West Branch School, PA

Sunny Day

S unshine on the grass,
P laying baseball in the spring.
R ide a bike in the spring
I n spring snakes come out.
N ice flowers come up.
G reen, tall grass comes up.

Aaron Shealy, Grade 1
Brookings Museum Magnet School, MA

Oh NASCAR, Oh NASCAR

How do you go so fast?
Doesn't it hurt when you crash?
How do you crash?
What are alleys like?
What is it like when you retire?
What do you do after the race?
What do you do during the off-season?
I accelerate in the corners.
I can breathe
And when I pit
The pit crews give me water or Gatorade.
Sometimes it hurts,
But you can still walk away.
By bumping into other people.
They help you
By drafting you on restrictor plates.
You get to be with your family.
I go test my cars after the season is over.

William Boyd, Grade 3
St Christopher's School, VA

Blue

Blue is a yellow belly daisy
Or a pillow under your head
Blue is eyes that glimmer in the dark
Little waves that shine
A blueberry that melts in your mouth
Cotton candy on a stick
Blue is the sky without a puff in it
Blue is a soft wave shining in the morning sun
    That is Blue

Emily Faraci, Grade 3
Jeffrey Elementary School, CT

A Valentine
A valentine, a valentine
I give to you today
To say that we're friends
The best of friends today and every day

A valentine, a valentine
I send this card to you
To say I like you very much
And hope you like me too!
Alexandra Theall, Grade 3
Memorial-Spaulding Elementary School, MA

Snow
Snow is falling down the park
Now it turns to ice
Outside it's icy
Turning white looking like frosty
Frosty is snowflakes coming down
Leaves are coming around
We play and love
Playing in the snow
Now it's summer
I got to say
Goodbye to winter and hello to summer
Joshua James, Grade 3
Public School 65 Mother Hale Academy, NY

The City
The city has lots of buildings,
One almost touches the sky.
That building is called a skyscraper.
There's a zoo called Franklin Park Zoo.
There are lots of things to find in the city.
Just come and find out.
Soad Tahlil, Grade 2
James M Curley Elementary School, MA

Spring
I love to go to the park.
There is grass everywhere!
Dogs are playing with their owners.
Spring is the best season of the year!
Heidi Cooke, Grade 2
Washington Park Elementary School, PA

Green
If I were green
I'd be a rattlesnake
Slithering to my prey.
Jake Vail, Grade 2
St Christopher's School, VA

Freedom
Freedom is like…
A bird flying in the air.
Fish swimming in the ocean.
Bees buzzing in the garden.
Relaxing on the sofa.
Sean Menges, Grade 2
St Christopher's School, VA

Seashell
It looks like
ripples in the sand
bumps on clouds
and on land.
It looks like the sun
with white beams of light
shining over all
day and night.
Drew Brockelman, Grade 2
Harry Lee Cole School, MA

The Kitten
My kitten loves
to meow
and hiss
and purr
and mew.
My cat loves me,
and she loves to
hiss, hiss and chatter!
She loves me a lot
And she goes
Purr, purr!
We like to sleep.
My cat likes to wear mittens.
She loves me.
Nora Ballotta, Grade 1
The Jefferson School, DE

Red

Red is my favorite color it is true.
Red shoes, red socks, red shirts, and red hair,
Red smiles at me so happily.
When I think of red it makes me think of red crayons, and red construction paper.
Red is made from you heart.
WAIT.
Hearts are red.
And that's all I know about red.
I really think red is cool.

Carolina Cruz, Grade 2
Ulysses Byas Elementary School, NY

The Best

I like the stores we have in Yonkers.
My favorite is Stew Leonard's, for this is the best!

I like the cow and mini chocolate chip cookies.
They are full of zest!

I like all the good parks and schools.
They all have high marks!

In Yonkers I have family, friends and good neighbors,
Surely, they are all the best!

Shaun Blute, Grade 1
Christ the King School, NY

Airplanes

Airplanes fly very high,
Like they are almost going to touch the sky.

If you fly backwards fast,
Would it take you into the past?

When you fly upside down,
You will definitely fall to the ground.

So fasten you seat belt on the plane,
That you may not fall down the lane.

Airplanes fly far and near,
May they take you to someone dear.

Sanjeev Jariwala, Grade 2
The International School at Rogers Magnet, CT

Candy, Candy, Candy
I know a person who likes candy
He eats candy day and night
But, I have a fact for you
Candy is not handy.
Sian K. Lum, Grade 2
Grace Miller Elementary School, VA

The Storm
I saw a hurricane smashing down.
It made me frown.
The storm was mainly in our town.
The street was flooded muddy brown.
David Patrick, Grade 2
JF Kennedy School, CT

Dolphins
D olphins are great
O h how they swim so fast
L ong, thin, and swift
P olite and careful
H onest and fair
I never saw just one
N o one swims like a dolphin
S o try to see one!
Ashe Hebrank-Ekas, Grade 2
The Jefferson School, DE

Mom
Mom
Happy, tall
Shopping, buying, cooking
She gets me candy
Real happy
Ralph Hicks, Grade 1
Daniel J Flood Elementary School, PA

Bugs
Bugs
Polka dots, red
Flying, crawling, hiding
Helping us learn where they live
Cool
Jenna Rhodes, Grade 1
Daniel J Flood Elementary School, PA

My Sister
I have a sister who is cute.
I call her a cutie pie.
She's a pumpkin pie.
She's the best sister in the world.
Hanna's adorable.
I love, love, love, her.
Taylor Adams, Grade 1
Williamstown Elementary School, NY

Moving
She moved when I was only three
I was sad
She was sad
She sent me a postcard
I wonder what she is doing?
Emma Finegan, Grade 3
Weston Intermediate School, CT

Cats!
A cat does MEOW at night
Meow, meow
Well, you can have it,
or not
Pout, pout
So, you cannot have a cat.
Sigh, sigh
I have a beautiful cat.
Smile, smile
My cat's name is Alex
Kiss, kiss
I love his soft fur.
Purr, purr
Caitlyn Nicole Schaffner, Grade 1
The Jefferson School, DE

Head Sense
A head is
how you see,
smell, taste,
and feel.
Heads
Kenneth McKee-Proctor, Grade 2
John Ward Elementary School, MA

Kite

It flies super high
It's soaring through the sky
It's going in circles
Oh no!
Towards a tree!
Boom!
It's in the tree!

Macala Leigey, Grade 3
Bradford Township Elementary School, PA

Food!

I love you,
You love me.
Let's go home and watch TV.
With a little bit of popcorn.
Buttery and sweet,
Now let's all enjoy this treat!
With a drink that's bubbly and clear,
That fizzles and sizzles like a glass of cheer.
Now mix the popcorn and soda together,
It will make the movie much better!

Tyler Miscannon, Grade 3
Ridge Park Elementary School, PA

Chocolate Is Sweet

Roses are red
Violets are blue
Chocolate is brown
And so good, just like you
The Earth is so peaceful
Just like Geckos and Labs too.
Geckos are so cute and so nice.

Alex Fisher, Grade 1
Media Childrens House Montessori, PA

Bunnies

Bunnies
Hopping, playing
Fluffy, soft, wiggly
Bunnies are so cute
Bunnies

Tory Padden, Grade 2
St Clement Mary Hofbauer School, MD

Dog

Dogs talk and walk
but don't really rock.
How many dogs
will it take to rock
a walky talky dog.

Nahida Alam, Grade 3
Public School 152 School of Science & Technology, NY

Sue and Roo

Sue loves the zoo.
Roo does too!
Together they see a kangaroo,
And a monkey too!
Together the old owl scared them with a boo-hoo
Roo and Sue have fun at the zoo!

Casey Friend, Grade 2
Christ the King School, NY

My Dog

My dog is brown and white
My dog's ears are white
My dog's paws are white
My dog's nose is brown
My dog's body is brown and white
My dog's nails are long
My dog's eyes are blue
My dog is a puppy
My dog is special to me

I love my dog very much
I love his blue eyes
I love his fluffy ears
I love my dog's wet nose
My dog's tail has brown and white
That's something else I love about my dog
I love my dog's fluffy tail
I love my dog because he is sweet
And his blue eyes help me go to sleep

My dog loves me and I love him too
But here's the thing, he knows how to tie my shoe
But in a few years, we'll have to get a puppy that's new

Tionna Taylor, Grade 3
Lyndhurst Elementary School, MD

Mad

Mad's face is red as can be.
Mad's hobby is fighting.
Mad has chains all over his room.
Mad brings a chain saw.
When he leaves his home, mad likes to fight.
Mad is bad towards everyone!

Jordan Cobbs, Grade 2
Maryvale Elementary School, MD

Springtime

Spring is the time when flowers bloom
Because the rain is watering them

Spring is the time when birds sing
Because the sun is getting brighter outside

Spring is the time when children play outside
Because it's the perfect weather

Spring is the time when people celebrate
Because it's

Spring!

Minhazul Bashar, Grade 3
Public School 131, NY

A Yellow Lab

There once was a frisky yellow lab.
While swimming got pinched by a crab.
Mom said to rest.
She thought that was best.
The yellow lab rests in a bright yellow cab.

Emily Pfau, Grade 2
Oakdale Elementary School, MD

I'll Miss You

Tim, I love you so.
But I have to go.
My mom and dad got a new job in California.
So I might not be able to see you any more.
So goodbye.

Taylor Waldron, Grade 3
Afton Elementary School, NY

Sports

I love sports.
there are all sorts.
In soccer,
you have a soccer ball.
In basketball,
you don't have to be tall.
In baseball,
you step on home plate.
I think sports are great.

Shannon Scott, Grade 3
Our Lady of Hope School, NY

Blue Bird

blue, wings fly so high
the cloud in the sky is blue
spread your wings and fly

Christian Rodriguez, Grade 2
Public School 148 Ruby Allen, NY

A Beach Day

A happy time
getting splashed by waves
MAKING HUGE SAND CASTLES
and letting the water wash
the whole sand castle away,
munching on snacks
playing with friends
on a hot summer day.

Alexa Shapiro, Grade 2
Dr Samuel C Eveleth School, MA

Cute, Cuddly, Crazy Cat

A cute, cuddly, crazy cat
was climbing a creepy car.
He packed a Coke and a candy cane
and truly looked bizarre.

There was a camel and a calf
already in the car.
They asked where he was going
and he told them "Mars."

Nate Strickler, Grade 3
Frenchtown School, RI

Bugs

Bugs are nasty!
I don't like bugs.
Bugs are insects too.
I hate bugs.
Bugs are very disgusting.

Jailene Martinez, Grade 2
Ulysses Byas Elementary School, NY

Summer

We're all at the pool in the summer.
We're here and it's not a bummer.
We get in the pool,
So now we are cool.
We're having fun!
We're all in the sun!
I look in a tree
Ahh! I see a bee!
Look at my sister in her new suit.
I think she looks really very cute!
I'm getting wet.
My sister has a net.
I'm not in the race
Because of my slow pace.
I'm sad the day's soon done
But we had lots of fun!

Madison Shuman, Grade 3
St Catherine Laboure School, PA

New Year's Eve

I can't wait until New Year's Eve
Because we always go to a big party.
We get to bowl almost all night
And try to beat our parents all right!
We also run around and have fun
And I love it a ton.

Jillian Foster, Grade 3
St Anastasia School, PA

Water

On a river of Canada
Swirling in lots of circles
One hot summer day.

Petros Giannaros, Grade 1
Public School 122 Mamie Fay, NY

Lollipops

Babies are blue, lollipops are pink.
Cupcakes are yellow and so are you.
The moon shines bright on a summer's night
and the sun shines bright on a summer's morning.

Alessandra Filippone, Grade 1
Media Childrens House Montessori, PA

Snowman

Cold
White
Scarf
3 Circles
Buttons

Bryan Horn, Kindergarten
Plainview-Old Bethpage Kindergarten Center, NY

My Class

22
children

13
boys

9
girls

and

I have fun with them
My class

Matthew Sala, Kindergarten
Plainview-Old Bethpage Kindergarten Center, NY

Green Is...

Green is the color of an oak tree's leaf,
a Granny Smith apple,
and some oceans, too.
Green is the grass stain on my pants,
also St. Patrick's Day across the USA.
Green is the spring grass with flowers blooming all around.
Green is an emerald in my mom's necklace
and a sparkling jade on my dad's ring.

James Mitchell III, Grade 3
Eli Terry School, CT

My City

Most of my family live in Yonkers.
I see them often here in Yonkers.

I love my school, Christ the King.
Here, I have many good friends,
And this give me zest!

Yonkers has good restaurants along the pier,
Families come together felling good and near!
John Cooper, Grade 1
Christ the King School, NY

God Has Room for All Animals

All animals big and small
all animals that are in our hearts
they still will go to heaven.

Even if they are mean or nice
they still will go to heaven
it doesn't matter what kind of animal they are
they all go to heaven.

Even if they're young or old
large or small
friendly or wild
their soul's go to God's golden gates.
Genevieve Keller, Grade 3
Klein Elementary School, PA

Fireflies

You glitter and glow
You twinkle like stars in the night
We like when you come.
Perri Chuska, Grade 3
Berry Elementary School, MD

Sweet Meat

A girl who did nothing but eat,
Cooked her dinner with carrots and meat.
When she went to the store,
She bought twenty more.
She thought it was the sweetest treat!
Elizabeth Robley, Grade 2
Oakdale Elementary School, MD

Easter Candy

Easter candy
Sweet, delicious
Making me glad
Melting in my mouth
Yummy!
Victoria Schultz, Grade 3
Penn-Kidder Campus, PA

Vacations

Hurray school is out.
We can go visit family.
Plane rides we will take!
Claudia Ricciardi, Grade 2
North Street School, CT

Space

Cold, empty
Dark as night
Huge, bleak, little light
Strange
Alex O'Connell, Grade 3
St Christopher's School, VA

Captain Underpants

C an save
A nd
P rotect people
T hat are
A lso in mortal danger
I f they are not human he
N ever loses in a fight

U ses special powers
N ow and then
D o you know that in
E very day life he is
R eally a
P rincipal
A lways
N eeds
T o
S ave the world
Shain McGovern, Grade 3
Afton Elementary School, NY

Storm

I see birds flying.
They fly high, they fear the storm.
The storm is coming.
Kyle Schultze, Grade 2
Calvary Chapel Christian School, NY

Dog

My dog's name is Ted
He is well fed every day
He runs in the park.
Lesley Zambrano, Grade 2
Public School 148 Ruby Allen, NY

Cats

Cats eat food and drink
Cats are soft and furry
Cats are playful too!
Rodrigo Ramirez, Grade 2
Public School 148 Ruby Allen, NY

Time

Time goes by so fast
It seems like ten minutes
When you have fun
And when you aren't having fun
It is not fast
Giovanni Fava, Grade 2
Cabot Elementary School, MA

Baseball

Windy as you run the bases to first
the next batter comes to hit
he hits it way in the outfield.
You run to second
and then third
you run home
the throw comes...

and you are safe!
Everybody cheers!
Hurray Hurray!
We won the game!
Peter Morrison, Grade 2
Dr Samuel C Eveleth School, MA

Spring

S pring flowers
P lants sprouting
R oses blooming
I nsects buzzing
N est-making birds
G rass growing greener
Ayanna Maxwell, Grade 2
Hebbville Elementary School, MD

Sports

Sports are what I like
I even like to bike
Up down left right done
A-Rod just hit a home run

Sports are so much fun
But now my poem is done
Liam McCarthy, Grade 3
Weston Intermediate School, CT

Water

Water
Cold, icy
Cooling, refreshing, energizing
Helping when I'm hot
H_2O
Rachel Landis, Grade 3
Hereford Elementary School, PA

Spring

Spring is here!
The sun is shining,
The rain is falling,
The flowers are blooming.

Spring is here!
The wind is blowing,
The children are playing,
The birds are singing.

Spring is here!
Sophia Davis, Grade 2
St Rose Elementary School, CT

Dolphins

D olphins are very smart
O nly live in saltwater
L ife span is 30 years
P eak seasons for mating are May and June
H unt with sound
I n the ocean, you may see one
N ice and kind — they will give you a ride

Sarah Montag, Grade 2
McQuistion Elementary School, PA

Gorgeous Colors

Rainbows and butterflies
Coral and fish.
Birds of great sizes
Pottery and dish.
Glass and a beautiful Christmas ball.
Flowers of wonderful colors
Standing straight and tall.
But the most dazzling, colorful object of all...
Are the magical colors of spring and fall.

Jamie Krouse, Grade 2
Mary Matula Elementary School, MD

Hockey

I love hockey
I love how the puck hits the boards hard
    BOOM!!!

I love hockey
I love the sound of a stick breaking
    CRACK!!!

I love hockey
I love the sound of someone stopping
    CHCHCH!!!

I love hockey
I love the sound of a stick hitting the ice hard
    CHCHCH!!!

I love hockey

Tim Kalinowski, Grade 2
Dr Samuel C Eveleth School, MA

What Is Pink?

Pink reminds me of soft, little piglets on a farm snorting all day long!
Hard chewing gum in my mouth.
Wearing my bright pink shoelaces on a light, sunny night.
At a carnival having sweet cotton candy on a Friday night.

Tyler Kling, Grade 3
Watsontown Elementary School, PA

Christmas

Thanksgiving was in November.
Now, it's Christmas in December.

I love my family with care.
And all the presents that we share.

In the morning we wake up out of bed.
To see the colors black, green, and red.

Christmas is about Jesus only
But on Christmas no one should be lonely.

Amanda Ashwood, Grade 3
Little Flower Day Care Center and Prep School, NY

Mystery Animal

It has a tail.
It has fur.
It has four legs.
It growls when it's mad.
It can climb a tree.

What do you think it is?
It is a cat.
That is the mystery animal.

Elvin Jose Suazo, Grade 3
Public School 152 School of Science & Technology, NY

Spring

Flowers start to bloom,
But I hate when they start to loom.
I see the moon,
But it's afternoon.
I love the sun,
But I hate to wait for fun.

Keith Hubal, Grade 3
Susquehanna Community Elementary School, PA

Days

Hey!
My little brother is getting away!
On Tuesday
My friends and I went outside to play.
On Wednesday my brother fainted.
My mom painted.
In May
It was my brother's birthday.

Kali Edwards, Grade 3
St Catherine Laboure School, PA

A Snow Day Is...

A day with no school.
A day to play in the snow.
A day to make a snow fort.
A day to make a snowman.
A day to throw snowballs.
A day to go sledding.
A day to finish your homework.
A day the lights could go out.
A day to have fun.
A Snow Day.

Joe McKeever, Grade 2
Dr Samuel C Eveleth School, MA

This Miserable, Horrible Day

Why me, why me,
On this miserable day
Did I go out to play?
I had no clue
About what to do
On this miserable, horrible day.
I went on the swing,
But it was hard on my rump.
So I went to play ball,
But I fell in a clump
Of weeds that gave me a lump
And a big, old bump
On my head.
So I couldn't play
On this miserable, horrible day.

Andrew Cragin, Grade 3
Middle Gate Elementary School, CT

Lemar

Lemar is a boy
He is tall with
Large feet
And dresses really neat

Lemar is in 3rd grade
He likes to run and jog
He has a pet hog
And a dog

Lemar likes P.E. class in school
Because he gets to move
Lemar is my best friend.

Maurice Johnson, Grade 3
Bensley Elementary School, VA

Trees

Trees gain back their shade
Leaves sprouting out of trees
Trees wake from their sleep

Brett Prochko, Grade 2
Long Meadow Elementary School, CT

People

People here, people there,
People everywhere.
People in the trees, people in the pond,
People going ha ha ha all day long.
People drive, people dive,
People are alive.
People sit, people knit,
People use emergency kits.
People catch, people throw,
People go to the Super Bowl.
People walk, people run,
People eat a hotdog bun.
People eat, people weep,
People cook with cookie sheets.
People legs, people arms,
People work on Christmas farms.
People fight, people write,
People use a light bulb light.

Brendan Correira, Grade 3
Frenchtown School, RI

Balloon

Smooth, squeaky
Oval, shape of your face
See through rubber material
All colors
Works with air or helium

Gabrielle DiRusso, Grade 2
Christ the Teacher Catholic School, DE

The School Rules!

School has rules in the hallway
where they tell you not to shout.
School has rules in the classroom
where they tell you not to pout.
The school has an important rule,
it is to not litter or to break the glass at Mass.
The school is fun for everyone.
Even though there's rules,
school is still cool.

Vanessa Dannecker, Grade 3
Holy Rosary School, NY

Spring

Spring spring I want to see,
What you bring for the bees;
Spring spring bring me sun,
I want to go for a long long run!

Camari Wilkerson, Grade 2
Georgetown East Elementary School, MD

Spring

There are trees and flowers.
Grass is green.
Flowers are different colors.
I love spring!

Spenser Anderson, Grade 2
Washington Park Elementary School, PA

Pets

Pets, cute and fluffy
Pets can be very furry
Pets are wonderful

Fiona Walsh, Grade 3
Christ the Teacher Catholic School, DE

Blue

Blue is the color of an empty sky,
Blue is the color of some person's eye.
Blue is the water in the spring,
Blue is such a beautiful thing.
Blue is of a rainy day,
You are blue if you can't play.
Blue is the color of the deep blue sea,
Blue is the color for you and me!
My favorite color is baby blue,
But I guess it can be yours, too.
In the rainbow blue is fifth,
Blue is very popular and that's not a myth.
There is a bird called the blue jay,
And it sings if it's a lovely day.
Blue is the color of some fish,
Blue is the color of a dish,
Blue is the color of Easter eggs,
And blue is the color of golfing pegs.
Blue is the color that I love,
And blue is the color when you look above.

Julia Okrant, Grade 3
Eli Terry School, CT

Friends

Friends draw with you,
Play, and talk with you.
Don't laugh at you if you get in trouble.
Sometimes you fight,
But if you are friends,
You make up.
Friends are nice, not mean.
But the important thing is
You like each other.

Melaina Cooke, Grade 3
James M Curley Elementary School, MA

Spring

Spring looks like flowers are blooming
Spring smells like warm air
Spring tastes like hamburgers on the grill
Spring feels like cool air
Spring sounds like birds singing

Tyler Sherrill, Grade 2
Ulysses Byas Elementary School, NY

My Favorite Brother

I have a brother.
He is a baby.
His name is Dylan.
I call him the Vylan.
He is lots of fun.
He likes to cry.
He is 3 1/2 months old.
I love him very much.

Courtney Ward, Grade 3
Holy Rosary School, NY

Airplanes

Airplanes
Jets, wings
Flying, piloting, soaring
Taking off from the airport
Planes

Dominic Campbell, Grade 2
St Rosalia Academy, PA

Catching

Cole caught computers
and cookies.
How crazy!

Robby Kwon Kessler, Grade 1
Seneca Academy, MD

New York

Long Island
Long, big
Walk, drive, work
Next to Fire Island
Plant, play, swim
Fun, busy
New York

James Broyles, Grade 3
St Joseph School, NY

The Thomas

Thoms taps Tom
and talks
to Tommy Tabs.

Brittany Noel Bostic, Grade 1
Seneca Academy, MD

Dance
Dance with me,
Do the salsa or the limbo.
Don't break your back
Or crack your feet.

Dance with me,
Dine on special treats.
Wear a fancy dress
And be my guest.

Dance with me,
We're going to roll.
Finish up.
Quick, jump in the car.

Jessica Lauv, Grade 2
Public School 152 School of Science & Technology, NY

My Yard
The sun is bright,
The birds are singing
The flowers smell good,
My yard.

Lina Enamorado, Grade 3
Public School 23 Carter G Woodson School, NY

Animals
Animals, animals, they're all around you.
Look, turn around, there's an animal behind you!
Do you see those mice?
Aren't they nice?
See those puppies run?
Boy they're having fun!
Animals can make great pets too.
They make me happy. How about you?

Jillian Kokernak, Grade 2
St Mary's Elementary School, MA

My Wishes
I wish I had toys.
I wish I could go to school on Monday.
Sometimes, I wish that my mom and dad were rich.
Most of all I wish that I could give love.

Julliana Mejia, Grade 1
Northeast Elementary School, NY

Green

Green is…
A frog that is chasing a fly.
Grass that is safe to run through.
Go — that makes cars keep going.
Sayeef Azgar, Grade 1
Public School 122 Mamie Fay, NY

Ping Pong Ball

Ping-pong ball,
Ping-pong ball,
I
 threw
  it
   in
    the
     air,
but suddenly, it stayed up there!
The vent, it sucks,
you said it would
BLOW!
That's not good,
Oh no, oh no.
I will turn off the vent.
It will drop to the ground.
But then it plunked on my head,
so I had to frown.
Michael Weymouth, Grade 3
Sunquam Elementary School, NY

Dogs

Golden retrievers
Rot Whilers, Collies, Pitbulls
Poodles, Yorkshire dogs
Luz Clementine Lim, Grade 2
Public School 148 Ruby Allen, NY

Horses

Cowboys ride horses
In Pennsylvania and Texas.
Police ride horses
In Newton and Boston.
People ride horses every place!
Nevin Ketchum, Kindergarten
John Ward Elementary School, MA

Spinning Leaves

Sudden whistling wind
Blowing leaves that twist and turn
Through the warm spring air
Dylan Anderson, Grade 2
Long Meadow Elementary School, CT

Fishing

We set our alarm
For seven o'clock.
We tell our friends
To meet at the dock.
First thing we do
Is go out for bait.
Next thing you know
It's already eight.
My dad says:
"What should we fish for Luke?"
I reply…
"Maybe today we'll try fluke!"
We drive to Old Orchard
And cast out our lines.
Now we sit and wait…
And hope a fish dines.
The sun is shining,
It's a beautiful day.
Too bad there are no fish
In Raritan Bay.
Luke McCann, Grade 3
Public School 5, NY

PSP

PSP My game
I like to play PSP
It is black and blue
Jason Cano, Grade 2
Public School 148 Ruby Allen, NY

Dog

A dog is furry
big, fat, noisy, funny dog
A dog likes to walk.
Wilmer Zhagui, Grade 2
Public School 148 Ruby Allen, NY

My Name Is Shane

Shane is my name,
Baseball is my game.
I have a dog named Molly
She is big and yellow and jolly.
I like to run and play
On a bright and sunny day.
My hair is brown and my eyes are green.
I am the happiest kid you've ever seen!

Shane McElwee, Grade 1
St Joan of Arc Elementary School, PA

Freedom

My dad is fighting for freedom
He says freedom doesn't come free
My mom agrees with him
I like freedom because if
We didn't have freedom we would be slaves
Freedom means that we can do what we want
Freedom is worth fighting for
I'm proud of my dad!

Kassity Hale, Grade 3
Hardwick Elementary School, VT

Snowy

Snowy
White flakes
Snowplow, kids playing
Hot chocolate and marshmallows
Winter

Matthew Rottaris, Kindergarten
St Stephen's School, NY

School

School is fun
School is great
School is good
Writing poetry
Playing outside
Circle time
Oh — I like school

Eleana Tsiamtsiouris, Kindergarten
Buckley Country Day School, NY

Names and Snow
One day I will play hockey
with Jeremy Shockey.
I ski
when people say "me."
I was outside using my stakes
when down came the first flakes.
Don and John
went skiing with Calvin Mon.
Tyler Stoner, Grade 3
St Catherine Laboure School, PA

Mud Season
Getting stuck
wheels spinning,
the motor roaring
my heart pounding
like crazy.
Will I get out?
Pushing
Rocking back and forth
back and forth
Gravel flies
I'm free!
Kristina Kish, Grade 3
Hardwick Elementary School, VT

Flower Grows
Seeds grow strong for me
Rain and sunshine help them grow
Flowers blooming — Spring!
Anna Hope Whalon, Grade 2
Killingly Memorial School, CT

Teacher
T hey teach you
E at in the classroom
A t trips they come with you
C an help you in school
H omework every night
E ven Friday
R esearch
Jocelyn Aldaz, Grade 2
Adelphi Academy, NY

Freedom/Slavery
Freedom
Happiness peace
Skipping humming playing
Friendly gentle painful hurtful
Running screaming crying
Fierce scary
Slavery
Maura Mulligan, Grade 3
Susan Odell Taylor School, NY

Waves
Waves so big and strong
Fish, seaweed, people, surfboards
Crashing, moving fast
Emily Sweeney, Grade 2
Long Meadow Elementary School, CT

Trains Go Fast
T rains go fast
R acing uphill
A train is sometimes slow
I want to ride a train
N ow trains are in their sheds
S ome trains go underground
Zachery Rice, Grade 2
Montessori Academy of Lancaster, PA

Nick
Cool friend to play with.
We play basketball all day.
We help each other.
James Sanchez, Grade 2
Public School 148 Ruby Allen, NY

Butterfly Fish
White and black
Eats fish
Sharp teeth
Fools predators
Lives in the ocean
A large fish
Can swim fast
Hunter Fuller, Kindergarten
St Christopher's School, VA

Blue

Blue are blueberries so tender and juicy
Blue is Pluto, so pretty, but cold
Blue is the American flag we cherish
Blue is the ocean, that's the shark's habitat
Blue are the jeans on our legs
Blue are Great White sharks waiting for prey to come

Morgan Moon, Grade 3
Enfield Station School, ME

Gossip Is...

Someone saying stuff behind your back
Telling people stuff that's not true
A friend talking about you
A sad feeling
Hurtful to other people's feelings
When someone you thought was a friend talks about you
The end of a friendship
A really bad thing

Brittany Chaison, Grade 3
Enfield Station School, ME

I Am Unique

I am almost 8 years old.
I wonder about if toys come alive.
I hear peaceful sounds outside.
I see the wind blowing at night.
I want to live longer and longer.
I am always playing with my toys.

I pretend I am a queen.
I feel God's rain on my skin.
I touch roses.
I worry about my mom.
I cry about sad things.
I am Louna. I have a very nice teacher.

I understand trying to be friends with an enemy.
I say silly things like Jamaican words to my friends.
I dream of waking up in Heaven with Jesus.
I try to keep my friends.
I hope one day, just one day, we will be living in a better world.
I am Louna. I am different.

Louna Joachin, Grade 2
Cornwall Terrace Elementary School, PA

Summer
S wimming in the pool
U nder the shade of a tree
M errily playing with friends
M arshmallow toasting
E very bird is singing
R iver flowing softly to music

Amber Litts, Grade 3
New Lane Memorial Elementary School, NY

Dance
Dance is a way to express yourself
You can put a trophy on your shelf
You can always show off your talent
Everything requires balance
Dance is a way to play on a hot summer day
Exercise and say olé
Dance is like you're floating in the sky
And every move passes gracefully by.

Payton Ackerman, Grade 3
Eisenhower Elementary School, PA

The Race
As soon as the beep tells me to go,
I'm off, speeding through the beautiful snow!
Oh! Here comes the first challenging gate!
Will I make it?
No! I'm too late!
The second, the third,
To slalom through,
I didn't make them!
I'm so blue.

But why am I sad on a day like today?
I should be happy in every way!
Who cares about gates or winning the race,
I think I'll ski at my very own pace.
I'll see trees covered in sparkling ice,
I'll smell air scented with woody pine spice.
I'll hear the wild wind whistling past,
The memories of today are sure to last!

Chloe Tinagero, Grade 3
Buckingham Browne & Nichols School, MA

Winter Is
Winter is the quiet sound of snow.
Winter feels icy cold like snow down your neck.
Winter looks like a big white blanket.
Winter smells like hot chocolate.
Winter is the coolest season ever.

Matt Bruno, Grade 1
St Teresa of Avila School, NY

Red Is...
Red is an apple freshly picked off a shining tree
on a blazing hot day in the summer

Red reminds me of the sight of a beautiful sunset
gazing right at me as the sun goes down

Red is a cardinal dreaming of a place it wants to be
so it's the happiest bird on Earth

Red is the sound of firecrackers
blasting away happily on the 4th of July

Red smells like a fruity, juicy strawberry
waiting to be picked

Red feels like a scared alone feeling
in a dark alley waiting to be found

Kyle Blanchard, Grade 3
Watsontown Elementary School, PA

I Have a Little Brother Who Acts Like a King
I have a little brother who acts like a king.
And when I'm watching TV.
He makes me do everything!!
Like sweep the floor
and open the door
for his best friends to come in.

But sometimes he's nice
like a couple of mice,
but when he acts like a king
he eats nothing but meat,
and won't be a person you would want to meet.

Anthony Fomin, Grade 2
Cornwall Terrace Elementary School, PA

Sun

I am the sun
That lives in the sky
I move up and down
Around the world
I make people hot
So hot
That they have to go swimming
In a pool
When they look at me
So dizzy, so dizzy
When the moon comes out
I am gone
To the other side of the world.
Sok-Vannary Prak, Grade 3
Meeting House Hill School, CT

Nature Tree

Oh tree, tree.
So special to me
Fruits grow on you
Animals live with you
People cut you down
And that's the end of you.
Maria Stogioglou, Grade 3
Public School 2 Alfred Zimberg, NY

Spring

Spring fling spring ring
Rain is falling from the sky
Clouds are hurrying, hustling by
Pittering pattering
What a shower
Watering every violet flower
Robins chirp in their nests
Mother birds take a rest
In the springtime
Flowers bloom tall
Blue jays yell their call
Nighttime in the spring
Crickets chirp from their legs or wings
Growing greener
Sprouting spring!
Sarah Oswald, Grade 3
Jeffrey Elementary School, CT

Mark Smith

Mark
Kind, nice
Colors in lines
Plays good with friends
Smith
Katelyn Walters, Grade 1
Mount Jewett Elementary School, PA

Under the Sunset

Under the sun
I like to play
I like to play on a hot summer day.

Under the sun
I love to tan.
I love to tan, as much as I can.

Under the sun
I like to swim.
I like to swim, with the prettiest grin.

Under the sun
I'm gonna play
I'm gonna play, for the rest of the day.

The sun is gone now
It is time for bed.
I know there will be
Another sun ahead.
Mattie Winowitch, Grade 2
Central Elementary School, PA

Shopping at the Mall

One cold day
We went away
To the mall
In the fall.
Let's get some money
And buy a bunny.
Thump Thump Thump Thump
Going through the mall was a blast!
Kaleigh Studdert, Grade 2
Pomperaug School, CT

Spring
I love to climb trees.
I can feel the leaves brush my face.
I climb the branches.
I love to go to the top.
Then climb down.
I love spring so much!

Tony Mazza, Grade 2
Washington Park Elementary School, PA

Periwinkle
The bluish on a Turtle Dove,
Also of a knitted glove.
The color code of depth in the sea,
The frozen dry wax of a bumble bee.
The frosty color of a chickadee's breast,
Until the winter comes to a rest.
Close to the color mingled with black in a fight,
The color on a face in the night.
A crisp stream in the sunlight,
The sky that holds up the kite.
Water in a clean marsh,
The enemy frost, which is so harsh.

Jonathan Bigos, Grade 3
Eli Terry School, CT

Nice Days
S unny days so hot you need a drink.
P ool says jump in.
R abbits say Easter is coming.
I love beautiful spring.
N ice days and daisies.
G reen, tall grass.

Paul Ingram, Grade 1
Brookings Museum Magnet School, MA

Ghost
Whispering around
On silent stages
To be pretending
Just a draft.

Blake Ardery, Grade 3
Bradford Township Elementary School, PA

Beautiful Star

Beautiful star shining bright
Beautiful star twinkling through the night
Beautiful star bring us light
In the dark silent night
Devyn Mufson, Grade 3
Weston Intermediate School, CT

A Cat in the Flowers

Once upon a time
there was a cat named Spooky
and he loved to play in the flowers
so one day Spooky went to the flower garden
and he fell asleep in the garden
and he lived happily after.
Miranda Spence, Grade 2
Media Childrens House Montessori, PA

Planting Flowers and Plants

Trees and grass in the summer,
The sun is out, trees are everywhere,
Wanting to grow everything.
No time to waste!
I want to grow trees, grass, flowers, and plants,
Every plant counts in this world,
Water and seeds make them grow,
One more thing, the most important…
The sun!
Dylan Sojka, Grade 3
Acushnet Elementary School, MA

Yellow

Yellow is sweet like a lemon
squeezed in my freshly brewed ice tea.

Yellow sounds like a duck quacking
in a pond on a hot summer day.

Yellow looks like a sunny day in the park
playing with my friends.

Yellow feels like corn fresh off the cob.
Yellow smells like sweet, buttery popcorn.
Daniel Weaver, Grade 3
Watsontown Elementary School, PA

All the Stars

All the stars
have a meaning.
Some form pictures.
Some tell stories of the past.

Stars are beautiful
to watch at night.
Lying underneath the stars
puts a smile on my face.

I love to look up
and count millions of stars
in the sky.
I love all the stars!
Kaitlyn Gutierrez, Grade 3
Sacred Heart School, MA

Football

Football! Football!
So hard at night…
Football! Football!
So easy in the light…
When I get the ball
I usually fall!
But that's OK…
I'll try another day!
Hey!!! I got good news…
We won! We won!
All because of that touchdown
After I fell down…
Football! Football!
Why can't I play
ALL DAY!!!
Christian Sullivan, Grade 3
Public School 5, NY

Orca.
Black, white.
Fast, jumps, eats.
It eats other whales.
Whale.
Michaela Griffin, Grade 1
Edna C Stevens School, CT

Colors

Colors are very pretty.
They make me happy.
Colors make the world better for me and you.
If there were no colors, the world would be black.
I use crayons every day to color my picture.
Crayons and colors are meant for you and me.
They are nice, colorful and beautiful.
I like colors and crayons.
They make the world a much brighter and fun way to live.

Claire Chaisson, Grade 3
Sacred Heart School, NY

If I Were a Snowflake

If I were a snowflake I would fly doing loop-de-loops and flips
I would be rolled up in a ball with all my snowflake friends
Then I would be jostled around bumping into everything
Then I would melt and evaporate
But sooner or later I would fall back down again

Amanda Green, Grade 3
Elkridge Elementary School, MD

Veranda

I am soft as clay, but hard as a throne
I am deep as a cascade that you see in a canyon
I am the drag you feel when you eat salt
I am warm like a veranda in the middle of Brazil

Jesse Bostic, Grade 3
McCleary Elementary School, VA

Killer Whale

K iller whales are small
I ndistinct beak
L arge paddle-shaped flippers
L argest member of the dolphin family
E stablish social hierarchies, and pods are led by females
R ounded head tapers to a point.

W hite patch behind each eye
H abitat is both coastal waters and the open ocean.
A verage length: 6.7-8 meters (males) 5.7-6.6 m (females)
L ife span of orcas is 30 to 50 years in the wild.
E ats dolphins and fish

Hannah Miller, Grade 2
McQuistion Elementary School, PA

Dogs
Dogs like to take baths
Dogs like to chase, bark and sleep
Dogs are really cute.
Stephanie Thompson, Grade 2
Long Meadow Elementary School, CT

An Amazing Sight
The Nutcracker is amazing,
amazing as can be.
People dance around,
among the golden valley.
The people are amazing,
especially their fancy clothes.
I wish some I'll know
I'll be good enough
to be in an amazing show!

The Nutcracker!
Caroline Fazio, Grade 3
Frenchtown School, RI

White Is Cool!
White is the color of a cloud
And snow that has just been plowed.
White is the color of a bloodhound
That cannot be found.
White is the color of a flower bud
In a spring flood.
White is the color of clay
So you can play.
White is the feeling of joy
For a nice behaved boy.
Brendan Cullinane, Grade 3
Eli Terry School, CT

In the Spring
In the spring
I play Saturday soccer.
I'm happy because my team
Scored the most goals!
I was the goalie!
Daniel Zhou, Kindergarten
John Ward Elementary School, MA

YMCA
soccer, swimming
diving, paddling, kicking
being a member is such fun
great time
Connor Prince, Grade 2
Marvin Elementary School, CT

Nephew
In the morning
My nephew is so noisy
That he wakes me up
And I get up so cranky
I wish he can be more quiet
I tell him to please, please, be quiet
Katie Umana, Grade 2
Ulysses Byas Elementary School, NY

Spring
S pring
P atrick
R obin
I reland
N ew
G arden
Margaret Vivian, Grade 1
Christ the King Elementary School, NY

Frog
I had a frog.
His name is Toes
and he is mad
He has no nose.
Danny Brandon Bishop, Grade 3
Afton Elementary School, NY

Snow
Snow, snow, look at it go!
Snow is like ice cream.
We like to go outside
And play in the marvelous snow.
Just like ice.
It is the best thing in the universe.
John Neal, Grade 1
John F Kennedy School, MA

Noise

I hate the noise it hurts my ears
I find there are times it brings me to tears

I love the quiet in the night
It is really a delight

Most of all I enjoy free time
Least of all I don't like to rhyme

Jake Pohl, Grade 3
Klein Elementary School, PA

School

I've never missed a day of school,
Even though I would like to go to a pool.
I hope I get good grades on tests,
And I hope I get time to rest.

Amanda Miller, Grade 3
Our Lady of Hope School, NY

Washington

W e celebrate President's Day in February
A brave man
S eemed to like horses
H e was the 'Father of Our Country'
I n American Revolution he was the leader
N ow he is not alive
G oing to war as a soldier when he was young
T hey lived at Mount Vernon
O n to win the American Revolution
N ow we have a free country

Rayna Stahli, Grade 2
Mount Jewett Elementary School, PA

Excited

Excited's face is as big as a cake.
Excited's hobby is to jump and play.
Excited has a lot of toys all over her room.
When she gets good news, excited hops.
When she leaves her home she brings toys.
Excited is nice to everyone!

Ashley Garcia, Grade 2
Maryvale Elementary School, MD

Islam

I am a Muslim
S preading the word to the people
L a illa ha il Lallah
A llahu Akbar
M ohammed is the messenger of Allah.
Ahmad El-Asmar, Grade 3
Islamic Academy of New England, MA

Big Balls of Sky

The sun is like the moon.
A circle I see most of the time.
They never see each other.
Both with the whole sky to themselves.
Blue likes yellow and black likes white.
Sun and moon are so alike.
Anna Giannuzzi, Grade 2
North Street School, CT

Dancing

D ancing in your dreams
A cro is great!
N utcracker is great ballet
C an't stop dancing!
I t's my favorite thing
N ot good it's great
G reat hobby!
Caroline Barone, Grade 2
Dr Samuel C Eveleth School, MA

Snowflake

If I were a snowflake,
I would drift down.
Down to the ground.
Where all the mortals are,
They will scream with excitement.
Then eat the snow.
Eat like it's ice cream.
All my snowflake friends will join.
When it is time to say goodbye,
Our cloud will fly away.
We will melt.
Thinking that felt good.
Katie Scarlett Eggleston, Grade 3
Elkridge Elementary School, MD

Black Is Back

Black is a cat at night
with a big fright.
Black is the color of some eyes
and scared spies.
Black is a cloudy day
when I don't get my way.
Black is the color of a scream
or a bad dream.
Black is a bruise
and a burnt cruise.
Black is the color of the sky
and the color of GOOD-BYE.
Michael Merrow, Grade 3
Eli Terry School, CT

Thunder Storm

Boom! Bang! Oh no it's that time.
Ting ting! Here it comes.
Boom bang crash crack here it is.
Snap, a branch fell onto the ground.
Heidi Mueller, Grade 3
Southwestern Elementary School, NY

My Dog Lazer

Lazer's my dog.
My dog has a chair.
My dog sleeps in his chair.

Bark, Bark, Bark...
My dog is hungry.
I give him a bone.
Lazer plays with a ball.
I love my dog Lazer!
Corinne Atkinson, Grade 1
Williamstown Elementary School, NY

Dreams/Imagination

Dreams
hopeful wish, waiting in anticipation
excitement, worry, and fear, confident
Imagination
Paul Vlahos, Grade 3
William Spyropoulos School, NY

The Pinewood Derby

Scouts race their cars down the track.
Mine is silver and green with wheels of black.
Some cars are fast, and some cars are slow.
The fastest will stay, and slowest will go.
The cars are lined up in lanes one, two and three —
Who's going to win? Will it be me?
They're off! There they go!
Uh-oh! Mine is too slow!
We worked hard on our cars, and we had lots of fun.
Maybe next year's car will have a better run.

Michael Falcone, Grade 3
Public School 5, NY

Winter

Winter is cold.
Winter is the sound of kids making snowmen.
Winter looks like a big white blanket.
Winter smells like smores and roasted marshmallows.
Winter feels like the best season to me.

Meghan Counihan, Grade 1
St Teresa of Avila School, NY

My Favorite Animal Questions

I want to ask you some questions about creatures
that have features.

I wonder if frogs
like the fog?

What if I saw a mole
That had the name Cole?

What if you saw a duck
stuck in muck?

Did you ever see a crow
wearing a bow?

Have you ever seen a monkey
that looked chunky
and was getting funky?

Cole Bevan, Grade 3
St Catherine Laboure School, PA

Spaghetti

Squishy, gooey, warm
Chewy, delicious
Mouthwatering
Red, white, wonderful
Do you like spaghetti?

Anna Desmond, Grade 3
Christ the Teacher Catholic School, DE

Make the World Beautiful

The grass is warm,
The sun is hot,
Butterflies are flying here and there,
The flowers are blooming in the breeze,
It's time for the seeds to grow,
And spread their roots in the blistering sun,
The world is a better place.

Adam Cambra, Grade 3
Acushnet Elementary School, MA

The Life of a Goose

Flying in the sky so high
Landing at ponds
Having colors of black, white, brown, and gray
Making a lot of noise.

Jessie Whitmer, Grade 3
Mary Walter Elementary School, VA

The Hydra

The hydra lived deep in the shade,
in a deep, deep cave.

It had nine hazardous heads,
an unpleasant monster to find under beds!

Kurt Phillips, Grade 3
Spotswood Elementary School, VA

Winter

Winter is white sparkly ground.
Winter is turning snowballs into snowmen.
Winter is making snow angels.
Winter is drinking hot chocolate.
Winter is a fun time to play.

Samy Diouf, Grade 1
St Teresa of Avila School, NY

The White House

Presidents live in it
Fame circles in
The White House

Luke Powell, Grade 2
St Christopher's School, VA

Star Wars

Star Wars is joyful.
Song and film are opposites.
Dramatic music.

Patrick Ryan, Grade 2
North Street School, CT

Spring

When it turns to spring,
Birds come out and sing…
But watch out for the bees.
They can really sting!

Kassondra Gonzalez, Grade 3
Our Lady of Hope School, NY

Mom

I love you mom
You are the bomb

You give me advice
Because you're so nice

I love you so
And you help me grow

But when I get mad
You don't get sad

I love you and you love me
Best friends we will always be

You are not mean
But sometimes you're keen

I love you and you love me
That's the way it will always be

Anna Brinling, Grade 3
Klein Elementary School, PA

Fire

Yellow, orange
Hot, dry
Popping, crackling
Musty, burnt
Smoke

Camille Brown, Grade 2
Christ the Teacher Catholic School, DE

Snow Angel

S nowballs
N ear freezing
O n the ground
W hite all day

A nother fun day
N ext we have hot chocolate
G o, go, go down the hill
E veryone loves snow
L et's make snow angels

Francesca Zink, Grade 2
St Clement Mary Hofbauer School, MD

School

School bells ring throughout the day.
Calling children in from play.
I have to keep my desk nice and neat.
So my teacher will not yell at me.

Baleigh Smalley, Grade 2
Washington Park Elementary School, PA

What Is Blue?

The sky is blue
When I dream in bed.
Blue is happy
When I think of my head.

Blue acts calm
Like the water and the snow.
I'll go inside
And drink cocoa.

Brittney Sollenberger, Grade 2
A.G. Richardson Elementary School, VA

What Is Purple?
Purple sounds like…
A sad song played on a violin,
Cries from a baby falling asleep,
A toddler pouting during timeout.

Purple feels like…
Gooey grape jelly in a jar,
A soft lavender blanket on my bed,
A bruise on my arm from a fall.

Purple looks like…
A dark night in June,
Some jam, on my sandwich,
Delicious grapes on a vine.

Purple smells like…
A mulberry bush in my yard,
Some violets in a big vase.
Sammi Rinehart, Grade 3
Watsontown Elementary School, PA

Candy! Candy! Candy!
Sweet, sweet, sweet
You're the best I like to eat
Gumballs, airheads and a gummy bear
Cotton candy in my hair!
Lauren Torre, Grade 3
Meeting House Hill School, CT

School
fun, talk, play, work, try
trouble, write, help and we share
draw; noise and teacher
Tom Yu, Grade 2
Public School 148 Ruby Allen, NY

Orange
Beautiful as the sunset
as bright as a burning fire
A pumpkin
Orange
Peter Kokias, Grade 2
Marvin Elementary School, CT

Rain
A really wet day
Puddles are made on the street
Umbrellas are up.
Ian Castrence, Grade 3
Berry Elementary School, MD

Wind
Wind makes tornadoes
Wind is very cold sometimes
Wind glides fast and slow.
Clara Behnen, Grade 2
Long Meadow Elementary School, CT

Ice Skating
I like to ice skate. It is fun.
I wear my hair in a bun.

When I jump I have power.
I practice for about an hour.

My coach's name is Luis.
He's teaching me to spin.
My friend Sara's coach's name is Allyn.

I started to skate
When I was seven, now I'm eight.

I like to compete but…
I have to wear skates on my feet!
Sydney Leonard, Grade 2
Warwick River Christian School, VA

Silly Sea Lions
Seven sea lions were swimming
sideways in the salty sea.
The small one turned to the bigger one
and said "I bet you can't catch me!"

The larger one said "I know I can.
I'm faster than you think!"
The little one turned and swam away
before the larger one could even blink.
Jonathan Volpe, Grade 3
Frenchtown School, RI

The Moon and the Sun
The moon will come up soon.
The sun will have fun making light for the Earth.
The time is up! The moon is up!
And the sun will have fun again tomorrow.
Everyone is in bed.
And the sun will pop up tomorrow
And the beginning of spring will start.
Flowers will bloom and the sun will shine
While the moon is waiting.

Andrew Kiley, Grade 3
Sacred Heart School, MA

Baby Blue
Baby blue makes me excited.
If I see the color baby blue I will be very, very happy, and surprised.
It will be great.
Baby blue shows me all of the blue in the world
like the baby blue sky, baby blue berries
And the baby blue birds too.

DeAnni Quill, Grade 2
Ulysses Byas Elementary School, NY

Spring
The colors of spring,
They make me want to sing.
I like to play outside in the sun.
It is fun.
The flowers start to bloom.
They are inside my mom's room.
It is so sunny.
My brother is so funny.

Ana Smith, Grade 3
Susquehanna Community Elementary School, PA

Spring
Spring, I love it so.
It brings new life to all the grows.
It makes me happy to play outside.
To feel the warm sun while I ride.
Through the garden as I go, up the hill and down.
Through the dandelions I go.

Bridget Weston, Grade 3
Frenchtown Elementary School, CT

Let's Think About Spring

Let's think about spring.
The weather is warm and nice.
I go home during Easter Sunday.
I will help with brownies and oatmeal cookies.
I will go to the Dairy Queen
And Old Country Buffet, and Bob Evans.
Let's think about spring.

Ashley C., Grade 2
Kanner Learning Center, PA

Summer/Winter

Summer
Warm, bright
Swimming, hiking, camping
Flower, sunshine, snow bank, gloves
Sledding, reading, snuggling
Cold, dark
Winter

Leanne Stephan, Grade 3
Our Mother of Perpetual Help School, PA

Spring

Spring is here,
let out a cheer!
I say Hooray,
spring is here!
The flowers bloom
out of the ground,
the birds make
a beautiful sound.
The fruits and vegetables really grow
and the best part of all? NO SNOW!
You see pretty colors everywhere,
I love the smell of the spring air!
Spring is such a beautiful sight,
that's why children's faces are so bright.
Spring is here,
let out a cheer!
I say "Hooray,"
spring is here!

Megan Grega, Grade 2
Waverly Avenue School, NY

Spring

S is for the sun that shines.
P is for pool to swim in.
R is for lots of rainfall.
I is for ice cream I eat.
N is for nest that birds live in when it's spring.
G is for great weather to ride my bike.

Tiffany Ashwood, Grade 1
Little Flower Day Care Center and Prep School, NY

I Like Summertime

I like to swim
I like to go out with my dad
I like to fish with Rudy
I like to drink Kool-aid
I like to play football outside
I like to eat ice cream and fruit
I like to go to the park

Kejon Jones, Grade 1
Urban League of Pittsburgh Charter School, PA

Summer

Summer is fun
School is done
Look at the sun
Let's go out and run

We have one more thing to do
Come on kids it is late
So go to bed now
So tomorrow we can skate.

Devon Atako, Grade 3
Little Flower Day Care Center and Prep School, NY

Spring

F abulous to see
L iving plants they are.
O h, so pretty to smell
W ith wonderful bright colors
E verywhere.
R unning, running all around,
S unny up above.

Leslie Castro, Grade 2
Public School 152 School of Science & Technology, NY

What Is My Favorite Candy?
Chocolate
Lollipops
Peppermint Patties
Reese's Pieces
M&M's
Candy Canes
Strawberry Licorice
Chocolate Eggs
Emily Frank, Grade 3
Montessori Childrens School, NY

Sunny Sun Shahana
Sunny sun Shahana
sells sunflower seeds by the seashore.
She showed me one while
sowing in the soil.
Talene Tse, Grade 2
Children's Village, PA

My Dog Rocky
Loves to
Eat
Sleep
Play
And swim

He loves to go to the
Bark Park
Dog Heaven
Squantz Pond
McDonald's
And his lazy boy chair

He has
Short brown fur
White paws and head
Hazel eyes
Stubby tail
Floppy ears
And a funny happy personality

I love my dog!
Nicole Itzkowitz, Grade 3
Meeting House Hill School, CT

A Snow Day Is…
Blustery
Snow
b
  o
    a
     r
      d
       i
        n
         g.
Jumps
bump, bump, bump.
Throwing
snowballs
at Maverick.
Sledding
crunchy snow
crunch, crunch
AN EXTRA DAY OF SCHOOL
Oh, No!
Julia Stockwell, Grade 2
Dr Samuel C Eveleth School, MA

The Lovely Leaping Llama
A lovely, leaping llama
found some licorice late one day.

He found it in the library
and ate it all away.

Just then a lively lion came
and liked it just the same.

He found out what the llama did
and wanted to make him pay.

The lively, laughing lion
lurched at the lovely llama.

He licked him like a lollipop
and gave him to his mama.
Liam Shaughnessy, Grade 3
Frenchtown School, RI

Dragons

If you thought dragons weren't long,
Then you are wrong.
They have fiery breath,
And I met one named Seth.
I saw a dragon's breath that turned into fire,
Then that dragon got hired.
I saw scales
Of dragon males.
I saw them in a fight biting each other's tails
I also hear their wails.
I looked my dragon in the eye,
And he said, "I will try."
All of a sudden, I saw a flash,
Then the dirt turned into ash.
Then all I saw were claws
With the dragons' giant paws.
This is all I have to say
It's too bad they passed away.

Arianna Flynn, Grade 3
St Catherine Laboure School, PA

Gentle Wind

Gentle wind
blows my hair but I don't care

Gentle wind
makes me happy like summer mornings
my kite won't fall to the ground
because your strength holds it up.

Gentle wind
keeps me cool all the time

Gentle wind
tries to make me fly

Gentle wind
is nice to play in
but I'll see gentle wind
until the next day.

Hilcia Argueta, Grade 3
Northeast Elementary School, NY

Healthy Water

Water is very healthy
Very, very healthy.
Some people like it,
Some people don't.
But I like it very much.
Don't you?

Marc Tyler Fagot, Grade 1
Public School 122 Mamie Fay, NY

Grandma

I hug my grandma.
She bakes cookies
And I can smell it on her clothes.
She bakes cakes.
We make chicken together.
We both clean dishes.

Madison Stickles, Kindergarten
South Side Elementary School, PA

Veteran's Day Is…

Marching and ceremonies
My birthday, yeah!
Gunfire honoring those who served
Our flag waving in the wind
Tents and camp outs galore
Crying when everyone comes home
Treats and parades
Stands and sodas
Having a good time

Alex Thompson, Grade 3
Enfield Station School, ME

A Bat

I want to be a bat at night
because bats fly high in the sky
I want to see at night
and I want to scare the birds that chirp
when I burp and fly higher than me
In July they take my apple pie
so I want to be scary to them
so they stop being mean to me

Aadam Abdullahi, Grade 3
Al-Rahmah School, MD

Meredith

Big, nice, cute, cool, doll
She is my favorite friend too!
Forever we are.

Meredith Rojas, Grade 2
Public School 148 Ruby Allen, NY

Winter

Guess what?
Winter has finally begun
Yes!
I watch it.
I see white snow
drifting silently
  down
    to
      the
        ground
Watching and seeing
The sounds of silence.
I wish I could stay longer and watch it.
I wish I could stay until spring.
Remember to watch the snow
When the trees are bold
And watching it never gets old.

Madeline Filoon, Grade 3
Ridge Park Elementary School, PA

My Best Family

My family is fun to play with.
My friends are nice to me
Just like my family.
I like to see my aunt and uncle.
They always take me to fun places.

Dominick Rossi, Grade 3
Our Lady of Hope School, NY

Spending Time with My Dad

Spending
Time with my dad
Is like flying in the sky.
We run together, play together,
And eat pumpkin pie.

Tanya Hatton, Grade 3
Afton Elementary School, NY

Thunderstorms

Have you ever looked up at a thunderstorm?
The sky is down and dark.
The clouds are gray and pale.
The fright is very sharp.
The rain is racing down to the ground.
Puddles are everywhere.
The thunder is very loud.
I am barely scared.

All of this is just nature's way.
This is just how it goes.
Looking at the leaves blow away.
That's what nature shows.

The fog walks down the window.
The rain doesn't want to stop.
The wind tries to whip my hair away.
The trees seem to hop.
A day like this is a day of rain.
A day like this is a day of clouds with form.
A day like this is a leaf in the face.
A day like this is called the mighty thunderstorm.

Pauline Ayer, Grade 3
Roger E Wellington School, MA

Fall

Looks like leaves swirling to the ground gathering all around me
Smells like smoke from leaves burning after we rake them
Sounds like geese honking their way to a new home in the South
Tastes like juicy sour apples just picked off the tree
Feels like cold wind blowing through my hair

Leiah Devenger, Grade 3
Hardwick Elementary School, VT

In the Winter

In the winter, I see trees sparkling with snow, waving with the wind.
In the winter, I hear the warm crackling fire dancing across the fireplace.
In the winter, I smell the dusty thick smoke slowly climbing out of chimneys.
In the winter, I taste the cold crisp snowflakes skating across the sky.
In the winter, I feel the hard, thick snow rubbing on my boots as I walk through
the snow.

Will Dougherty, Grade 3
Broadneck Elementary School, MD

Spring

Spring is very pretty,
Spring is very nice,
It doesn't cost you anything,
It doesn't have a price.

The sun is very warmful,
The sun is very hot,
It heats you up, oh yes it does,
But cools you down does not.

So much rain falls
Down in the spring
It makes a funny sound
It goes ping, ping, ping.

Lots of pretty flowers
Start to bloom and grow
They stand oh so beautiful
In a nice little row.
Nicole Harney, Grade 2
Clara Byrd Baker Elementary School, VA

Earth

E arth is where people live
A frica, North America, South America,
    Europe, Asia, Australia, Antarctica
R ivers, lands, oceans, deserts
T he perfect place to be
H ow well do you like the Earth?
Mariah Little, Grade 2
The Jefferson School, DE

The Volcano That Never Exploded

One day there was a volcano,
And people used to bake.
They got really annoyed,
When someone dropped in a cake.

Then the people dropped in a computer,
Filled with water from the lakes.
Then, the volcano went "BOOM,"
And the people realized it was a fake.
Matthew Petrouskie, Grade 3
Montessori Childrens School, NY

My Brother

My brother and I
Playing tag outside
After school
In my backyard
So we can have fun.
Jack MacDonald, Grade 1
Cornerstone Academy, MA

Snow

Snow blows in the wind
like dancers in the sky
going down.
Katie Lewis, Grade 2
Pomperaug School, CT

Foxes

F urious
O utstanding
X inging
E lectrical
S neaks
Emily Greenwood, Grade 3
Afton Elementary School, NY

My Cats That Have Hats

I have a cat his name is Nat.
He sleeps on a mat.
He has a hat.
He likes me to lay on the mat.
I have another cat.
Her name is Pat.
She likes me to pat her back.
She likes Nat.
Caitlyn McCaslin, Grade 2
Cambridge Day School, MD

Olympics

Olympic athletes
Playing games
On February 10th
At a stadium
Because they're the best at it.
Simon Stock, Grade 1
Cornerstone Academy, MA

Flowers

Flowers
are red
flowers
are blue
flowers
are pretty
and so are
you!

Osida Richards, Grade 1
Baltimore White Marsh Adventist School, MD

My Guinea Pig

P erky
E ats a lot
A ctive
N utty
U nhappy when called a rat
T oo handsome
S illy

Mackenzie Griffin, Grade 2
Washington Park Elementary School, PA

Mesa — My Dog

I like playing with Mesa
Because she is fun.
We play ball
And pull with her pull toy.
It gets slimy!

Shannon Romanchak, Kindergarten
South Side Elementary School, PA

Garfield Is…

An orange cat that fools people
Scared of all dogs, but he loves his dog, Otis
Really, really tricky a lot of the time
A lot of fun
Really mean sometimes
Really smart sometimes
A fast runner
A safe cat

Dustin Smith, Grade 3
Enfield Station School, ME

Deep Snow Is...
Powdery
Floating in the winter breeze
Snowball fights
Building secret tunnels
Snowboarding
Skiing
Sledding
Snow forts
Igloos
Drinking hot chocolate
Deep snow is...
André Schneider, Grade 2
Dr Samuel C Eveleth School, MA

Pigs
curly tail big ears
little fur, pink
and rough skin
the pig likes to snort
Gabriel Sencion, Grade 2
Public School 148 Ruby Allen, NY

The Spring Is Here
The spring is here.
The butterflies are flying.
The flowers are growing.
The bees are flying.
Ella Palmon, Kindergarten
John Ward Elementary School, MA

Snowwoman
Snowwoman, don't get in a fight
'Cause it won't be a happy sight
Snowwoman, so lovely, so light
Winking at the snowman tonight.
AnnaMarie Fiducia, Grade 3
Penn-Kidder Campus, PA

Devan
Devan, active, cool
Dodge ball, baseball, basketball
Smart, strong, brave, student
Devan Singh, Grade 3
St Mary's Institute, NY

Allah
Allah Allah
You gave us light
And You are always in the right
You even taught us how
To read and write.

Allah Allah
Please lead us
To everlasting Jannah,
Your paradise.
Ali El-Gabri, Grade 3
Islamic Academy of New England, MA

My Dog, Mrs. Claypole
C ourageous
L oving
A mazing
Y ou could never imagine
P arting with her
O n her first snow day
L iking chasing the truck, she was an
E lf of a dog but she was fast.
Caleb Shapiro, Grade 3
Weston Intermediate School, CT

Pigs
A pig is as pink,
As strawberry ice cream,
Eyes like little pieces of gum,
Fur goes back and forth,
When the wind blows.
Stephanie Haas, Grade 2
St Rose Elementary School, CT

Basketball
Basketball is fun,
when you're passing the ball,
we are dashing down the court.
At the end of the game,
it was a shame,
because we lost.
Sean Genoino, Grade 3
Holy Rosary School, NY

Pigs

Pigs are very nice.
Do not make them into food.
Give them lots of care.

Chelsie Alexandre, Grade 2
Public School 152 School of Science & Technology, NY

Underground Railroad

Slaves escaped,
Harriet Tubman started it,
Long, with conductors,
Slaves escaped at night,
Many hiding spots,
Many special signs,
Slaves escaped to freedom.

Noah A. Sinclair, Grade 2
The International School at Rogers Magnet, CT

Springtime

The sun stays longer.
The trees get leaves.
The flower blooms.
It gets warmer.
The bird sings.

Alexandria Lee-Robinson, Kindergarten
Little Flower Day Care Center and Prep School, NY

Spring

Spring is a wonderful time
to spread some wings and shine.
Birds are flying
through the air.
Up to the sun,
like a sweet little bun.
People are in the park going on the swings
jumping out flying with wings.
Seeing the world all around,
Sometimes sitting down.
Then, making your way to town.
"I love spring!"
It's a beautiful season.
It's time to celebrate the reasons!

Shaquille Mclean, Grade 3
Public School 397 Foster Laurie Elementary School, NY

Winter Is...
Winter smells like pine trees.
Winter feels snowy and icy.
Winter looks like the Northern Lights.
Winter is the time when people ice skate.
Winter is so much fun!

Will Doody, Grade 1
St Teresa of Avila School, NY

Animals of the Jungle
Lions hide in the grass.
Waiting for prey to pass.
Can you see them in the dark?
Look out!
They found their mark.
Do you see jaguars jumping tree by tree?
They are glad they are free.
Tigers sneaking in the night.
They don't need any light.

Lukas Murray, Grade 2
Hyman Fine Elementary School, MA

Spring
S unflowers growing
P laying outside
R unning
B **I** king
Hiking to my gra **N** dmother's house
Jog **G** ing downtown for lunch

Johnathan Gates, Grade 3
Hardwick Elementary School, VT

Water of the Sky
Water of the sky
Pours from the crystal clear atmosphere
Gently hammering from the big blue
If you're lucky
You can see it drifting
Very gently
To the hard ground
Rain makes a huge puddle.

Jack Driscoll, Grade 3
Jeffrey Elementary School, CT

My Little Brother's Sound Effects

We all say, "Lime,"
My little brother says, "Time"

We all say, "May I,"
My little brother says, "Way I"

We all say, "Hola,"
My little brother says, "Audios"

We all say, "Grapes,"
My little brother says, "Napes"

Sometimes my brother's words are mysterious,
But we just think he is hilarious!

Abreanna Washington, Grade 3
Urban League of Pittsburgh Charter School, PA

On My Way to School I Saw a Dog

On my way to school I saw a dog
It was a black dog
It was a medium, black dog
It was a hairy, medium, black dog
It was a scary, hairy, medium, black dog
It was a hungry, scary, hairy, medium, black dog
And it wanted to chase me home.

Taylor Bizzaro, Grade 2
Cornwall Terrace Elementary School, PA

Beautiful

My mom is beautiful
My mom is nice
My dad is nice
My sister is beautiful
My brother is beautiful
My grandma is beautiful
My aunt is beautiful
My aunt is beautiful
My aunt is beautiful
My aunt is beautiful
My aunt is beautiful
My uncle is beautiful

Leeana Bolden, Kindergarten
Public School 23 Carter G Woodson School, NY

Snakes
Have different colors.
Have no legs.
Have no hands.
Have ears, but you can't see them.
Have no hair.
I like snakes.
Katherin Renderos, Grade 1
Northeast Elementary School, NY

My Day
I like to go outside to play
I play all day
Then I go inside to eat
Then I go to watch a soccer meet
Then I come home and brush my teeth
And then I go to sleep.
Dennis Farley, Grade 3
Public School 5, NY

Colors
Green is the color of the grass
Brown is the color of the dirt
Yellow is the color of the sun
Blue is the color of the sky
Red is the color of poinsettias
Gray is the color of a mouse
White is the color of the clouds
Do you like colors?
Joshua Johnson, Grade 1
The Jefferson School, DE

Pain
pain pain
makes rain
many many tears
it feels like you've been hit by a tree
or got stung by a bee
ow! it hurt
then my sister will blurt
that I got hurt badly
Brian Kaplan, Grade 3
Eisenhower Elementary School, PA

Cheerleading
Cheerleading is fun
But sometimes it is scary too!

But for me it is really easy
So I don't have to worry
About being scared

We use skirts
And shirts
And paint ourselves so pretty

Our coach tells us to get ready!!
Karla Lizama, Grade 3
Bensley Elementary School, VA

Make a More Beautiful World
I wish
I wish
Penniless people could have
Money like you
I'll help them
And you should too
I'll help them be
As they should be
Melissa Peets, Grade 3
Acushnet Elementary School, MA

Beyond this Door
Beyond this door is a castle
That has a magical mat
Put your feet on the floor
You will be allowed
And the mat will whisk you away
James Wohlsen, Grade 3
St Mary School, NY

Fly Down Leaves
Catch the leaves
Run for them.
We love leaves and so do you.
Leaves, leaves swoop them creep them
Pile them up. Hooray! Hooray!
Ilana Zeldin, Grade 2
Shaloh House Hebrew Day School, MA

Abe Lincoln

A be didn't like slavery
B efore being president he was a farmer
E verybody trusted Abe

L incoln stopped slavery
I n 1860 he became our 16th president
N ow we honor him
C ivil War ended in 1865
O ften was poor
L incoln liked reading
N ow people remember him

DiAnte Swartzfager-Santiago, Grade 2
Mount Jewett Elementary School, PA

Friends

My friend's name is Tom
We build forts out of the couch
We always have fun
Buddies

Alexis Peabody, Grade 2
Christ the Teacher Catholic School, DE

Food

Hot juicy food
creamy mashed potatoes
and freezing ice cream
there's more, steamed hot chicken
and cream donuts with jelly inside.
Now that's a delicious dinner!

Tayler Wisor, Grade 3
Bradford Township Elementary School, PA

Different People and Different Languages

China, Russia, Italy
They're all a different place.
Russia speaks a language called Russian.
China speaks a language called Chinese.
And Italy speaks a language called Italian.
But somehow they're all the same.

Rebecca Rooks, Grade 1
Glover Elementary School, MA

The Colors of a Rainbow
Up in the sky,
So way up high,
With colors of red, orange, and green
It's the most beautiful thing you've ever seen
The clouds are so fluffy and so very puffy,
It's not even funny,
It's worth a lot of money,
Because of the gold in the pot.
So what is this thing you see?
It's the most beautiful thing that could ever be!
Erin Ruggiero, Grade 3
Middle Gate Elementary School, CT

Butterfly
One day a butterfly was happy.
Her birthday was coming up soon.
She went to her big sister's house.
She had fun playing games.
She had fun playing with her sister.
She had so much fun in her sister's house.
She saw a kitten outside.
She asked her mom and dad.
Her mom and dad said "yes."
So she went to the park
With her mom and dad.
Michelle Maik, Grade 1
Children's Village, PA

Cancer
F inding medicine
I n need of help
N urse
D reaming of getting better
I ll
N o hair!
G rowing older

C aring
U nhappy being sick
R eading the hospital books over and over
E very day at the hospital
S till waiting for a cure
Kristen Flynn, Grade 3
Acushnet Elementary School, MA

Spring Is Here
Spring is here
Everyone will cheer
Here is spring
We all will sing
Bring love
Like a dove
Spring is here
Katie DiColandrea, Grade 3
Our Lady of Hope School, NY

Hammers
Hammers pounding down
A noisy job for a day
Nails rushing in wood.
Amir Hopkins, Grade 3
Berry Elementary School, MD

The Fat Cat
The cat is fat.
I'm scared of that fat cat!
That cat sat on my hat.
My hat is flat!
Kyle Strang, Grade 3
Linden Hill School, MA

Snow
Snow, snow, snow is so fluffy
Like a pillow.
I like snow so much.
But it comes one time a year.
Snow is fun.
Snow is so good.
Kevin Swain, Grade 1
John F Kennedy School, MA

Spring
S pring is fun
P lants grow
R iding on a scooter
I play with my friends
N esting birds
G orgeous flowers bloom
Eugene Sugarman, Grade 1
Adelphi Academy, NY

I Knew It Was Spring

I knew it was spring
Because the sun was very bright!
I needed to wear sunglasses.
Lukas Alexander, Kindergarten
John Ward Elementary School, MA

My Sister

Jennifer is my sister
She is not a mister
Although she gets bad grades in school
I still think that she is cool

Although my sister is lazy
She is never ever crazy
Sometimes we play the PS1
When we both play, it's really fun

She talks a lot on the phone
And also plays a saxophone
She is better than the rest
I think that she is the best
Michael Morgan, Grade 3
Klein Elementary School, PA

Spring

S pring makes me happy
P lay outside
R ide my bike
I see trees bloom
N o more snow
G rass
Bryce Kotnick, Grade 1
Mount Jewett Elementary School, PA

Spring

Flowers bloom in spring,
Beautiful birds that sing,
Bees that buzz and sting,
Church bells ring on Easter morning,

Oh, what a wonderful thing!
Amanda Lyons, Grade 2
Timberlake Christian School, VA

Gymnastics

Gymnastics is a fun way to exercise,
It is a pretty sport,
That's why I do it in a squort,
I jump on the trampoline,
Then I balance on the beam,
I have to practice on the mat,
And I very much look like an acrobat,
On the bars I do a flip,
Then I have to get a grip!
Rachel Mazzie, Grade 3
Eisenhower Elementary School, PA

Love

Love is green.
It sounds like a summer rain.
It smells like baking bread.
It tastes like your favorite food.
It looks like flowers.
Love feels warm.
Samuel J. Saar, Grade 2
West Branch School, PA

Thankful

T hankful for my family
H ouse
A pples
N ature
K ind people
F riends
U mbrellas when it rains
L ove of my family
Richmond McDaniel, Grade 1
St Christopher's School, VA

Thunderstorm

Crash Boom Bang
there is a thunder storm.
And it is a bad one.
Crash Bang Boom
it is as loud as a lion.
Storm Hartmann, Grade 3
Southwestern Elementary School, NY

I Am

I am a football player.
I wonder what I look like inside my body.
I hear coyotes.
I want a dirtbike.
I am a football player.

I pretend I am a monkey.
I feel cool.
I touch a pencil.
I worry about my clothes.
I cry when I don't get my way.
I am a football player.

I understand my sister.
I say, "Can I go with you?"
I dream of having a mini bike.
I try to do my best!
I am a football player.

Christian Miller, Grade 3
Susquehanna Community Elementary School, PA

Spring

In the spring I like to play
I like to run.
Why don't we stay
To have some fun.

Spring is cool
Spring is nice.
Don't be a fool
Just get your bike!

Shawn Dawkins, Grade 3
Little Flower Day Care Center and Prep School, NY

M Is for Marisa

M y parents have just one precious child
A nd though I behave, my mom thinks I'm wild.
R unning through rooms all over our house,
I squeal when I'm happy like a cute furry mouse.
S ometimes I read when my legs tire out,
" **A** nd I love you Mom and Dad!" is what I always shout.

Marisa Balanda, Grade 1
St Joan of Arc Elementary School, PA

Summertime

Summertime is nice.
Playing in the pool, having fun with friends.
Licking chocolate ice cream cones.
Camping in a tent,
Playing tennis and going to the beach.
Summertime is nice.

Michael Foley, Grade 2
Montessori Children's Community School, PA

If I Were a Butterfly

If I were a butterfly
I would float with the clouds
Making the world an endless place
For many other wings and flies
The world would be perfect
Just as it should
Even if one butterfly vanished
There would be a next
Our life cycles are short
But still very peaceful
Egg, larva, pupa
And then adult
I would take my beautiful purple wings
Everywhere I went
So everyone could enjoy them
The sweet nectar would taste like
A delicious cooking melting in my tiny mouth
That's how it would be if I were a butterfly

Meghan Wood, Grade 3
Jeffrey Elementary School, CT

The Meadow

Let's go play outside in the meadow.
In the beautiful flowers of different colors:
Yellow, red, orange and purple.
The meadow smells like honey.
Busy buzzing bees, sipping sweet nectar.
Fluttering dots of color,
Butterflies in the air.
The meadow is full of life.

Shannon Frost, Grade 2
Montessori Children's Community School, PA

Rabbit

There once was a rabbit named May
Who hopped in the garden all day
She liked to have fun
Playing in the sun
And eating all of the way

Vanesa Benavides, Grade 2
Ulysses Byas Elementary School, NY

Butterfly

Caterpillars form
The tall leafy grass has grown
A butterfly comes

Alex Laforest, Grade 3
Acushnet Elementary School, MA

Daniel

D oes like dogs
A nd likes games
N ever hurts anyone
I am thankful for my family
E verything is nice
L ate nights at home are the best!

Daniel Lepera, Grade 2
George L Cooke Elementary School, NY

Becca

Becca is so cool
She is not a fool
Becca is so cool
She is a real jewel

Even when she leaves me in the dust
I do not fuss
Becca is my friend
Until the very end

Even though she leaves me behind
This is not a crime
Becca can be kind
She's the best friend I can find

Laura Ann Niedzielski, Grade 3
Klein Elementary School, PA

Flowers

beauty, garden
blooming, growing, raining
flowers growing everywhere
colors

Alexus Phillips, Grade 2
Marvin Elementary School, CT

Football

Tackle, touchdown
Kicking, running, scoring
Playing Pop Warner is a dream
Best sport.

Brian Quick, Grade 2
Marvin Elementary School, CT

Rainbows

rainbow
colorful, bright
shining, changing, stretching
rainbows are way up in the sky
streamers

Hanna Tomlinson, Grade 2
Wells Central School, NY

Summer

Summer is fun,
I like to play in the golden sun.
When the sun is bright,
I like to fly a kite.
I like to swim in a pool,
I think it is cool.
School is done,
Now we can play in the sun.

Lauren Urbano, Grade 3
Our Lady of Hope School, NY

Dream/Nightmare

Dream
Mind's picture
Sleeping at night
Excitement, worry, and fear
Nightmare

Stephen Spiridakis, Grade 3
William Spyropoulos School, NY

Sunshine
The warming sunshine gold and yellow,
Makes my tummy shout, "Hello!"
The flowers bloom bright colors in the meadow.
Oh, nothing can live without sunshine.
Sunshine, sunshine.

Like a blooming garden,
Sunshine glows bright in my heart.
When night takes over,
The meadow sleeps and blooming stops.

At night we sleep with hope
That sunshine will glow tomorrow.
When we wake up,
The sun wakes up,
Just like a bright glowing cup.

Dawn is the word
For when flowers yawn.
Now the flowers bend,
For nightfall comes again.

Dianne Lee, Grade 2
John Ward Elementary School, MA

School
School is cool.
Who wants to be a fool
flying kites,
taking hikes,
and wasting time all the time?
Don't be a fool,
stay in school.

Owen Zeng, Grade 2
Public School 152 School of Science & Technology, NY

Jamieson Bailey
J. Bailey was a little puppy born in October.
He came to us for three weeks, then went to my sisters.
You see he was a Christmas gift but not for me.
We just took care of him a little while.
We get to see him all the time for lots of days and nights.

Stefani Moore, Grade 2
St Mary's Elementary School, MA

Enzo

Who in Enzo?
Enzo...
Was born on May 16th.
His family and he moved to America.
He has a little and big brother.
He likes to play games and going to school.
That is Enzo.

Enzo Pereira, Grade 3
Central Avenue School, CT

What Is Blue?

August is blue
before blueberries grow
when they are ripe
and people know.

Blue sounds like
the ocean floor
when the waves rush
across the seashore.

Rachel Henry, Grade 2
A.G. Richardson Elementary School, VA

Day and Night

Day
Awake, bright
Eating, reading, swimming
Sun, colors, scared, moon
Sleeping, dreaming, snoring
Dark, tired
Night

Christina Kizeik, Grade 3
Our Mother of Perpetual Help School, PA

Love That Dog

I love that dog
like a person loves G-d.
Said I love that dog
like a person loves G-d.
I like to bark at her in the morning and say
"Hey Bella, you're the best!"

Alexandra Brostoff, Grade 3
Weston Intermediate School, CT

Christmas at Nanny's

We always like to go,
To Nanny's in the snow.
It's a special Christmas treat,
For breakfast we will eat.
Then we go downstairs,
For presents everywhere.

Celia Mongeluzi, Grade 3
St Anastasia School, PA

Autumn

Leaves
are
falling
down
on
the
sidewalk
softly.

Dallas Ellis, Grade 3
Afton Elementary School, NY

Rabbits

Cute, fun
Jumping every day.
They feel so soft
Funny!

Stephanie Weidner, Grade 3
Penn-Kidder Campus, PA

My Dog Wilbe

Green eyes looking up
Jumping chasing butterflies
A dog comes to play

Aulden Beckett, Grade 2
Killingly Memorial School, CT

Carnival

Sounds like happy yells
Looks like happy people
Tastes like cotton candy
Feels like getting dizzy
Smells like popcorn

Parker McGlauflin, Grade 3
Enfield Station School, ME

Spring

Spring, spring
You're so sunny.
I go to the playground
And play on the swing.
Bike, bike
Can I take a hike?
Bees, bees
You go in the breeze!

Keontè Downs, Grade 2
Georgetown East Elementary School, MD

Spring

S hiny green grass shining in your eyes.
P laying nicely under the bright yellow sun.
R unning, running all around my backyard.
I 'm so tired from running in my backyard.
N eed to take a nap for a little while.
G ee should we?

Emily O'Connor, Grade 2
Hyman Fine Elementary School, MA

Little Star, Little Star

Little star, little star
Are you very small?
Little star, little star
Be careful from the sun
It is very bright and don't come next to it again.
Little star, little star go in the space
If you don't you will get hurt in morning.

Rija Ahmed, Grade 2
Public School 205 Alexander Bell, NY

Carolyn

C heerful
A te macaroni and cheese today.
R ainbows are something Carolyn likes.
O wls are cute.
L emonade she drinks.
Y ellow is my favorite color.
N ice to Jess.

Carolyn C., Grade 2
Kanner Learning Center, PA

Dancing

Jazz, tap, ballet
I'm great at them all
even if I'm not so tall

D reaming to be on TV
A cro is fun!
N utcracker
C an't stop too much fun!
E veryone can do it

    it
      is
        dance
Marissa Massaro, Grade 2
Dr Samuel C Eveleth School, MA

Earth

The Earth is so fun,
The Earth has a lot of things,
The Earth is so big,
God created this planet,
The Earth is a sphere,
The Earth moves around the sun,
The Earth is so fun.
Nicholas DeFranco, Grade 3
Holy Rosary School, NY

Fishing

Bucket, shovel
Catching, cutting, cooking
Fishing with my friend is super
Flip, flop
Elvis Canahui, Grade 2
Marvin Elementary School, CT

The Sun

The sun is like…
  A flaming sphere
  A glowing jack-o'-lantern
  Orange juice in a clear cup
  A yellow apple
  The sun
Cailey Bussiere, Grade 3
Houghton Elementary School, MA

My Camera

My camera captures happy times
that I could look at any time
My friends and family bring me joy
that's better than getting a new toy
My camera looks so cool
but I can't bring it to school!
Megan Morabito, Grade 3
Booth Hill School, CT

TV

TV can be crazy.
You watch it if you're lazy.
The people who made it
Are millionaires.
If you watch it much longer
You'll be gasping for air.
I hope you take the hint.
If you don't
You'll be turned into a mint.
Joshua Steinkopf, Grade 3
Central Elementary School, PA

White

Clean snow
Mean snow
Vanilla ice cream
Paint
Shaggy dogs
White
Is not the color of logs.
Lily Sutton, Grade 3
Weston Intermediate School, CT

Baseball

Baseball is fun,
You hit the ball and run,
It's hard to see with a ton of sun,
None of us won,
But we got a bun.
Well done everyone!
Amanda Diaz, Grade 3
Holy Rosary School, NY

Wrinkle

I am the haunt of a ghost in a scary house.
I am a beautiful café on the island of Hawaii.
I am a warm smooth cup of cappuccino in the light of the morning.
I am the north who fought in the battle against the south.
I am the dusty porcelain doll in the corner.
I am a leprechaun who will vanish if you take your eye off of it.
I am a big canyon that is as hot as the glittering, sparkling sun.
I am a wrinkle in the lumpy, hard bed.

Brianna Via, Grade 3
McCleary Elementary School, VA

Sick Day

There was a boy named Tom who played every game,
He hated each one just the same.
He listened to a song.
He played some ping-pong.
Being sick is such a shame!

Michaela Buckwalter, Grade 3
Marlborough Elementary School, PA

Silly Sarah Saint Bernard

Silly Sarah Saint Bernard sat on a sandy beach.
She socialized in the sun while eating a juicy peach.
She dug for sea shells at the shore,
While her owner ate her lunch.
All Silly Sarah heard was "Crunch, crunch, crunch!"

Sarah Migliori, Grade 3
Frenchtown School, RI

Horse Showers

Horses' hooves are stomping.
Clip, clop, clip!
I hear whinnies from the field.
The horses neighing.
Flowers on the ground.
It is like a flower shower.
Clouds up overhead rumble.
Whoosh! Went hooves
In all directions
The rain comes down.
Drip, drop, drip.

Bailee Hastings, Grade 3
Southeastern New Hampshire Christian Academy, NH

The Blow-Up B-B-Q Sauce
Loose top,
Pop, splat B-B-Q sauce
On my glasses,
On my hair,
It is everywhere.
Slimy, slimy B-B-Q sauce.
Hayden Kimber, Grade 1
Williamstown Elementary School, NY

Spring
S ome birds come back
P eople ride bikes
R ain falls from clouds
I t is sunny
N ew nests are made
G reen grass grows
Danny Eschrich, Grade 1
Mount Jewett Elementary School, PA

A Visit to the Zoo
I want to go to the Bronx Zoo!
Don't you?
We could see cuddly bears
And lions that give us a scary stare!
We could see many mammals,
And ride on a camel!
I want to go now to the Bronx Zoo!
Don't you?
Brian McCatella, Grade 2
Christ the King School, NY

Bird
The bird is as...
 beautiful as a morning sun
 swift as a fox
 sharp as a needle
 quick as a blazing fire
 soft as a cloud
 oh, if I could have one
 The bird.
Sarah Gianos, Grade 3
Houghton Elementary School, MA

Christmas
Christmas is...
Decorating
lights
giving gifts
family
toys
Santa
friends
visiting Grandma and Grandpa
Christmas is exciting!!!
Ben Holloran, Grade 2
Dr Samuel C Eveleth School, MA

Irish
I rish dancing
R un catch that leprechaun
I rish dazzling gold
S heep all around
H appy Saint Patrick's Day!
Brett Rotatori, Grade 2
Long Meadow Elementary School, CT

Green
If green had a smell
it would smell like fresh cut grass
in my grandpa's yard.

If green were a taste
it would tastes like
sour pickles in my sandwich.

If green had a feel
it would feel like
a spring day.

If green had a sound
it would sound like a frog
croaking in a pond.

If green had a look
it would look like ivy
all over the house.
Brandon Ranck, Grade 3
Watsontown Elementary School, PA

Blue

Blue is the color of the light sky
Blue is the color of a baby's cry
Blue is the color of a shadow in the snow
Blue is feeling way down low
Blue is the color of a sapphire ring
A blue jay's wing
And on winter mornings the dawns are blue
Blue is my eyes
Blueberry pie
A blue tie
A robin's egg
Blue jeans leg
And on winter mornings the dawns are blue

Bobby Lanza, Grade 3
Jeffrey Elementary School, CT

Moths

I very much do not like moths
Because they eat right through the cloths.
They are the most annoying bug
I like to see them squished on a rug

My mom does not like them too
One time a moth made a cow moo
A moth can eat an entire mat
I once saw a moth go SPLAT

Moths make clothes look like Swiss cheese
A moth had one time made me sneeze
Moths go flying through our halls
Thank goodness for those great mothballs

Robert Malmgren, Grade 3
Klein Elementary School, PA

Hookstown Fair

We got stuck at the top of the ferris wheel.
There was a spinning ride.
I used my fingers to eat cotton candy.
I got to feed the sheep.
I liked the fair.

Joe Lally, Kindergarten
South Side Elementary School, PA

Christmas Eve
A Slovak dinner on Christmas Eve,
With grandparents we know believe,
That Mary and Joseph had no meat,
Only mushrooms, bread, garlic, and honey so sweet,
One by one we pass around,
To taste the food, even the hound.
When dinner is done we all sing,
A birthday song for Christ the King.

Shannon McHugh, Grade 3
St Anastasia School, PA

Nature's Color
The leaves and trees of nature
Are usually green
Light green, dark green, apple green, just green
The leaves and trees are green.

The flowers of nature
Are red, orange and blue,
Yellow and purple
Maybe pink too.

The soaring birds of nature
Are red, brown, blue
Some with feathers so green
As the morning dew.

Animals are any color
Maybe even blue
Those are the colors of nature
And people too.

Giovanna Armstrong, Grade 3
Public School 152 School of Science & Technology, NY

Spring
S is for the sunny days
P is for the precious and pretty animals that move around
R is for the roses in the garden
I is for the ice cream we eat
N is for the noises of the birds and bees
G is for green grasses in the meadow

Kaziah Clark, Grade 1
Little Flower Day Care Center and Prep School, NY

Spring

Spring, spring it's finally here
So let's all get up and cheer.
It will be a nice day so let's go out and play.
The wind is light
The sun is bright
So let's go and fly our kite.
Soon the pretty flowers will grow
I'm so happy there's no snow.
I like to hear the birds sing
And the gentle wind that makes the chimes ring.
But best of all, why I like spring
Because I get to watch baseball like a king.

Salvatore LaRussa, Grade 3
Our Lady of Hope School, NY

What Is Blue?

The sky is blue
On a cold spring day
When kids are at home
Then they go out to play.

Blue sounds like a blue bird singing
Blue acts like a bell softly ringing
For a little angel singing
Kings bring gifts to Jesus.
Blue is a very beautiful thing.

Morgan Brown, Grade 2
A.G. Richardson Elementary School, VA

Grass

I am the grass
So green and fresh
I sway back and forth
When the wild wind comes
I live in the mid-west where my friends are
When the horses come
I get matted down, but I am okay
Baby sprouts are born every day
I am light and long
That's how I stay

Aislinn O'Connor, Grade 3
Meeting House Hill School, CT

The Sad, Sad Dog
There was a crazy dog named Lad.
He was extremely so, so sad.
But he lost his great bone,
So he came home with a cone.
Now Lad is not extremely sad!
Cameron Pitts, Grade 2
Oakdale Elementary School, MD

Water
Water makes your hand cold
When you dip it in a river
Water makes your hand hot
When you put it in a warm bath
Michael Puglisi, Grade 1
Public School 122 Mamie Fay, NY

Spring
The sun is shining, shining bright
The clouds are crying, crying light
The stars are flashing, flashing fast
The plants are popping, popping up!

Bunnies are hopping in a field of green
The wind is nice, the wind is mean
You are running, running fast!
Dog is chasing
Home at last!

Drinking, drinking lemonade
Eating ice cream and a parade
Drop the cone on the street
Oops, another
Bon appétit!
Ruby Mayer, Grade 2
Cabot Elementary School, MA

Turtles
Turtles
Green, rough
Crawling, swimming, eating
Hide safely in their shells
Pretty
Jamir Brown, Grade 1
Daniel J Flood Elementary School, PA

April
A ll the birds come out singing.
P lay outside in the sun.
R un in the grass all day long.
I will get ice cream.
L et's have fun in April.
Danielle D'Oliveira, Grade 3
Central Avenue School, CT

Multiplication
M ultiplication is so fun
U nusual math problems
L oopy math problems
T errific math problems
I nteresting math problems
P erfect math problems
L aminated math problems
I s this an adding problem?
C reative math problems
A mazing math problems
T errible math problems
I t is fun
O h is this a multiplication problem?
N ature math problems
Ryan Soule, Grade 3
Frenchtown School, RI

Dog
big large furry dog
likes to play games
and jump too!
My big furry dog.
Jasmine Amigon, Grade 2
Public School 148 Ruby Allen, NY

Summer
Summer
Whales swim
Riding my bike
Flowers grow in summer
Warm
Hannah Kurek, Kindergarten
St Stephen's School, NY

Summer

My favorite season is summer,
Because I have fun in the sun.
It surely is not a bummer
I know because I get to run.

I travel to different places,
And do so many things.
I wish that summer could be longer,
With all the fun it brings.

Jelani Sealy Greigg, Grade 3
Little Flower Day Care Center and Prep School, NY

Red and the Five Senses

When I see red,
It reminds me of rubies and cardinals.
I hear red in angry words.
Red tastes like a plump, juicy tomato.
Red feels hot, and smells of ketchup.

Saskia De Borchgrave Niblett, Grade 3
Lycée Rochambeau (French International School), MD

I Am

I am a good dancer.
I wonder what costumes look like.
I hear people dancing.
I want a nice year of dance.
I am a good dancer.

I pretend to be a famous dancer.
I feel very excited.
I touch other people.
I worry about cartwheels.
I cry when one of my animals die.
I am a good dancer.

I understand that it is hard for my dance teacher
to think what we should do for dance.
I say "Can we do a bridge?"
I dream about a famous dancer.
I try not to mess up.
I am a good dancer.

Allison Ryder, Grade 3
Susquehanna Community Elementary School, PA

Colors
Red is like the color of a beautiful rose.
Yellow is like the color of the shining sun.
Blue reminds me of the bright sky.
Purple reminds me of my special shirt.
Colors! Colors! Colors!
Curtis Odom, Grade 1
Northeast Elementary School, NY

Soccer Is…
Soccer is…
athletic
it's just a time to be free
letting the wind blow in your face

scoring goals in the net feels good
especially when your team is cheering for you

it's a satisfying feeling to win
to be a good sport if you lose,
shake hands with the other team
and say "good game"
you have a celebration after you win
have the time of your life
Soccer
Katie Rodger, Grade 2
Dr Samuel C Eveleth School, MA

Birds
Birds
Big, little
They build nests
Lay small fragile eggs
Hatch
Michael Pappano, Kindergarten
St Stephen's School, NY

Daffodils
Daffodils
Swaying, dancing
Pretty, early, yellow
Pick them and smell them
Daffodils
Jenine Vivar, Grade 2
St Clement Mary Hofbauer School, MD

Neopets
Toys
Soft, furry
Walks, talks, swims
I like this toy
Flies, sinks, floats
Crazy, funny
Neopets
Brandon Rodriguez, Grade 3
St Joseph School, NY

Hockey
Skating and shouting
Fans are holding lots of things
They can play good games.
Jonathan Tsarouhis, Grade 3
Our Lady of Hope School, NY

Soccer!!
S occer is fun,
O h it is cool,
C loudy is cool when wet,
C atch the coach,
E xcellent when we win,
R efreshments are good.
Gianna Russo, Grade 3
Holy Rosary School, NY

Flying
I am just a boy
That wants to fly.
Zooming by and by.
It would be just glorious
To see all of the florias
From high in the sky.
Billy Thomas, Grade 3
The Jefferson School, DE

Summer Is Coming
Summer is coming,
We can all have fun.
We can play a game today,
We can run all day today.
Maryam Ahmad, Grade 1
Al-Rahmah School, MD

Winter
Winter looks like snow and heavy jackets.
Winter smells like marshmallows.
Winter tastes like hot chocolate.
Winter feels like cold air.
Winter sounds like fireworks.

Briahna Harris, Grade 2
Ulysses Byas Elementary School, NY

Anger
Anger is red
It sounds like mortars hitting the ground.
It smells like dead stuff.
It tastes like poison.
It looks like a battlefield.
It feels like nothing.

Justin Lee, Grade 3
Christ the King Elementary School, NY

My Mom
my mom is like a charm on my arm
there's something great about my mom
I don't know what it is
but all I know is she's my mom!

Cherelle Parkes, Grade 3
St Joachim and Anne School, NY

The Love Bug
T iny car.
H erby.
E xcited.

L ovely car.
O ily and old.
V iolent is the
    opposite of Herby.
E xtravagant.

B eautiful car.
U gly car.
G lad.

Alexa Canamucio, Grade 2
Bucks County Country Day School, PA

Trucks

Trucks
Big, Shiny
Beeping, driving, stopping
Picking up stuff and going places
Loud
Adam Eddy, Grade 1
Daniel J Flood Elementary School, PA

Snakes

Snakes are
green,
curvy,
long,
strong,
        but not
            dangerous.
Oscar Panezo, Grade 1
Northeast Elementary School, NY

Going to the Beach

Splishing, splashing at the beach.
Having fun — what a treat.
Playing ball, flying kites…wow
Look at those heights!
Aw…time to leave.
Come on, hurry,
Get in the car.
I do not want to be late for supper!
Alyssa Fleming, Grade 2
Pomperaug School, CT

Spaghetti

Spaghetti, Oh Spaghetti
I love you a lot.
I bought you at the store
And my mom boiled you in a pot.
I sprinkled sauce and cheese on you.
Oh how my face is a mess!
Every time my mom says,
"You have to have less!"
Ryan Kirk, Grade 3
Meeting House Hill School, CT

Music

I love music!
The sound so beautiful,
Mozart, Bach, Beethoven.
Play it!
Sing it!
Enjoy it!
So wonderful! So alive!

Music fills me with love and pride,
My bow dances on the strings!
Notes fly from my violin!
Marvelous musical masterpieces,
Bring pleasure, hope, and joy,
To everyone around the world!
Kanade Shibata, Grade 3
John Ward Elementary School, MA

Green Grass

G etting to
R ide
on th **E** lawn
mow **E** r when it
N eeds cutting

roarin **G**
th **R** ough the
gr **A** ss
make **S** me
S mile
Garrett Mayo, Grade 3
Hardwick Elementary School, VT

School

I go to school to learn
I learn a lot at school
I learn math and reading and gym
I really like to sing

I really like to learn all these things
They are important life skills
I love my teacher Mrs. Brown
I go to school to learn
Chelsea Wallace, Grade 3
Klein Elementary School, PA

What Is Aqua?
Have you ever seen aqua?
Aqua looks like a bright blue sky on a summer day or a huge, frozen, silent lake.
But, I think it's a bright, radiant, smiling face.

The smell of aqua is a large ocean breeze in the fall.
It's a silent morning wind in the spring.
But, mostly a small child's tear when they are sad.

Aqua feels like getting wet in the huge and wonderful ocean.
And the very cold ice of an iceberg in the freezing ocean.
Aqua tastes like nothingness in water or the bad taste of yucky blucky blueberries.
And even small particles of mist landing on your sensitive tongue.

Do you know the sounds aqua can make?
Aqua can sound like the majestic waves in the wide and vast ocean.
Or maybe a little drop of rain pitter-pattering all over the wide road
And a big long flood that just knocked down the tallest, largest, oldest tree
On the shoreline of beautiful Rhode Island.

Laura Kessler, Grade 3
Watsontown Elementary School, PA

I Am a Horseshoe Crab
I am a horseshoe crab.
I have two compound eyes,
And I don't even try to hurt flies.
I try not to get picked up by my tail,
But because of people, I fail!
My favorite foods are shellfish, clams,
And worms that I get in the sea.
I lay 4,000 eggs in the sand,
But not nearly that many survive.
My eggs feed the shorebirds,
So they have energy to migrate.
Scientists use my blue blood to
Diagnose human diseases.
I burrow in mud when the temperature is low,
So that is where to find me if it should snow.
I am more closely related to spiders,
And scientifically known as Limulus polyphemus.
So you see, I'm as harmless as can be,
And am truly a help to nature and humanity.

Andrea Cygan, Grade 3
McQuistion Elementary School, PA

Amazing Life

Life is fun
It is never done
I want all
Not some
To you, me
And all to be
Life should be fun
And never will be done.

Ramya Iyer, Grade 3
Public School 148 Ruby Allen, NY

Winter Is...

Winter is the sound of jingles.
Winter looks like snow on the ground.
Winter feels like a long nap.
Winter smells like hot chocolate.
Winter sounds like people singing.
Winter is when Santa comes.
In the winter you play in the snow.
Winter is so much fun.

Jacob Citone, Grade 1
St Teresa of Avila School, NY

My Dog, Buckeye

My dog, Buckeye has brown fur,
With a little white on his tail.
His ears are sort of black.
We like to play soccer —
He cheats!
He bites the ball.

Wyatt Patterson, Kindergarten
South Side Elementary School, PA

Peace

Peace is lollipops dancing
In the sky.
Peace is the wind
Blowing and circling in the night sky.
Peace is quiet days
On the beach.
Peace is the sound of whistling.

Olivia Fusegni, Grade 1
Glover Elementary School, MA

Phill

There once was a bird named Phill.
He lived with his wife named Jill.
They made a big nest,
It was the very best.
Now they have a baby named Bill!

Santiago Gutierrez, Grade 2
Northeast Elementary School, NY

Looking

I am looking at the sun.
I am looking at the flower.
I am looking at the grass.
I am looking at the water.
I am looking at the butterfly.
I am looking at the book.
I am looking.

Angelys Vargas, Grade 1
Northeast Elementary School, NY

Springtime

Springtime
Springtime is so sweet

Springtime
Springtime, time to play

Springtime
Springtime, time to rest

Springtime
Springtime, time to watch TV

Springtime
Springtime, time to clean

Springtime
Springtime, time to watch the birds

Springtime
Springtime, time to go to school

Erick Alonso, Grade 3
Public School 131, NY

Friends

A friend is like a brother or sister.
It is fun because two is better than one.
I can do lots of things with friends.
Friends can help me with my homework.
Pick me up if I fall.
And play with me.
It is fun to have a friend,
But sometimes they make you mad.

Mateusz Zezula, Grade 3
Our Lady of Hope School, NY

Red, White, and Blue

Red as the apples I go to pick in the fall
Red is what I see when I'm standing on Mars
White as the chalk I write with on the board
Blue as the sky in the day
It's the water in a pool
Sometimes it's the fences painted blue
Blue is a good one to pick

Cameron LaVertu, Grade 3
Enfield Station School, ME

Red

Red is blood that runs through you.
Red sounds as loud as a fire alarm at school.
Red smells like sweet roses in a bowl.
Red feels like a giant ruby at a store.
Red tastes like fresh picked cherries.
Red looks like shining fire in the night.

Jenesis Analiz Rodriguez, Grade 3
Elkridge Elementary School, MD

March

March, oh March, you are the best.
The month of March is the best
because sometimes it snows in March.
Why is March the best you ask?
The reason why March is the best
is because you can go ice skating, sledding
and have a snowball fight.

Salvatore Monico, Grade 3
Holy Rosary School, NY

It's Time to Play

It is time to play on swings.
It is time to go hiking.
Field trips and field day are coming soon.
Cooking outside and riding a bike.
Squirting water guns
Oh what fun!

Gene K., Grade 2
Kanner Learning Center, PA

Snow Day

Snow day! Snow day! Snow day!
Sleep in late!

After breakfast,
Rush to get our blue and yellow suits on
And head outside with our tubes!

Play lots of games
And sled all day
Snowball fights and contests

How far can you dig a tunnel?
How high can you build a snowman?

I love snow days!

Brian Harkins, Grade 3
Meeting House Hill School, CT

Sunset

The sunset is my favorite part of the day
because the sun is shining.
It is beautiful and shining so pretty
that it almost makes me cry.
It is bright.
I love the sunset!

Chloe Egbert, Grade 1
Media Childrens House Montessori, PA

Ants

Ants are great and special too, well to me.
If you touch them they will get you.
Some are happy. Some are mad.

Sabrinna Guardado, Grade 2
Ulysses Byas Elementary School, NY

Fly Eagle Fly

Roars like a volcano
Eats like a fat pink pig
Mean as a vulture.

Hunter Pratt, Grade 2
Killingly Memorial School, CT

Pugs

Pugs
Brown, small
Sleeping, running, prancing
White, medium
Pugs

Delia Sipe, Grade 1
Seneca Academy, MD

Cookie

I wait 'til
the cookies
are done,

smell the
aroma from
my room,

to see the
wonderful
and tastiest
cookies ever,

and wait for
more tomorrow,

But there's no more
tomorrow.

Annie Reing, Grade 3
Fulton Avenue School #8, NY

Snowman

Snowman, he's so fun.
Oh no, here comes the sun!
No, oh man, don't you go!
I will miss you so!

Alexus Capone, Grade 3
Penn-Kidder Campus, PA

Butterflies
A beautiful butterfly
flying across the sky.
So peaceful
just singing a lullaby.
Feeling the wind
blow my hair,
rush my way.
Well —
maybe I'll fly like the butterfly.

Sadia Rahman, Grade 2
Public School 152 School of Science & Technology, NY

Curious George
I like
him

I like his
books

I like his
title pages

I like
the man
with
the yellow hat

I like
him

Danielle Burkheimer, Kindergarten
Plainview-Old Bethpage Kindergarten Center, NY

I Like Lions
I like it when the lion roars and chases the ostrich.
I like lions' loud power.

Lions roar like tornadoes
They're fierce, strong and brave.

Jumping, roaring, sneaking, pouncing
Proud lions. I like lions.

Kevin Reyes, Grade 2
Children Studio School Public, DC

Crickets

Crickets chirp loudly
Crickets are thin green creatures
Jumping in the wind
Jaden Brodeur, Grade 2
Long Meadow Elementary School, CT

Baseball

I love baseball!
It's my favorite sport.
I like to hit the ball and run!
I like catching the ball.
I like my uniform.
It makes me feel good.
Casey Jones, Kindergarten
South Side Elementary School, PA

Super Snake

I'm poisonous
And scary too.
Look at me!
I'm shedding.
I have new shiny scales
And really big fangs.
Beware!
Hector Gutierrez, Grade 1
Northeast Elementary School, NY

The Ocean

Look at the ocean.
Its waves are very wavy.
The ocean is nice.
Sydney Scripture, Grade 2
Marlborough Elementary School, PA

Dogs

Dogs
Run, bark
Sleeping in cage
My dog is brown
Loud
Victor Freeman, Kindergarten
St Stephen's School, NY

Details

The important thing about a poem
is that is has details.
It is sometimes imaginary but
it can be real.
It has big words and small words.
Something special is anybody can do it.
But the important thing about a poem
is that is has details.
Kaylie Schiowitz, Grade 1
Glover Elementary School, MA

Friends

They're there when you need them
They go ahead
They leave you behind
You need to let them go
You have to say goodbye
She'll turn up soon
In your head
Lorenzo Manuali, Grade 1
Buckley Country Day School, NY

Getting Glasses

Went to get new glasses —
Only the store was closed.
Went up to the door
And I partly froze.

Now what should I do?
Without my glasses,
I can't see for the rest
Of my classes.

I had to wait a long time,
My eyes were really blurry.
It is the last day,
I have to do it in a hurry.

I got my glasses,
Went to school,
I thought
I looked really cool.
Christopher Wright, Grade 3
Hamilton Elementary School, PA

Shamrocks
I've definitely seen enough of shamrocks,
And the color green.
My baby-sitter brought cupcakes,
With green frosting.
So boring!
And on them what I see,
Those dancy, prancy, jumpy, bumpy,
Jiggly, joggly shamrocks!

But, I really do like shamrocks,
Very much, in fact I had a cookie
Shaped like one for lunch!

Emma Waldor, Grade 2
John Ward Elementary School, MA

Do You Know What Color Is?
Do you know what Spring Green is?
It is a flower blooming.
It is a bird singing a peaceful song.
That is Spring Green!

Do you know what Wild Strawberry is?
It is a dream,
It is a swirl of color.
That is Wild Strawberry!

Do you know what Midnight Blue is?
It is a slick cat creeping upon a mouse.
It is a colorful painting.
That is Midnight Blue!

Do you know what Pine Green is?
It is a soft moss bed.
It is dewy grass with the sun shining down.
That is Pine Green!

Do you know what Sea Green is?
It is an artist painting a picture.
It is someone reading an insightful book.
That is Sea Green!

Jillian Ridler, Grade 3
Susan Odell Taylor School, NY

Sleepover

My cousin Tyara was sleeping over,
I wished we had a four leaf clover.
Her mom called with some really bad news,
"We're moving to Florida," I felt so blue.

I didn't want my cousin to move so far,
We were so close, like best friend movie stars.
But she was very happy
and I was for her.

She went home and started to pack.
She called me and said her brother was moving back.
I said, "Why don't you?"
Then she felt blue, too.

I felt bad for her,
I didn't know what to do,
So I asked my mom, she said
"There's nothing I can do."

When my cousin Tyara was in Florida,
I knew that was it — I knew she wasn't coming back
She called me and wanted to come back,
I was happy.

Selena Garcia, Grade 3
Hamilton Elementary School, PA

Mom

Mom is very sweet.
She can be funny sometimes
When I am so sad.

Denice Griffith, Grade 2
Public School 152 School of Science & Technology, NY

The Light and Roars of My Dream

Day and night
I get confused
Every night I follow my path
Going to a place
Where thunder and lightning occurs over and over
Searching for their way to their light and loud roar.

Diego Guallpa, Grade 3
Public School 41 Greenwich Village School, NY

Candy Is Pink

Candy is pink, lollipops are purple,
Chocolate is sweet and so are you!
Cakes are yummy;
Cupcakes are too,
Like candy in a bowl of sweets.

Jeffrey Pak, Grade 2
Media Childrens House Montessori, PA

Spring

Spring, Spring, bring me leaves;
Spring, Spring, I love your breeze.
Fireflies, fireflies, I love how you glow;
Fireflies, fireflies, I love to catch you though.
I ride my bike all day long;
I ride my bike for oh so long.
Clear blue sky, I can see your clouds;
Clear blue sky, you're a mile high!

Kory Outlaw, Grade 2
Georgetown East Elementary School, MD

Cookies

C ookies are so yummy
O h I love chocolate chip cookies the most
O h I love cookies so much
K atie likes cookies too
I love making cookies too
E verybody in my family likes cookies
S tep on a cookie and I'll still eat it

Eileen O'Connor, Grade 3
Sacred Heart School, MA

I Am

I am little but the world is big.
When I grow up I could be a paleontologist
And dig, dig, dig.
I have a sister who is tall
She likes to carry me down the hall.
I like to play with my ball
It's fun to kick, but not to fall.

Michael Lapioli, Grade 1
St Joan of Arc Elementary School, PA

My Family
My family is great
My sisters are nice to me
My family is cool
Victor Montoya, Grade 3
Public School 148 Ruby Allen, NY

Cats
Cats
Soft, nice
Running, meowing, walking
My nice pets
Cats
Kenan Parent, Grade 1
Daniel J Flood Elementary School, PA

Oceans
Looks like clear glass,
Tastes like salty French fries,
Feels like very cold snow,
Sounds like thunder.
Patrick Briscoe, Grade 2
St Rose Elementary School, CT

Apples
Apples are tasty.
They are colorful,
Red, green, yellow.
They have a stem.
They grow on trees.
You can eat them.
YUMMMMMMMY.
Oren Schouten, Grade 1
Williamstown Elementary School, NY

Ode to Mittens
She's sweet and loving,
But at the same time,
She's as feisty as a 2-year-old brother.
Mittens is a wonderful miracle,
Born to help my 16-year-old cat.
She's a black calico,
With little, white paws.
Maggie Wilcher, Grade 3
McCleary Elementary School, VA

Spring Is Here
Have no fear spring is here.
The flowers grow every year.
We see the trees and leaves.
And we hear the humming of the bees.
Arianna Olivier, Grade 3
Our Lady of Hope School, NY

Germ
You're nasty, vile, evil, mean,
But you are never seen.
Why are you wicked?
Can't you be nice?
Your heart must be like ice.
You're not kind.
In fact you're bad.
And you make people sad.
You make the evil spread
When the children are in bed.
You're a nasty, vile, evil, mean, bad
Germ.
Madeline Guth, Grade 3
Thoreau Elementary School, MA

My Friends Anthony and Andrew
My friends are funny.
Their names are Anthony and Andrew.
I like them just as they are.
A lot of fun and kind.
Sadia Brown, Grade 2
Ulysses Byas Elementary School, NY

My Friend and Me!
I love softball!
You love gymnastics!
I have brown hair.
You have blonde.
I love May!
You love March!
We are different,
But love each other!
Bridgett Holman, Grade 3
Oakdale Elementary School, MD

In the Cafeteria

In the cafeteria, the tables are as shiny as a new glass mirror.
In the cafeteria, I hear people talking as loudly as an earthquake.
In the cafeteria, I feel my rough, soccer lunch box.
In the cafeteria, I taste the fresh saucy pizza.
In the cafeteria, I taste the fresh spicy chicken nuggets.

Tyler Gabarra, Grade 3
Broadneck Elementary School, MD

Four Seasons

Spring is fun under the sun,
the night comes, it feels cool,
but don't go in the swimming pool.
Summer comes, go to the beach!
Eat a sandwich with tomatoes and a peach.
The night comes, catch flies,
then the night goes by.
Fall comes, rake the leaves and jump in a pile,
maybe you could walk a mile.
The night comes, stay in and watch the wind blow,
and make cookies with dough.
Winter comes, make an angel and put it on a tree.
The night comes, stay in and make some hot cocoa, and some cookies too,
and the snow turns from white to blue.

Priya Govil, Grade 3
Media Childrens House Montessori, PA

Blue Waterfall

Blue tastes like a delicious blueberry
freshly picked in the summer.

Blue sounds like the ocean singing to a beautiful lake
that dances with a lovely waterfall.

Blue feels like a person that is blue
and a singing blue jay dancing with a pretty bluebird.

Blue smells like bubble bath
over filling the tub after a long day.

Blue looks like the waterfall
splitting from a jutting rock on a summery day.

Haley Keiser, Grade 3
Watsontown Elementary School, PA

Baseball

Baseball is fun,
Baseball is cool.
We play baseball
After school!

My brother and I
Play on a team.
We like to hear our friends
Cheer and scream!

Michael Malherek, Grade 2
Mary Matula Elementary School, MD

Spring

S weet
P eppermint
R oses
I ce cream
N ickel
G uitar

Brianna Dowling, Grade 1
Christ the King Elementary School, NY

How Was Your Day?

How was your day May,
was it nice and gay?
Was it bad?
Did it make you mad?
How was your day May?
May? May? May!

Dustin Harris, Grade 2
Grace Miller Elementary School, VA

Spring

S is for spring which is very pretty.
P is for purple grapes.
R is for red juicy apples.
I is for I love spring.
N is for spring never ends.
G is for green grass in the spring
shining in the sun.

Cassandra Barber, Grade 2
Hyman Fine Elementary School, MA

My Friends

I have friends,
they are kind,
they helped me get baskets in
during basketball.
My friends are really nice to me,
and I am nice to them too.

Alexandria Altieri, Grade 3
Holy Rosary School, NY

Spring

Flowers grow, now we know,
Spring is here.

Birds come home,
Bears awake, now we know,
Spring is here.

Buds come up,
Then they grow, now we know,
Spring is here.

And I'm glad!!

Emma Siegel, Grade 2
St Rose Elementary School, CT

Football

Football
Brown, pointy
Flying, bouncing, scoring
My favorite sport to play.

Zachary Earley, Grade 1
Daniel J Flood Elementary School, PA

Peace

I wish the whole world
was peaceful.

If the whole world was peaceful,
imagine how it would be?

So quiet and peaceful
what a safe place to be.

Youssr Attia, Grade 3
Islamic Academy of New England, MA

Gold

Gold is the sun, shining in the air.
Gold is blond, yellowy hair.
Gold is a star in the middle of space.
Gold is the number one in a relay race.

Victoria Lin, Grade 2
Cornerstone Academy, MA

The Moon

The moon is up at night
It beams extra bright.
Its shadow on the pond shines.
We remember all the old special times.

Jaclyn Joseph, Grade 3
The Jefferson School, DE

My Name Is Thomas

T rickster,
H ilarious,
O ne that likes school.
M usial is my last name.
A nimal lover,
S illy.

Thomas Musial, Grade 2
Montessori Children's Community School, PA

Winter

I love winter, yes I do
I love winter
You should, too.

Winter's good
Winter's great
It's something I appreciate.

After playing in the winter snow
It's time to watch a TV show.
Slurp! Slurp! Slurp!
Hot chocolate in my cup
Now it's time to cuddle up with my little pup.

Don't you agree that winter is just meant to be?

Olivia Pesce, Grade 3
Middlebury Elementary School, CT

Spring
S unny
P retty
R obins
I s nice outside
N ot cold
G lad spring is coming
Jackie Baker, Grade 2
Bucks County Country Day School, PA

The Bumpy Toad
If brown had a sound,
It would sound like
A horse galloping in the fields.

If you tasted the color brown,
It would taste like a Three Muskateers bar
Floating down from above.

The smell of brown reminds me of
Butterscotch ice cream
At an ice cream stand.

Have you ever seen brown?
Brown looks like a bumpy toad
Hopping down a country road.

It feels like an old shoe
Stored away for a hundred years.
Mitchell Keiser, Grade 3
Watsontown Elementary School, PA

Spring
Spring is here the air is warm,
One more year until another snow storm,
I cannot wait to run and play,
On a nice hot summer's day,
When I get hot I'll jump in my pool,
With all my friends I know from school,
We'll laugh and play the whole day long,
And sing our favorite children's songs,
I hope this day will never end,
Until next time goodbye my friends.
Jilliann DeGon, Grade 2
St Mary's Elementary School, MA

Bird
Bird
Peaceful, graceful
Wading, flying, eating
Walking in the water
Crane
Leah Fisher, Grade 3
St Rosalia Academy, PA

The Seasons
I am an autumn.
All of my friends are winter.
Now it's really hot.
Meredith Morris, Grade 3
West Branch School, PA

Spring
Roses are red,
Violets are blue,
I love spring!
How about you?
Paul Marzan, Grade 3
Public School 164, NY

Music
Music is so playful,
Music is so nice,
Music is a great sound
That I can dance to all night.
Music brings me pleasure,
Music brings me calm,
Music is my favorite sound
That makes me feel so warm.
Austin Tan, Grade 3
Sacred Heart School, MA

Spring
S inging girl.
P laying soccer.
R ainbow
I t is a sunny day.
N ational park
G etting my bicycle.
Kayla Carrelo, Grade 3
Central Avenue School, CT

Gold

If gold had a sound, it would sound like a royal king
sitting down on his throne or servants letting down the drawbridge.

Gold looks like a lion's mane that is so golden it shines brighter than the sun.
Gold is a gold trophy that I won in a race and a king that rules the land.

Gold sounds like crispy golden brown toast sitting on my plate
or a gold juicy pineapple freshly picked from a bush.

If gold had a taste it would taste like caramel that's my mother's favorite treat
or like butterscotch and caramel smothering over ice cream in my bowl.

Gold feels like a smooth block of gold in a king's castle
or a hard chunk of gold hidden in the ground.

Tyler Meehan, Grade 3
Watsontown Elementary School, PA

Gold

Gold feels like warmth in the hot, summer sun,
Gold looks like Steelers getting ready to score,
Gold sounds like mustard coming out of the bottle,
Gold smells like fresh, hot muffins coming out of the oven,
Gold tastes like corn on the cob in the summertime.

Nathan Keiser, Grade 3
Watsontown Elementary School, PA

Buddy's Treats

Buddy is my cat
He catches all the mice
Buddy is getting fat
And he is very nice

Buddy doesn't like other cats
He likes to hide behind my bed
Buddy never wears funny hats
And he really likes to be fed

Buddy brings in all types of "treats"
Like dead frogs, mice, and birds
Buddy scares everyone, (I think it's kind of neat)
And my sister's scream is the loudest I've heard

Zach Prather, Grade 3
Klein Elementary School, PA

The Checker Board Colt
Click clack the colt went
Like black and white checker board
It trots on the field
Chace John Wood, Grade 2
Killingly Memorial School, CT

Summer
Summer is cool!!!
You can go in the pool!!!
Playing with your friends...
The fun never ends!
Eating ice cream is a blast!!!
But you have to eat it fast...
Swimming is a lot of fun
With your cousins in the sun!!!
Pretty flowers everywhere...
I like to put them in my hair!!!
Summer is really cool!!!
I think SUMMER RULES!!!
Elena Erica Tornabene, Grade 3
Public School 5, NY

Trucks
Trucks
Go fast
Very fun
Are really loud
Gas
Bradleigh Batchelder, Grade 3
Enfield Station School, ME

People, People
People, people, everywhere
even in their underwear
some go here,
some go there,
people, people, everywhere.

Some people have short hair
and others like teddy bears,
people, people, here and there,
people, people, everywhere.
Ashley Mateer, Grade 3
Frenchtown School, RI

Michael
one day my dog
Michael
he turned tall
he was so big
I had to give him away
to someone else
my tears rolled down my cheeks
I was sad
Rebecca Cabral-Brockway, Grade 1
Glover Elementary School, MA

Ode to the Flag
The flag stands for justice
It gave us our freedom
It has red, white, and blue
We fought a hard war
Just to be free
You can see the flag
Almost everywhere you go
The flag should be honored
In a very special way
The flag is special
To each and every one of us
Today it stands for us
It is very special to me
The flag stands for courage
It stands for heroic people
Who fought for freedom
It stands for braveness
For those who gave us freedom
The flag should be special
For every one of us
Amber Bradley, Grade 3
McCleary Elementary School, VA

What I Like
My dad makes chocolate
and I eat a lot of it!
I am a boy and football is my game.
When I play I have a good aim.
Kevin Mazick, Grade 1
St Joan of Arc Elementary School, PA

Page 225

In the Cafeteria

In the cafeteria I see smiling faces. I also see tables that look as shiny as new glass plates.

In the cafeteria I always hear the cash register open and almost make a ching ching sound. I hear the kids munching on their food.

In the cafeteria when I get my food I feel the foamy lunch tray. I also feel the key pad when I put my number in. When I need to get my napkin I feel the softness that almost feels like a brand new fur coat.

In the cafeteria on pizza day I smell the cheese on the pizza that tastes wonderful. I sometimes smell the French fries that smell like fries that just came out of the oven.

In the cafeteria where I taste the sweetness of the chocolate milk. I love the chocolate that is so yummy.

Julia Poerio, Grade 3
Broadneck Elementary School, MD

Where Do All the Leprechauns Go?

Where do all the leprechauns go?
Do they live in the trees? Do they live in the snow?

Do these small people live in a stream?
When they see a snake, do they start to scream?

Where do all the leprechauns go?
I don't think anybody will ever know.

Where do the leprechauns hide their gold?
Do they hide their gold in the deep, deep cold?

Do they hide it in the stars?
Do they keep it in jam jars?

Where do the leprechauns hide their gold?
I don't think anybody was told.

Danny Palumbo, Grade 3
Davidsonville Elementary School, MD

Peace

Hello, my name is Dr. King.
I'm so very wise.
When I walk down the street
Everyone I meet
Asks, "When will there be peace?"

Abigail Blaise, Grade 2
Public School 152 School of Science & Technology, NY

Fall
Fall is a season.
The leaves fall off the trees.
The leaves change colors.

Ciara Cunningham, Kindergarten
Little Flower Day Care Center and Prep School, NY

Three Things I Love About Yonkers
I love my school because I have many good friends,
And it's really cool!

I play on the swing in my favorite park,
Until it's almost dark!

I love shopping and buying clothes in all the Yonkers stores.
Happily, I go in and out of all their doors!

Let's give Yonkers a big cheer!

Alexis Fernandez, Grade 1
Christ the King School, NY

About Me
I play soccer in the fall and softball in the spring,
I like to go outside and play on the swing.
I'm in first grade and I really like school,
I like to go to Disney World because it is cool.
My birthday is in June and my hair is light brown,
my family and I live in Middletown.
I like gymnastics and dance too,
my favorite color is pink and my eyes are blue.

Kayla Strohecker, Grade 1
St Joan of Arc Elementary School, PA

The Thanksgiving Show
Our tradition is a talent show.
Why? Nobody really knows.
Now, we can't wait
Until Thanksgiving to celebrate.
Today I think I will sing
But, I always change my mind when the bells ring.
It doesn't matter who's number one.
But we always try to make it fun.

Alexa Andrisani, Grade 3
St Anastasia School, PA

When It Snows

When it snows it's as white as a cloud
When it snows it feels as cold as Alaska
When it snows I want to go outside
and play football and have flaming hot chocolate
When it snows I want to play video games all day long
When it snows if you're lucky, but only if you're lucky,
You won't have school.

Zachary Kulliver, Grade 3
Ridge Park Elementary School, PA

I'm a Snowflake

I'm a snowflake big or little.
I feel gravity
Pushing on me.
Falling.
Slowly,
And slowly.
I smell water.
I see other flakes falling under, above, and beside.
Imagine where I could go.
Where could I end up?
Why would I be there?
Who knows where the answer lies.
Beneath me,
Above me.
I wonder.
As I ask these questions,
I fall onto a hand.
On a glove.
I slowly melt…
Until I'm water.
Snowflake.

Shalimar Azima, Grade 2
The International School at Rogers Magnet, CT

Spring

S winging
P laying
R iding bike
I s still school
N ice weather
G oing fishing

Katie Greene, Grade 3
Susquehanna Community Elementary School, PA

Soccer
Soccer
Running outside
Playing indoor soccer
Soccer makes me happy
Goalies
Nicholas Falbo, Kindergarten
St Stephen's School, NY

Rock Star
I'm going away forever,
Somewhere very far
I'm gonna go (when I grow),
To be a rock star!

I'm on the stage
The folks all cheer
I play my guitar
For people to hear!

I'm very happy,
But also sad,
I like being a rock star,
But miss my mom and dad!
Danny Perry, Grade 3
Meeting House Hill School, CT

Orange
Orange is the color of the sun
Or a knitted sweater that is done.
It's a quilt on my bed
Or a hat on my head.
Maybe the color of a box
Or someone's chicken pox.
The color of your lips
Or the color of your clips.
Orange is the color of some tea
Or the color of an orange tree.
It's the color of a shirt
Or the color of a skirt.
Orange is my favorite color.
Olivia Tracy, Grade 3
Eli Terry School, CT

Blue
Blue
Foggy Sky
Soggy Sky
Ocean
Water
Blue Jay
Blue
Is the color of the water
In the bay.
Simeon Okoro, Grade 3
Weston Intermediate School, CT

April Flowers
A pril showers bring May flowers
P etunias are beautiful
R oses are amazing
I love how flowers bloom
L auren waters flowers
Bryce Katch, Kindergarten
Montessori Academy of Lancaster, PA

Summer
Summer
Sunny hot
Swim in pool
Plant flowers for Mom
Fun
Dominic Nappo, Kindergarten
St Stephen's School, NY

Things That Ducks Do!
Ducks fly
Ducks preen
Ducks quack, quack, quack!

Ducks dive
Ducks swim
Ducks migrate, migrate, migrate!

Ducks eat
Ducks eat
Ducks waddle, waddle, waddle!
Veronica Washington, Grade 1
Northeast Elementary School, NY

The Sun

Sun.
the sun is yellow, hot and big,
the sun is round, bright and warm,
the sun lights up the Earth,
it looks like a star,
it looks like a ball,
very far away.
it makes me happy.
it makes us warm when we are cold.
it makes the snow melt.
it makes fire.
I really like the sun.
the sun is so good!

Itzel Guerrero, Grade 2
The International School at Rogers Magnet, CT

Getting Great Clothes

I'm going shopping. I think I'll look great.
After shopping my mom said I could skate.
First I got a shirt with dragons on it.
It didn't scare me one little bit.

Next I got pants. They were so cool.
I think I'll wear them on the first day of school.
Then I got socks. They were the best they can be.
Maybe they made them just for me.

Last I got shoes. They were covered in green.
If I look closely they look mean.
Now I'm done. They look great.
Now I could go on and skate.

Steven Aronow, Grade 2
Thomas Fitzwater Elementary School, PA

Fall into Fall

When the leaves turn yellow, red, and orange,
What does it mean?
It means fall! Yes, fall is on its way!
Let's rake a pile of the colors yellow, red, orange, and
Let's jump!
WEEEEEEEEEEEEEEEEEEEEEEEEEE!!!

Olivia Martins, Grade 3
Harrison Road Elementary School, VA

Butterflies
Butterflies
Flying, fluttering
Beautiful, colorful, quick
Lightly touching the ground
Butterflies
Chidera Iwudyke, Grade 2
St Clement Mary Hofbauer School, MD

What Is Black?
Dark is black
When a big storm comes
There is a tornado
Down go thumbs.

Black tastes like sour apples
Black acts like it is scared
Like a ghost is chasing him.
Black thinks I cared
Mike Sprinkel, Grade 2
A.G. Richardson Elementary School, VA

Marshmallow
Sticky, fluffy
White, puffy
Sweet, tasty
Delicious
Jose Fontano, Grade 3
Christ the Teacher Catholic School, DE

Teddy Bear
My teddy bear is nice and soft
It comes in handy when I'm scared
He follows me wherever I go
That's something that I know
Leanna Chester, Grade 1
Our Lady of Perpetual Help School, NY

The Eye of the Tiger
Fierce, deadly when the tiger arrives.
The tiger tells you when you're about to die
So you better run and you better hide
Because here comes The Eye of the TIGER!!!
Rhys Gilkenson, Grade 1
Home School, RI

Lion the Licker
Lion licked lemons
with lots of
lemon limes.
Nate Goonasekeram, Grade 1
Seneca Academy, MD

My Snickers
Ponies
brown, small
swimming, eating, sleeping
white, black
Ponies
Emily Gebhardt, Grade 1
Seneca Academy, MD

Jones Beach
Beach
Warm, cool
Surf, rest, run
It is so relaxing
Eat, play, tan
Fun, sandy
Jones Beach
Julia Biscardi, Grade 3
St Joseph School, NY

Spring
S pring is hot
P retty
R omantic
I ncredible season
N ice, too and
G reat
Jocelyn Calixto, Grade 3
Public School 164, NY

Flowers
flowers
sweet, beautiful
growing, blooming, picking
blooming daffodils all over
tulips
Carly Luck, Grade 2
Wells Central School, NY

Mrs. Levisy

She loves kids
She is cool
She is nice
She is beautiful
She is wonderful

She has curly hair
And beautiful clothes

She is fun
But not all the time
Especially when we take tests

We love Mrs. Levisy
She is the best!

Mariah Kelley, Grade 3
Bensley Elementary School, VA

Horse

H appy
O wners
R eally know a good horse when they
S ee one
E specially a trained one

Julia Knapp, Grade 3
Afton Elementary School, NY

Snow/Precipitation

Snow
White, cold
Many snowflakes fall
We can make snowman
Precipitation

Trey Wennerstrom, Grade 1
Mount Jewett Elementary School, PA

Basilisks

Basilisks
Fast, scaly
Sprinting, walking, running
Like to sprint on water
Wow

Matthew Malenovitch, Grade 1
Daniel J Flood Elementary School, PA

When Heavy Snow Falls

When heavy snow falls
Windy
Whirling
Destructive
Powerful
Falling
Disturbing
Moving strongly.

Jeff Stern, Grade 2
Dr Samuel C Eveleth School, MA

Money

Money is shiny

Some are big
Like the half-dollar

Some are tiny
Like the penny

Some are kept in our wallets
Like the 100 dollar bill

I put my money in my pocket
And carry it everywhere!

Roberto Romero, Grade 3
Bensley Elementary School, VA

The Woods

I could see a squirrel
Up in a tree
I could hear the birds
Singing to me
I could smell the flowers
Scattered on the ground
I could taste the breeze
Blowing all around
I could feel the fresh spring air
Blowing in my hair
When I was walking in the woods

Rachel Coe-Scharff, Grade 3
Scott M Ellis Elementary School, NY

How Basketball Is Awesome

B asketball is a cool sport
A ll people cheer
S ome people, like me, love basketball
K eep practicing foul shots
E arning money to play basketball
T homas is also in a basketball team
B asketball is fun
A ll 5 basketball players are playing
L ay ups are tricky
L ooking at the players makes me want to play too

Anthony Padro, Grade 3
Growing Life Christian Academy, NY

What Is Red?

Red is the beautiful sunset, painting the sky.
Red sounds like the first hurry of the wind, rushing over the trees.
Red smells like the ripeness of apples.
Red feels like the wonderfulness of love.
Red tastes like the freshly picked cherries of the orchards.

Alina Wieprecht, Grade 3
Elkridge Elementary School, MD

Animal Alphabet

I wrote a poem about animals
I wrote it just for fun
I wrote a poem about animals

A is for alligator
B is for bunny
C is for cat
D is for dragon
E is for elephant
F is for ferret
G is for giraffe
H is for horse
I is for iguana
J is for jaguar
K is for kangaroo
L is for lemur
M is for monkey

N is for North Atlantic Lobster
O is for octopus
P is for panther
Q is for quail
R is for rhino
S is for snake
T is for turtle
U is for Ursus Maritimus (we call it a polar bear)
V is for viper
W is for water bug
X is for xiphosura
Y is for yak
Z is for zebra

And now my poem is done.

Riley Chilcott, Grade 3
Klein Elementary School, PA

Nature
As the sun shines on the
rivers
trees
birds
and animals
I look at the swans
swimming and eating,
the lions
running, eating and playing
the sun leaves,
the moonlight comes,
the animals go to sleep
they say goodnight.

Sarai Rondon, Grade 3
Public School 152 School of Science & Technology, NY

The Little Cowboy
The little cowboy lived in the desert
He traveled and traveled and traveled
Until he spotted a hotel

He needed a room but he had no money
He walked and walked and walked
Until he spotted a gold rock

He gave the gold to the hotel owner
Then he slept and slept and slept
Until he heard a shot come through the window

Then he said "It is ON"
He grabbed his hat and ran and ran and ran
Until he spotted a bull

The bull charged at him and the cowboy grabbed his horns
And rode and rode and rode the bull
Until he busted out of the hotel and rode into a group of mean cowboys

The little cowboy took off his hat and said "Howdy ya'll!"
And the mean cowboys laughed and laughed and laughed
Until they realized that the little cowboy was the one who took their gold
Then they said "It is ON"

Jonathan Jackson, Grade 2
Urban League of Pittsburgh Charter School, PA

Winter Snow
The snow is falling.
It looks like fur on a lamb.
Then it starts to melt.
Miranda Katz, Grade 3
Ridge Park Elementary School, PA

Writing
Papers turning
Teacher talking
Kids whispering
Footsteps walking near
People tapping pencils
Children thinking
Quietness has come
Rocking chair rocking
Computer typing
Chairs wiggling
Pencils dropping
Books closing
Writing time is done
Katie Maleckar, Grade 3
Jamestown Elementary School, VA

Water
Water is...

a whirlpool,
a big sea,
a small pond,
a short lake,
a long river.
Felisa Artas, Grade 1
Public School 122 Mamie Fay, NY

20 Chickens and 3 Hens
20 chickens lead 3 hens;
They lead them to the barn.
When they got to the barn
They sat down talking
About how hens and chickens grow up.
Erik Uebelacker, Kindergarten
Bel Air Elementary School, MD

Snake
Snake
Long, dangerous
Hissing, slithering, biting
Finding all kinds of prey
Sneaky
Srivatsav Challa, Grade 1
Daniel J Flood Elementary School, PA

About Snow
I love snow
Because it is soft and cuddly
Like my dolly Pooh

When I walk in the snow
The snow feels squishy squashy
Under my feet

When I walk in the snow
It feels funny.
Leila Bruske, Kindergarten
Children Studio School Public, DC

Snowmen
Still, frosty
Standing, staring, waiting
Memories of all blizzards
Then melted
Noah Taylor, Grade 3
Acushnet Elementary School, MA

Spring
Spring is here let's cheer
we are going to the park
we will have fun there.
Amanda Dennison, Grade 3
Public School 148 Ruby Allen, NY

Volcano
Volcano, volcano so tall and high
You look like a painting in the sky,
So powerful and strong.
Volcano you are long.
David Baker, Grade 3
The Jefferson School, DE

Chocolate

Once I met a man who ate chocolate
for breakfast, lunch and dinner and sometimes brunch,
but when he eats it for brunch he always eats it on a raisin banana split.
One day he asked me if I wanted some chocolate...
and I said no.
I don't like chocolate.

Steven Brooks, Grade 2
Grace Miller Elementary School, VA

Lovely Walk

Roses are red, violets are blue,
And I love you.
So come with me on a walk to see some pretty flowers too.
And may we see lovely butterflies too,
Look at those pretty bugs
They're spotted ones, green and yellow and purple too.
Do you see those pretty birds in the sky?
How about those cute little bunnies that lie in the grass.

Paul Weaver, Grade 3
Maynard P Wilson Elementary School, NY

Reading

Reading is like going anyplace
Every book could be an ace
Every book could be something different
You will not forget it if you just go and get it
When you open a book something exciting happens
When you start reading a book it is like starting a race
When you stop reading a book it is like winning first place

Doug Hapeman, Grade 3
Eisenhower Elementary School, PA

Summer

Summer is here
I get to go in the pool.
We get to go on summer vacation
And now I'm out of school.

Summer is here again
Here comes the fun.
We get to go on a picnic
We get to play in the sun.

Darean Fortune-Lee, Grade 3
Little Flower Day Care Center and Prep School, NY

Horses

Horses, horses, what are you doing in the field?
We are grazing and talking to each other.
Master, master, what are you doing in the field?
Watching you graze you silly horses.
Rebekkah Gull, Grade 3
Oakdale Elementary School, MD

Blue

Blue is sports in the autumn sky
The winning high
The Blue Jays' caps
Olympic laps
Lakers' jerseys are old light blue
A Yankee homer, the sky is glittering blue
Jason Kidd sinks a three pointer shot
From gym floor spot

Michael Jordan
In Carolina blue
UConn blue
Dolphins' blue
Patriots' blue too
All of these sports
Have a shade of blue.
Luke Nolan, Grade 3
Jeffrey Elementary School, CT

Slick Sam the Snake

A slick snake is not so great
for a pet or for a friend.

It's slow and stick
won't catch a stick and slides all over it.

You should stay still
as he slides all over you.

Slowly slide away from him
now he will not slide again

Well just until June starts
then he's free again.
Joseph Angolano, Grade 3
Frenchtown School, RI

All in One

It's all in one
tiny ball
of China.
You can see
a new world.
Rachael Duval, Grade 1
Harry Lee Cole School, MA

Abigayle

Abigayle, kind, fun
Sweet, cool, amazing, super
Smart, fun, beautiful
Abigayle Dybas, Grade 2
St Mary's Institute, NY

Friends

I like my friends,
With them the fun never ends.
We are true to each other,
And never hurt one another.
Our friendship will be forever.
Ariana Gopal, Grade 3
Our Lady of Hope School, NY

Macramé

Strings go back and forth
back and forth
watching my fingers go
back and forth
back and forth
as I do
macramé
making the four
gifts for friends
bright different colors
in the string
going under
and pulling its way across
the big wooden desk
as I listen to
the noisy room.
Hannah Avant, Grade 3
Mast Landing School, ME

Playing with My Family
Trucks with my
Brother

Polly Pocket with my
Mom

Game boards with my
Dad

Crawling with my
Hamster
Katelyn Rodriguez, Kindergarten
Plainview-Old Bethpage Kindergarten Center, NY

Rain
The rain and sun together makes rainbow.
Rain. Rain is good.
The lightning glows. Rain is fun.
The storm flying in the air. Rain is water.
The rain glows in the night. I like rain.
The rain makes storms and lightning. Rain.
The sun is good and the rain is bad. Good rain.
The sun shines. Rain.
Mud mud puddles are fun you can jump in them.
You play in them you could get dirty.
It is fun to play in rain.
Rain is fun to play outside.
I like big rain. You can drink rain.
I like rain. Rain. Rain. Rain.
Play in rain. I love rain.
Good rain! Good rain! Good rain.
Rain is mud.
Dima Belov, Grade 2
Shaloh House Hebrew Day School, MA

Poetry
P oetry so soft
O kay I like that poem
E nough to show how I feel
M ake poetry into a song
S mooth and nice
Kionna Romans, Grade 3
Public School 152 School of Science & Technology, NY

Meow

I have a tall cat.
He catches a mouse.
Runs down the hall,
Runs into a wall, meow!
Molly Moore, Grade 2
Calvary Chapel Christian School, NY

Wind

Wind can be speedy
Racing through the leaves on trees
Sh! Sh! Sh! — blows you away!
Ryan Skeean, Grade 2
Killingly Memorial School, CT

The Crazy Day!

I hit my head
And I'm turning blue,
I have a dollar and fifty-two
I like to eat, but never meat
Or else I'll go achoo!

My brain is bouncing like a ball
I think I just jumped off the wall
I can't stand it anymore!

I need to go to sleep
Or else I might even weep!
Aaron Karasik, Grade 2
Cabot Elementary School, MA

Moon

Moon, moon,
    As pretty as a loon,
On a lake —
    Black and white.
Sometimes full, sometimes half.
I see mist and fog —
    Steam that rises into the air.
The water is warm, the night is cool.
    A still life painting,
        Peaceful
Moon, moon.
Max Ranzato, Grade 3
Viola Elementary School, NY

A Thingamajig

A dog who did nothing but dig,
Dug a hole so very bid.
A wig that was red,
Blew up on his head.
Now he's known as a thingamajig!
Dustin Crummitt, Grade 2
Oakdale Elementary School, MD

Sounds of Summer

I'm looking out my window,
I'm hearing the birds sing,
I'm hearing the waves crashing,
Going cling!

What is this?
Could it be?
It's the sound of summer,
Yippee!

Waves crashing on the shore.
Kids yelling, "There's school no more!"
It's the 20th of June,
And I'm hearing the tune!
Brianna Gershkowitz, Grade 3
John Ward Elementary School, MA

Christmas Eve

Every year on Christmas Eve
We get together to read
'Twas the Night Before Christmas.
We are so excited we cannot wait.
Until morning, which will be so great!
Christmas is here again!
Shane Dougherty, Grade 3
St Anastasia School, PA

Snow

Snow is really fun.
Snow, snow angels and snowmen.
Snow is cold and bright.
Luke Lane, Grade 2
Calvary Chapel Christian School, NY

Shadows

S unny days my shadow follows me.
H ow the sun shines on me and makes a black clone of me.
A pesky clone that copies me and follows me.
D oooooooooone!!! I can't take it anymore!
O kay I am not going out on sunny days.
W hen I go inside, the sun shines on my and I see my shadow.
S o I realize my shadow is my friend.

Osiel Orellana, Grade 2
Hyman Fine Elementary School, MA

Cuisenaires

They are colorful

They are
rods

They are
wooden

They are
fun

Cuisenaires

Jack Gross, Kindergarten
Plainview-Old Bethpage Kindergarten Center, NY

Candy

Candy, candy, candy
Candy is sooo sweet
It is a heavenly treat

Candy, candy, candy
I wish I can eat it every day
But my mother will scream and shout and take it away.

Candy, candy, candy
I love it so much
But for now I have too many cavities, toothaches and such

Candy
Candy
Candy

Sanjidah Chowdhury, Grade 2
Public School 205 Alexander Bell, NY

Spring

S pringtime is fun.
P eace on earth.
R ain falls in spring.
I love spring.
N ests are built in the spring.
G od created spring.
Joseph Corkindale, Grade 3
Central Avenue School, CT

Spring

flowers blooming
wind blowing
sap running
grass growing
birds chirping
a new beginning
Axl Errington, Grade 3
Hardwick Elementary School, VT

Clouds

Clouds can look
like fluffy pillows in the air.
Clouds can look
like dragons and knights.
When you look at a cloud,
you can see whatever you want to see.
Grace Archer, Grade 3
Afton Elementary School, NY

My Dog Buddy

Going to the park
Watching buddy catch Frisbees
This spring was awesome
Logan Doring, Grade 2
Long Meadow Elementary School, CT

Rain

I am very fast
I make thunder and lightning
I can make mud too.
Cullen Huffines, Grade 2
Long Meadow Elementary School, CT

Cats

At the pet store
scratching in its litter box
as the store closed.
Evangelia Angelis, Grade 1
Public School 122 Mamie Fay, NY

Dear Fish

Dear Fish,
How are you
Down under the water?
What is it like swimming
All the time?
Is it fun?
Well, see you soon.
Love, Megan
Megan McCarthy, Grade 1
Glover Elementary School, MA

Flowers Are Fun

One flower
Two flower
Three flower
Four
Five flower
Six flower
Seven sunflowers
Stout and tall
Too much to count
I can't count 'em all!
Jesse Bukera, Grade 2
Central Elementary School, PA

We Are Third Grade

Third grade is the best
Because we're always good in tests
Our teacher is Sister Nur
The best teacher in the school.

In the school
There is not a pool,
But if there is
Our life will be extra cool!
Amal Adra, Grade 3
Islamic Academy of New England, MA

Books
The pictures
illustrators

The words
authors

The front
cover

The back
cover

I like books
Lillian Garfinkel, Kindergarten
Plainview-Old Bethpage Kindergarten Center, NY

Fly
Once I saw a fly.
It was in the sky.
I tried to kill it,
but it buzzed away.
I tried to spray,
but the water couldn't stay.
Ksawery Surdel, Grade 3
Public School 160 William T Sampson School, NY

What Is Red?
Red tastes like
sweet strawberries eaten in the summer sun,

Red sounds like
people yelling stop because there are cars,

Red feels like
a smooth, ripe apple in the fall,

Red looks like
firecrackers in July, bursting in the sky,

Red smells like
a sweet batch of Valentine cookies coming out of the oven.
Miranda Smith, Grade 3
Watsontown Elementary School, PA

Martin Luther King

F ootball was Martin's favorite sport
A great leader
M any blacks were slaves
O nly whites could do certain stuff
U nfair people attacked him
S omeone threw a bomb in his house

Willard Cobb, Grade 3
Susquehanna Community Elementary School, PA

My Nest

Yonkers is the best,
Because it is our nest!

I go with my mom to ShopRite,
Our time together is fun and bright!

When it rains,
We ride the trains!

Together, my family and I go to Sprain Ridge Pool,
Where it is really cool!

Nicholas Gaschler, Grade 1
Christ the King School, NY

Mother

Mother is not mean.
She does not scream.
She plays with me every time,
Until I go to sleep.
She's always quiet,
When I am asleep
Mother is very kind to me.

Baleria Guzman, Grade 2
Public School 397 Foster Laurie Elementary School, NY

Spring

The flowers start to bloom.
I have flowers in my room.
There are flowers in my yard.
I smell them hard.
I play under the sun.
I have a lot of fun.

Tiara Leonard, Grade 3
Susquehanna Community Elementary School, PA

Sunset

Sunsets are blazing with colors of light with chirping birds.
A dog answers with a howl.
Seeing a dog fetch a ball when night like a blanket rules the land.
The noise of barking dogs is softened with the chirp of birds.
Night is as soft as a dog's long droopy ear.

Abigail Kohler, Grade 2
Head O'Meadow Elementary School, CT

Do You Know Mrs. Red?

Red listens to romantic music.
Red celebrates Valentine's Day...every day!
Red's temper erupts in fiery explosions,
Red enjoys sweet strawberries and juicy tomatoes.
Red kisses when in love and blushes when embarrassed,
Red screams louder than the siren of a fire truck!
Red's touch feels like a hot sunburn.
WARNING!! Watch out for Red!

Thomas Bernhardt-Lanier, Grade 3
Lycée Rochambeau (French International School), MD

Juan Ponce de Leon

When Juan Ponce de Leon was on his first voyage,
he went searching for the fountain of youth.
Sadly he did not succeed, but he did discover Florida.
He died in search of the fountain of youth.
I like that Florida is always nice, except when it rains.
But it is still kind of fun in the rain
because you can still go swimming,
and you can go on those fun waterfalls.
If Juan Ponce de Leon hadn't discovered Florida,
we wouldn't have Disney World or Universal Studios
to go on rides like Men in Black, Jaws,
Back to the Future, or The Tower of Terror.
We wouldn't have Disney characters
to sign autographs in our books.
And we wouldn't get to see what Mickey Mouse,
Daffy Duck, Minnie Mouse, and Goofy look like.
Florida is like the fountain of youth
because it makes everybody feel younger and happier.
So maybe Juan Ponce de Leon succeeded after all.

Neil Hailey, Grade 3
Old Bridge Elementary School, VA

Dogs

I like frogs and I like hogs
but most of all I like dogs
She sits on my lap
I give her a tap
saying goodnight
While the moon shines bright
Abby Zadrozny, Grade 3
Eisenhower Elementary School, PA

Dolphins

Dolphins
Gray, pretty
Playing, eating, swimming
Happily splashing through the waves
Sparkly
Victoria Obitz, Grade 1
Daniel J Flood Elementary School, PA

Mouse

Mouse
Gray, small
Eating, running, squeaking
Lives in a hole
Little
Bryona Pega, Grade 1
Daniel J Flood Elementary School, PA

My Adorable Puppy, Mr. Mojo

Soft baby pup
Black and white little Shih Tzu
My cute puppy Moj
Kirsten Sluyter, Grade 2
Killingly Memorial School, CT

Snowman

S now is falling.
N o school today.
O utside I made a snowman.
W hat a stormy day!
M aybe he could wear a scarf.
A hat for him too.
N othing makes a sound.
La Faith Youngblood, Grade 1
Frenchtown Elementary School, CT

Killer Whale

Black body
White circle on top of his eye
Lives at Sea World
Type of whale
Eats dolphins and seals
Swims with big flippers
Jumps really high
Splashes you with his flippers and tail
I rode on him!
Wils Hosken, Kindergarten
St Christopher's School, VA

About Me

I like to read books.
I like to dance a lot.
I like to paint my art work.
But, I don't like to eat fatty foods.
Folasade Bailey, Grade 1
Northeast Elementary School, NY

Mud Season

M ajor
U ndertaking to
D ig out of

the **S** limy
E arth
A s it
S ucks my boots
O ff
It **N** eeds to dry up!
Monica Kerr, Grade 3
Hardwick Elementary School, VT

Fall

Fall
Leaves fall
Yellow, red, orange
Rake leaves into piles
Autumn
Elizabeth Strott, Kindergarten
St Stephen's School, NY

Park

I went to the park
The sun was hot
I saw my friend and we had a chat
We played with a ball
my friend had a fall
The ball rolled in some hay
and that where it is today

Aaron McMeo, Grade 3
Public School 152 School of Science & Technology, NY

Winter Is

Winter is the season of hot chocolate mustaches.
Winter is the sound of the crack, crack, crack
that goes on in other people's fireplaces.
Winter feels like the warmth of the blankets that we wear at night.
Winter looks like frozen frosting.
Winter smells like hot chocolate.

Angus Crowley, Grade 1
St Teresa of Avila School, NY

Stars

Stars are bright
You can see them in the night
Too bad you can't see them in day.
In the day time you can't see them because they are too bright.
Stars are small
So you have to use a telescope to make them big.
Stars are amazing in every way.
There are a lot of stars around you.
You just can't always see them.
Stars are up high in the sky
You will never be able to touch them.
Stars make a lot of pictures.
Stars are very far away.

Dominique Stromple, Grade 3
Eisenhower Elementary School, PA

My Pet

I like my pet cat.
My pet cats listens to me.
I walk my pet cat.
My pet cat is friendly.

Chantia Murphy, Kindergarten
Little Flower Day Care Center and Prep School, NY

My Fish
My parents gave me 3 fish,
My fish are very brave,
They swim, back and forth in a blaze,
I watch them getting food,
They go so fast they create a wave,
Sometimes I doze off wishing I was a fish
Brianna Kaplan, Grade 2
Public School 205Q, NY

Heather
Heather is my cat.
She is so soft,
Just like a feather.
She has stripes.
The colors are white and gray.
She has a cute pink little nose!
She says meow.
Emmy Jo Toogood, Kindergarten
South Side Elementary School, PA

If I Were a Snowflake
If I were a snowflake
I would float to the arctic
And see the polar bears, seals, and penguins
Then I would jump on a cloud and sing:
I'm a snowflake
I'm a snowflake
I see all the wonders
I'm a snowflake
I'm a snowflake
How happy I am.
Alexandra Anakia Paul, Grade 3
Elkridge Elementary School, MD

Spring
S is for the beautiful sunshine.
P is for pretty flowers.
R is for the rain that falls
I is for insects in the grass
N is for the nice trees that have green leaves
G is for the green growing grass
Malik Tobias, Grade 1
Little Flower Day Care Center and Prep
School, NY

Fall Is...
Trick-or-treating,
Fall Festival,
Jumping in leaves,
Reading scary stories,
And Thanksgiving.
Bo Williamson, Grade 1
St Christopher's School, VA

My Dog
My dog
Black, furry
Pulling, barking, playing
Walking with me
Blackie
Kayla Rizzo, Grade 3
St Rosalia Academy, PA

If I Were a Noodle
If I were a noodle
I'd take a bath of cheese.
I would get eaten by a kid.
I would be plopped on a plate.
I would be cooked.
I would taste of cheese.
It would be fun.
David Ballowe, Grade 3
St Christopher's School, VA

Spring
Winter is over
Baby animals are born
Flowers are blooming.
Katie Polk, Grade 3
Berry Elementary School, MD

Beach
Beach
Beautiful, amazing
Swimming, climbing
Looking for shells
Ocean
Olivia Rowe, Grade 2
St Rosalia Academy, PA

Secrets About Me

I am as happy as a birthday
I am as playful as a puppy
I am sometimes as sad as a cry
I can be as lonely as someone with nobody to play with
I am as fierce as a cheetah
I am as angry as a snorting bull
I am jealous when children get to play
And they don't let me go to recess.

Fidel Ramirez, Grade 2
Children Studio School Public, DC

Dogs

Dogs are cute.
Dogs are fun.
Dogs can play when you don't have anyone to play with.
I love dogs!

Christina Mack, Grade 1
Jamestown Elementary School, VA

The Amazing Dolphins

Dolphins are amazing.
I love dolphins.
I love their nice smooth skin.
I kiss the tip of her nose.
I ride on her back.
We play 'til sundown.
At night we cuddle and look up at the stars and the moon!
Sometimes we play in the warm water in the summer.
Sometimes I play mermaid with the dolphin
and we pretend like she is my sea pet.

Asiyya Ferguson, Grade 2
Al-Rahmah School, MD

Nature's Call

Nature calls the wind over the land
Nature calls my name through the summer rain
Nature calls freedom for the world
Nature is the gift of life
Nature calls the spring flowers through the winter's light shade of snowy ground
Hold onto your soul while nature calls the sun to rise

Meredith Shepard, Grade 3
Weston Intermediate School, CT

Names
My name could be Hesley,
It could be Gesley,
It could be Sesley or Presley,
It could be Besley,
But, my name is Wesley.
Wesley Simmons, Grade 2
Calvary Chapel Christian School, NY

Flying
I fly
Up in the deep
Blue sky.

I hate to lie
When I am
In the sky.

Up or down
Here or there
I love to fly

Everywhere!
Sabrina Salameh, Grade 3
Islamic Academy of New England, MA

Fall
F all is fun.
A jump in the leaves is fun.
L ittle people play in the leaves.
L ets go rake the leaves.
Alexis Savage, Grade 3
Central Avenue School, CT

Friendship
When I think of you
I am not blue
When I think of you
My heart is true
I like you for who you are
Because you are my shining star
Shahirah Khan, Grade 3
Al-Rahmah School, MD

Spring and Winter
Spring
Sunny, warm
Playing, laughing, singing
Tulips, birds, snowflakes, snowballs
Snowboarding, snowing, playing
Snowy, cold
Winter
Lacie Dube, Grade 3
Central Avenue School, CT

Friendship
I feel friendship in the sky.
In the clouds too.
And there is a friend for me and you.
There are good times and bad times.
And when you say sorry.
Then they forgive you.
Now we are friends again today.
Let's play!
Leah Wilk, Grade 3
Sacred Heart School, NY

Color
Brown is the color of a penny
Yellow is the color of the sun
Red is the color of a bird
Orange is the color of a basketball
Black is the color of the night
Green is the color of the grass
Colors are pretty!
Cheyenne Poe, Grade 2
The Jefferson School, DE

Teachers
Teachers teach children everywhere
Teachers even look in your hair
Teachers always check your tests
Teachers see who's the best
Teachers sometimes use a printer
Teachers make a book for the winner
This is what teachers do
Maybe you can do it too!!!
Semir Sheikh, Grade 3
Al-Rahmah School, MD

The Cow

I saw a cow
he always took a bow
he went to town
but he did it upside down
oh wow!

Kristen Foye, Grade 3
Public School 23 Carter G Woodson School, NY

My Dreams

I often dream of being in the big diamond!
And wishing for a ball to come my way.
I think of being a star!
And, when I dream I want to dive and catch the ball,
I feel like I am weightless.
I often dream of being in the big diamond!

Jeffrey Hayek, Grade 3
Oakdale Elementary School, MD

About Me

I like to go shopping at the mall.
I like to read lots of books.
I like to eat pizza.
But, I don't like to play football with my brothers.

Ashanti Albert, Grade 1
Northeast Elementary School, NY

Spring

Spring is here
Let's have some fun.
Lots of ice cream,
Sweet and good.
Now too much now,
Time for good foods, too.

Kirby LaGuerre, Grade 2
Public School 152 School of Science & Technology, NY

My Hands and Feet

I use my feet to walk the path of life.
I use my hands to swim in the pool of life.
I use my feet to bounce on the trampoline of life.
I use my hands to paddle the boat of life.
I use my hands and feet for joy and struggle.

Hunter Briccetti, Grade 3
Susan Odell Taylor School, NY

Hockey
playing
scoring
winning

shooting
and
passing

checking
goaltending
lifting the puck
into the net

diving shots
icing the puck
in back of net

Hockey
Neal Patrick Murray, Grade 2
Dr Samuel C Eveleth School, MA

French Fries
Boiling hot
Look at them bubble
Oh my gosh
See all the smoke
I may want one
Tasty
Chewy
Crunchy
Oily
I love this all so much
I'll eat a whole bag
No, I'll eat every single one
Chelsea Lopez, Grade 3
Meeting House Hill School, CT

I Don't Like Snakes
They are dangerous.
They eat rats.
They have no legs.
They slither.
Jesus Peguero, Grade 1
Northeast Elementary School, NY

Spring Comes
Easter bunny comes
Butterflies drink sweet nectar
I have fun in spring
Anya Lowe, Grade 1
Montessori Academy of Lancaster, PA

Storms
Wind, lightning
No sun
Thunder
Like drums
Rain, wet
Jump in
Snug in my bed
I like storms
Emma Deutsch, Kindergarten
Buckley Country Day School, NY

At the Beach
I see sand
I see boats
I see a lighthouse
I see waves
I see fish
I see a crab
I see a lifeguard
I see the sun
I see an airplane
I DON'T see a robot!
Anthony Pineda, Grade 1
Northeast Elementary School, NY

Friends
F riends are fun.
R emember we were friends.
I like being friends with
E lvie and Anthony so much!
N ow we start being friends.
D id you say friends?
S o let's be friends.
Jose Diaz, Grade 2
Ulysses Byas Elementary School, NY

The Basketball Game

Dribble, pass
Run fast,
Try to block
Then make the shot.
Yes, we scored
Swoosh some more!
Now they steal
It's no big deal.
Oops, out of bounds!
Our ball now.
Go for the layup
Just got fouled.
Shoot for two
Me not you!
We're winning by four
Then...they even the score.
Time for some tricks
The players are mixed.
A quick pass, then a walk only 30 seconds to go!
I steal the ball and dribble down court
And slam dunk, baby! The score is 6 to 4!!!

Cody Gunther, Grade 3
Public School 5, NY

Winter Is

Winter is the smell of hot chocolate.
Winter is the sound of roasting marshmallows.
Winter feels like building a snowman.
Winter looks like a bunch of bumpy hills covered by a blanket.
Winter is fun!

Dorothy Shi, Grade 1
St Teresa of Avila School, NY

Sister

My sisters are annoying every day,
They bother me in every way.
Both of them are very loud,
They don't make my mom and dad very proud.
My family isn't very happy about the noise my sisters make.
I say stop for goodness sake!

Jennifer Frappa, Grade 3
Ellicott Road Elementary School, NY

The Special Fork

There once was a young man from Cork.
He eats chops with his special fork.
But now it is lost.
He forgot that he tossed
His chops away with his fork!

Noah Leadore, Grade 2
Oakdale Elementary School, MD

My Sister

I love my sister.
I will kiss her on the cheek,
And I love her a lot.

Jennifer Hoffman, Grade 2
Bucks County Country Day School, PA

Dolphins in the Sea

Dolphins, dolphins in the sea,
Can you grant a wish for me?
I want to swim by your side,
As far as we can ride.
Beneath the ocean blue,
I'd love to stay with you.

Sarah Goble, Grade 2
Georgetown East Elementary School, MD

That House

There is this house that's by the road
I don't know who lives in it, though.
My little bear must think it weird
To stop this very second here.
But I just love to spy and see
The things that aren't meant for me!

Siobhan Haggett, Grade 3
Vergennes Union Elementary School, VT

Rigs

I'm trucking in a rig breathing diesel smoke.
Enjoying the view.
I need more money.
Because I spent it on diesel fuel.
I'm banned from some highways.
All the other truckers and me.

Jarod Flood, Grade 3
Bradford Township Elementary School, PA

Fall Is...

Seeing leaves fall,
Hearing owls hooting,
Smelling pumpkin pie,
Tasting pumpkin pie,
Touching cold noses.

Cole Eck, Grade 1
St Christopher's School, VA

I Pray

I love Islam.
I pray with Iman.

I pray to Allah.
I pray Salah.

I pray Fajr
I pray Thuhr.

I pray Asr.
I pray Maghrib

I pray Isha
I make Dua.

Salmaan Mubeen, Grade 3
Al-Rahmah School, MD

Our Class

Our class is so cool
Our class really rules
We know how to do it
We know how to get to it

We are all so strong
Just like King Kong
We all stand so tall
We help each other not to fall

We are very handy
Sometimes we get candy
Our class is so funny
We love recess when it's sunny

Jacob Anderson, Grade 3
Klein Elementary School, PA

Rainbows

Rainbows are beautiful
Rainbows up in the sky
with beautiful colors
that fills me with joy
I get so excited,
I run around and...
Look at them until they fade.
Then, I go to my shade.

Jordan Bowen, Grade 2
Public School 397 Foster Laurie Elementary School, NY

My Grandma

My grandma is pretty
My grandma is funny
My grandma is happy when I am learning
My grandma is busy every day
My grandma had a brown closet
My grandma had a yellow clock
My grandma had a green chair
When I was little, my grandma taught me how to talk
When I was little, my grandma taught me how to walk
My grandma helps me with math
My grandma helps me with my homework
My grandma lives in China
My grandma knows how to write Chinese
My grandma knows how to read Chinese
But my grandma can't write English
But my grandma can't read English
I miss my grandma
I miss my grandma

Xudong Zheng, Grade 3
Public School 173, NY

Sweet Stuff

It's funny how I saw a rain cloud coming by.
But then, I saw it was raining apple pie!
It started snowing ice cream with tops of whipping cream
and then there came a root beer float in a glazing brown beam!
Then there was some chocolate cake, and sugar cookies in lots of pounds
lots of chocolate bunnies in some melting chocolate mounds!
It's funny how I saw a cloud of apple pie that was really gonna pour
but then I heard my mom say: "Get up!" Aw, mom, just five minutes more.

Aidan Quigley, Grade 3
General Wayne Elementary School, PA

P.S. 148

It is the best school
nice, very good place to be.
I love this great school.

Moaz Khan, Grade 3
Public School 148 Ruby Allen, NY

Saying Good-bye

Mrs. Joslyn,
Do not go, for the learning amount
will become slow.
I remember that happy glow
when you started teaching so long ago.
I am becoming sore
but, just to tell you that I adore
the way you teach and so much more.
(But I really am becoming sore.)
You are the greatest teacher
the best and beyond
so I really am quite fond
of your magic teaching wand.
I like you very much
You have that special touch.
For when you leave
I will receive sadness that will stay
because you went away.

Nina Lindenbaum-Grosbard, Grade 3
Jenkintown Elementary School, PA

Cats

They love balls of yarn
Cats are cuddly and cute
Cats are fast to play.

Joey Ceccolini, Grade 2
Long Meadow Elementary School, CT

Christmas

Christmas is joyful.
Christmas is nice and giving.
Christmas feels so warm.

Kaylee Rhinehardt, Grade 2
Fonda-Fultonville Elementary School, NY

Air/Smog

Air
clean, clear
blowing, breathing, flowing
trees, plants, dump, smoke
polluting, destroying, coughing
thick, dirty
Smog

George Triantafillou, Grade 3
William Spyropoulos School, NY

Lost

My dog likes to wander
And I have to look for her.
Why does she wander?
I don't know.
I think she looks for food,
Grass and sticks.
I wish she didn't wander.

Jill Kirson, Kindergarten
John Ward Elementary School, MA

Stars

Stars are like…
little night lights in the sky
small specks of sparkling sand
a shining diamond on a ring
Stars.

Erin Orsini, Grade 3
Houghton Elementary School, MA

Recess

Bell rings,
Run out,
h
scotch
p
"jump rope"
whatever you want.
A kid yelling
TAG YOU'RE IT!
Bell rings,
get in q u i c k!

Julia Klopfer, Grade 2
Dr Samuel C Eveleth School, MA

Because of Poems
Magic is overwhelmed
Hurricanes hide
And tarantulas cower.

Because of poems
Words meet together
Perfectly
Like *drizzle* and *fog*,
Even simple ones
Like *cat* and *dog*.

Words have a match
To see which is better.
POW!
The ball hits the word *letter*.
He breaks into twenty-six parts —
Only to make the new words, and capture new hearts!
Isabel Feinstein, Grade 3
Thoreau Elementary School, MA

Spooky Rhythm
I am a haunt, scaring people away from the darkness where I live
I am a rhythm of spooky sounds
I am an ash in the fireplace of the dark house
I am a blur in the bright sun that I hate
I am ice on a hot day
I am the throne of a king
I am oil dripping from a car
I am a click that comes from nowhere
Katie Flinchum, Grade 3
McCleary Elementary School, VA

My Five Senses About Yellow
Yellow smells like a buttercup in a fresh garden with daisies.
Yellow tastes like a fresh lemon squeezed in my lemonade.
Yellow sounds like a bright yellow duck quacking in a big sparkling pond.
Yellow feels like fresh corn from the barn.
Yellow also feels like a banana on a bright green tree.
Yellow looks like a firefly lighting up the dark night sky.
Yellow looks like a candle melting the hot yellow wax on a cold winter night.
Tyler Hornberger, Grade 3
Watsontown Elementary School, PA

Baseball

Baseball is fun like a baseball time.
Baseball is cool because it's so much fun.
Baseball is enjoyable when someone gets a HOME RUN!
Baseball is easy to play at any time of day.
Baseball — it's break time!!!
Baseball

Veecheat Sim, Grade 2
Hyman Fine Elementary School, MA

Yellow

Yellow is like the taste of
a sweet banana sliced on top of a hot fudge sundae.

Yellow is like the taste of
a fresh pineapple on a summer day,

Yellow is like the sound of
a bus dropping kids off after school,

Yellow is like the feel of
a soft buttercup blooming in the meadow.

Cheyanne Hollenbach, Grade 3
Watsontown Elementary School, PA

Spellbound

I feel like I'm in a trance, as though I've been polished by the golden ray of the
sun. I feel as though I've been touched by the soft gleam of the moon. The
elegant folds of my gown flutter rapidly in the wind. I soar across the lake
leaving a foot path of my soul. My mind and spirit have fled across a lake of
silence, illuminating the waters surrounding me. Then I reach lakeside, my
damp gown has tears of magic rain upon it. I pace across the blue dewy grass
and into the still, calm, peaceful forest — never to be traced again.

Hannah Willig, Grade 3
Conestoga Elementary School, PA

Blue

Blue is the color of birds in the sky.
Blue is a color of the big blue sea.
Blue is a color of lakes, ponds, rivers, and oceans.
The ocean has blue sharks, eels, and whales.
Blue is a color of big airplanes.
Blue is my favorite color of all colors.

Long Phan, Grade 3
Eli Terry School, CT

Gucci

Gucci, Gucci, Nana's purse dog,
Is with us for three weeks.

He's wild like a bull,
But as sweet as a kitten.

He has squeaky toys that look like meat.
We throw them, but we have to chase him to get them back.

When I get home he jumps all over me.
He'd like to bite my ear off!

He has wavy white hair,
Pure white like snow.

He is always there for me.
When I'm in trouble he is like my guard dog.
He watches out for me.

Elizabeth Murtagh, Grade 3
Meeting House Hill School, CT

Yellow

Yellow looks like the sun beating down on me on a hot day in July
Yellow tastes like juicy buttery popcorn
That just came out of the microwave when I am watching a scary movie
Yellow feels like juicy squishy butter that I spread on my toast
Yellow sounds like a school bus roaring down the road
Yellow smells like a yellow daisy that just blossomed in the spring

Miranda Acor, Grade 3
Watsontown Elementary School, PA

I Was Mad

I was mad
When I asked my dad,
Are you sad?
But my brother was bad,
My little brother cried,
I thought my grandma died —
What was in my mind?
But of course all of the above.

Hifza Ahmed, Grade 3
Public School 160 William T Sampson School, NY

Useless Things

A locker with no lock.
A car with no engine.

A shoe with no lace.
A person with no face.

A poster that does not post.
A toaster that does not toast.

A picture with no drawing.
Birthdays with no cake.

A person with no name.
A car with no airbags.

Ciarra Jae Olivera, Grade 3
Northeast Elementary School, NY

The Snake

A snake can harm you
If it is afraid.
A snake can find good hiding places.
Some snakes can be long
And some snakes can be short.
I like snakes.

Jefferson Castillo, Grade 1
Northeast Elementary School, NY

Figure Skating

Figure skaters are so lucky.
They spend their days on the ice,
Twisting, turning, jumping,
Must be really nice

Wonder if they feel happy,
Or nervous, too
Maybe they'll make a mistake,
I wonder what they will do.

The music finally starts,
Will they make it or not?
Here comes the first jump,
I don't want it to stop…

Megan Schreiner, Grade 3
Hamilton Elementary School, PA

My Daydreams

In my daydreams I'm a dragon
flying way up high,
breathing red hot fire
as I race across the sky.
Or else I am an astronaut
soaring into space,
collecting ruby red rocks
in my rocket called the Ace.

Thaddeus Harbaugh, Grade 1
St Joan of Arc Elementary School, PA

My Cat

My cat likes to cuddle
He sleeps a lot in the day
He's active at night
Very fast and wants to play
He's a little orange fluff ball
That is why I like mine
Do you like your furry feline?

Thomas Crivelli, Grade 3
Eisenhower Elementary School, PA

Winter

Winter
Snow falling
Dogs barking loud
Snowflakes falling from the sky
Winter

Ruby Benz, Kindergarten
St Stephen's School, NY

Useless Things

A person with no name
A book with no pages
A computer which does not work
Glasses with no lenses
Shoes with no laces
A world with no people
A sky with no clouds
A car with no engine

Jailene Rivera, Grade 3
Northeast Elementary School, NY

Winter Is...

Winter is a cold season.
Winter is the sound of air blowing over the snow.
Winter is freezing hands.
Winter is a snowy season.
Winter smells like hot chocolate.

Janine Mae Bariuan, Grade 1
St Teresa of Avila School, NY

Spring

S unny out
P retty flowers
R ain falls
I ce cream is delicious
N ature is beautiful
G arden

Jacki Wheeler, Grade 3
Susquehanna Community Elementary School, PA

Vermont

Maple syrup d
      r
       i
          p
           p
            i
             n
              g out of maple trees.
Trees with buckets under them for fresh maple syrup. Wild turkeys, bears,
turtles, deer, almost all of the animals you could
think of are in the Vermont woods. Strawberries, raspberries and maybe even
blueberries in my Grammy B.'s garden.
Beautiful flowers in the spring.
Marvelous h
      i
        l
         l
           s to go sledding
d
o
w
n.
Vermont

Risa Berman, Grade 2
Dr Samuel C Eveleth School, MA

Spring Sounds
Spring sounds are everywhere.
I can hear the children laughing.

The trees are blowing
In the air.

The bees are buzzing,
And look out!
They may sting you.

The birds are chirping.
The dogs are barking.

The mothers are calling,
And those are the
Sounds of spring.
Annie O'Connor, Grade 2
St Rose Elementary School, CT

Buddy
Scurries out through the yard
Never bothers
Always listens
Crazy when I come home
Prances around
Doesn't chase squirrels
Always in my heart
I love him 100%
Kenny Sahinovic, Grade 3
Meeting House Hill School, CT

Snakes
Snakes are
yellow,
strong,
long,
scaly,
curvy,
but not
furry.
Andrea Mauricio, Grade 1
Northeast Elementary School, NY

Winter Days
It is cool in snow.
In the winter it is fun.
The winter is fun.
Jahcorie Norworthy, Grade 2
Ulysses Byas Elementary School, NY

Rain
Rain, Rain
Go to Spain
I don't care I'm in Rome
It's too hot
I wish I could go home

With my mom
But she's with Christopher Columbus
In a boat
I will send her a note

The rain comes from the clouds
It drops on the earth
And the river gets more water
For the fish to swim

It's time to go to bed
I dream in my head.
Kevin Perdomo-Pavon, Grade 3
Bensley Elementary School, VA

A Girl Named Sherree
There once was a girl named Sherree,
Who had a very loving family.
She had two brothers and a sister,
And they called her dad mister.
Her mother was a woman of love,
Because she knew the Lord God above.
Anah Taylor, Grade 2
Warwick River Christian School, VA

Steven
Steven, kid, weird, nice
Baseball, basketball, dodge ball
Football, soccer, cool
Steven Killeen, Grade 2
St Mary's Institute, NY

Animals
This is a butterfly
This is a goat
This is a fish
This is a bud
This is a panda
This is a horse
This is a dog
This is a cat

Timothy Perez, Kindergarten
Public School 23 Carter G Woodson School, NY

Steelers
The Steelers are a football team.
They are going to the Super Bowl.
They huddle and run with the football.
They run fast like deer.
Steelers are fun to watch.
They need helmets, gloves, pads, sweatshirt and socks.

Zach Dudas, Grade 3
Eisenhower Elementary School, PA

Me and My Brother
We play

Toys
Legos
Race cars
Tracks

We play

Andrew Kholodny, Kindergarten
Plainview-Old Bethpage Kindergarten Center, NY

Spring
S is for the shining sun.
P is for playing with the leaves.
R is for running with friends.
I is for ice cream people eat.
N is for nice things we wear.
G is for great things we do.

Alyson Kiara St. Omer, Grade 2
Little Flower Day Care Center and Prep School, NY

Spring Is...

Spring is the aqua blue sky opening its arms
Robins singing spring charms

Spring is dragonflies darting through the sky
Butterflies lifting their wings and starting to fly
Spring is animals waking up
A beautiful blossoming tulip
Spring is warm air
Shining blue water everywhere
Spring is the sun so bright
The stars that float above us in the night
Spring is Easter with rainbow eggs
Bunnies hopping on strong legs
The low tide calming the sea
And children running happily

Spring is the aqua blue sky opening its arms
Robins singing spring charms!
Spring!
Kelsey Richard, Grade 3
Jeffrey Elementary School, CT

Lollipop Flip-Flop

I have a little bunny and she loves to hop.
One day my bunny went out to hop
All of a sudden she ran into a Cyclops.
That big old Cyclops was wearing a Flip-flop
Made out of lollipop.
My little tiny bunny took that Cyclops' flip-flop
Made out of lollipop
And took it to IHOP.
My bunny hid that Cyclops' lollipop flip-flop
And no one saw it again.
Daniel Walton-Barahona, Grade 2
Cornwall Terrace Elementary School, PA

Ice Cream

Soft, cold
Creamy, sweet
Smooth, round
Crunchy, crackly
Chocolate delicious
Kathryn Paller, Grade 2
Christ the Teacher Catholic School, DE

Tiger

Faster than the wind
Pattern of stripes on its back
Tiger has sharp teeth
Kyle Crossman, Grade 2
Killingly Memorial School, CT

The Sand Dollar

It's a flower
growing on a shell
and it's sewn on
picked fresh
from the ocean floor
Lauren Kelley, Grade 2
Harry Lee Cole School, MA

Spring

I like spring.
It makes me want to sing.
Flowers blooming.
Birds zooming.
Sunshine bright and warm.
I can't wait until it's here.
It won't be very long.
Joseph Haufe, Grade 3
Our Lady of Hope School, NY

Science

Chemistry
Dangerous, scientific
Mix, pour, create
Chemistry is very hard
Test, discover, help
Amazing, fun
Science
Andrew Hughes, Grade 3
St Joseph School, NY

My Mat

My mom
made a
magnificent mat.
Lewis Byrd, Grade 1
Seneca Academy, MD

Orange
Orange sounds like…
Lassie barking up a deafening storm.
It also sounds like flames crackling at a camp in a starry night.
I hear a tiger snoring as it is turning into night.

Orange feels like…
The inside of a mushy, squishy pumpkin getting ready for Halloween.
It also feels like a soft tiger lily on a bright spring day.
Also, a warm fire in the chimney to keep us warm.

Orange looks like…
A swift fox looking for some food,
A beautiful sunset on a summer day,
Something too swift and wild for me to see.

Orange tastes like…
A super, juicy orange on a warm summer day.
It also tastes like crunchy carrots in my salad.
A tasteless apricot with a pit inside of it.

Orange smells like…
A nice, big melon waiting to be cut.
A fiery bonfire about to explode!
A fresh peach about to be picked.
Madelyn Baker, Grade 3
Watsontown Elementary School, PA

Spring
S un shining
P urple flowers
R unning with the wind
I ce cream with chocolate
N othing more beautiful
G orgeous sky
Shirlynne Wademan, Grade 3
Susquehanna Community Elementary School, PA

Springtime Is
Springtime is when flowers bloom.
Springtime is when animals come out.
Springtime is taking your dog for a nice long walk.
I'm happy in spring.
Maria Baca, Grade 2
Northeast Elementary School, NY

In My Dreams
In my dreams I'm a Hollywood star
With a fancy car

In my dreams I am able to sing
And mostly when I wear a ring

In my dreams I dance every day
Especially by the bay

In my dreams I write a memo
And I feed my little Nemo

So bye for the day
I'll be here every day
Raniya Sheikh, Grade 3
Al-Rahmah School, MD

A Cat
A cat was walking on the side
Then the cat saw a rat
The cat said "Here comes the rat"
Then the cat ran to hide
Then the rat said "Hello" to the bat
Then the rat and bat were friends.
Celine Yu, Grade 1
Children's Village, PA

The Snow Moon Is...
Round
and
sphere
like
sometimes
cloudy
with
horror movie looks.
A bright face
for dogs to howl at
lighting
up
the
ground.
Julia Marsden, Grade 2
Dr Samuel C Eveleth School, MA

My Mom
I love my mommy.
I miss her a lot.
She gives me hugs at night.
She tucks me in.
My dad gives me kisses at night too.
My mom plays tea party with me.
Julieann Day, Kindergarten
South Side Elementary School, PA

My First Step on Ice
O how good it feels to glide on the ice.
So go to the rink and try.
I feel so great when I spin around,
Around, and around I go.

Skate, skate, and skate. I love to skate.
O how good it feels to glide on the ice.
So go to the rink and try.
Skate, spin, jump, swirl, twist, twirl...

I love to skate.
Sssssssswoosh!
Lindsey Ball, Grade 3
Warwick River Christian School, VA

A Boy Named Tracy
There was a boy named Tracy
And he played with his friend Stacy.
And they played ball all day
Through the month of May
And liked to shop at Macy's
Kymani Morris, Grade 2
Ulysses Byas Elementary School, NY

Hockey
Hockey
Goalie, slap shot
Shooting, skating, hitting
Playing hockey is fun to do.
Ice rink
Gavin McCallum, Grade 2
Marvin Elementary School, CT

That Silly Ole Dog

It was a sunny day,
I went out to play.
I found a dog,
He was on a log.
He made his own home,
It was under a dome.
He had pictures of frogs,
They were dancing on logs!
For show-and-tell, I took him to school.
Immediately he started to drool!
The teacher threw him out and the doors she did lock.
Then everyone mocked.
That dog met a flea
He found her on a tree.
Then they had babies,
I hope they don't have rabies!

Taylor Shoun, Grade 3
St Catherine Laboure School, PA

Springtime

Springtime is here again
because rain is in the air.
The flower will soon be budding and blooming.
The birds will then come zooming in the trees.
Singing and chirping flying from tree to tree.
As they make their nest living high above.
Tell us to look up.
Behold the beauty as spring is in the air.

Kyle Codougan, Grade 3
Public School 397 Foster Laurie Elementary School, NY

Class

They care about me
They play with me
They eat with me
I love my class
They love me too
And my teacher loves me too
I love everyone in my class
My teachers and my classmates

Sharleen Camacho, Kindergarten
Public School 23 Carter G Woodson School, NY

Spring
M ay
I n the sun
K ayaking in the spring
A beautiful flower
Y ou can make a garden
L eaves
A pril

Mikayla Hargett, Grade 3
Susquehanna Community Elementary School, PA

June Birthday
J umping in the air.
U p I go, round and round.
N icely diving into the pool.
E xcitement in the air!

Hooray, Hooray! It's my birthday!
I'm turning 8!

Veronique Bazelais, Grade 2
The International School at Rogers Magnet, CT

Lucky and Princess!
L ucky and Princess are my
c **U** ddly friends. They are my
C at and
K itten! Lucky is black with some white on his chest. He is
Y oung no more, he is older than 4!

A calm,
N ice, and
D ecent cat as you may see.

P rincess is a female. She
R eally is only half a year old! She
I s a good friend, though she's not too bold! She
N ibbles away at her food. She's
C ute and
E nergy filled.
S he's also white on her body.
S he has a gray-brown face and black nose. Her eyes are green.
    She has black details on her forehead.
    I love *them* so much!!

Catherine Medaglia, Grade 3
Meeting House Hill School, CT

The Runt

I heard the rooster crow.
I leaped right out of bed!
I ran to the shed.
I saw a little runt,
His head was a little blunt.
I heard squeal, snort, shuffle.
The runt got knocked off
The mother's belly.
I decided to name her Nellie!

Kylene DeSmith, Grade 3
Southeastern New Hampshire Christian Academy, NH

Spring

I watch flowers,
it seems like they grow every hour.

I see big birds,
and they travel in herds.

I throw my hat,
and it lands on my cat.

I see a dog,
and it looks like a hog.

You see a bug,
and you give it a hug.

I saw a bear,
and it had hair.

Emily Stark, Grade 3
Susquehanna Community Elementary School, PA

Spring

S is for the sunny days
P is for the pretty flowers in the garden
R is for the roses I smell
I is for the ice that melts away
N is for the nest that birds build
G is for the good times I have in the spring

Athina Thomas, Grade 1
Little Flower Day Care Center and Prep School, NY

Ice Skating
Skating on ice
With new skates
Jumping
Spinning
And twirling around.
Lessons twice a week
Always beginning with
Stretching
Working hard and
Having fun
Skating on ice!
Emily Roesch, Grade 2
Spring Hill Elementary School, VA

My Mom
she is my hero
she is so special to me
nice, caring, happy
Erika Santos, Grade 3
Public School 148 Ruby Allen, NY

Star Wars
S tar fighters fly
T roopers run
A nikan beats Count Dooku
R epeating blasters shoot

W ars with clone troopers and droids
A dvice from Red Leader
R epublic is in danger
S olar power is in the "Ark Destroyer"
Thomas Terino, Grade 3
Growing Life Christian Academy, NY

A Walk in the Wind
I went for a walk in the wind one day.
I wanted to play,
but my teacher said, "No way, Jose!"
So I picked up a leaf,
and I threw it away!
Karen Rodriguez, Grade 2
Northeast Elementary School, NY

Turkey Day
Hi turkey! Now you're here.
Today's my favorite day of the year.
I can't wait until the feast begins
With all my family and my friends.
Alyssa Lemons, Grade 3
St Anastasia School, PA

Ready to Play
My sky is all blue.
Oh how 'bout you.
The sun is all shining.
Just come out and play.
I'm ready to go.
Are you ready to play.
It's a beautiful day.
No time to feel lazy.
This is the end of my poem.
Just come out and play.
Lisa Giannini, Grade 3
Frenchtown Elementary School, CT

Octopus
Octopus
smart, camouflaged
hiding, swimming, sneaking
have eight tentacles
sea creature
Octopus
Matthew Wallace, Grade 2
Dr Samuel C Eveleth School, MA

Summer
Heat waves in summer
People will play in lakes, rivers
The pool will not shine.
Christopher Bilcheck, Grade 2
Long Meadow Elementary School, CT

Dog
Her ears are floppy
She lives in a pretty house
Her name is Nasa
Maria Forero, Grade 2
Public School 148 Ruby Allen, NY

Brown
Brown tastes like a hot Hershey brownie
just coming out of the oven

Brown feels like a dirty toad
jumping into a cake I made for my sister's birthday

Brown smells like cinnamon
when you open a new pack of Big Red gum

Brown sounds like a loud, huge dog barking at a cricket
in the woods at midnight when the moon is bright

Brown looks like an old, rustic, log house on a country road

Casey Aunkst, Grade 3
Watsontown Elementary School, PA

The Feeling in My Soul
I believe I can fly
I believe a lot of things
in my soul
Like if the water in the ocean
would let me float on it
'til I reach my destiny

I believe in my

SOUL

I feel powerful inside
I believe that I can go to Pluto
I believe
I believe in my SOUL

Natasha Mora, Grade 3
Public School 152 School of Science & Technology, NY

The USA
USA a big county! People from here. From there people everywhere.
There are states everywhere too. From California to Maine.
In each state are rivers, beaches, mountains, forests and animals too.
It's great being in the USA there are towns and cities all around.
Come to the USA! You'll have a happy life here in the USA!
Come! Come! Come to the United States of America.

Jason Amaral, Grade 2
Hyman Fine Elementary School, MA

Spring and Winter
Spring is hot and winter is cold
In the springtime you swim in the pool
And in the wintertime you build snowmen, too!
Jill Latanowich, Grade 2
Cabot Elementary School, MA

Beautiful Spring
Spring
Flying through the swift air.
Spring is fresh juice.
Spring is courage for jumping off the swing
Spring
Fresh flowers growing
Fairies scampering
Butterflies emerging
Glistening and glimmering sand,
Blooming bears,
Amusement,
Leaves growing,
Chicks and ducklings hatching,
And fruit mounting to it peak of ripeness.
That is the feeling of spring.
Kendall Ackner, Grade 2
Susan Odell Taylor School, NY

Beautiful Snakes
Some are scary.
There are different kinds.
They grow a new skin under the old one.
Some are not poisonous
And can be good pets.
I like snakes.
Andy Amaya, Grade 1
Northeast Elementary School, NY

A Bear
He's finding a friend in the woods.
He's swimming in the water.
He found a friend.
He played with him.
They went to get something to eat.
Then they went home to see their moms.
Kaitlyn Knox, Kindergarten
South Side Elementary School, PA

Summer/Winter
Warm
Fun, outside
Wet, splash, sunny
Beach, waves, winter, boots
Snow, ice, blizzard
Ski, snowboard
Cold
Casey Russell, Grade 3
Cornerstone Academy, MA

Soccer
Soccer
Cool, tough
Run, shoot, kick
What an exciting game
Dribble, catch, pass
Listen, practice
Football
MaryKate Kenny, Grade 3
St Joseph School, NY

Volvo
Cars
Cool, fast
Make, learn, move
We learn about them
Fix, drive, wash
Big, small
Volvo
James Noyes, Grade 3
St Joseph School, NY

Seashell
The tallest tower of a castle
mountains and starfish
ripples in the silent water
smooth white curves
as silent as the night
the secret of the shell
is that…
the ocean lay inside it
Katelyn Murphy, Grade 1
Harry Lee Cole School, MA

What a Day!
Brady is my name
And soccer is my game.
My dog is Clancy.
He is very antsy.
I like to draw and swim.
Dom is my friend, ask him.
Watching the Steelers with my dad
Makes me really glad.
My poem is done now.
I think I'll take a bow!

Brady Baker, Grade 1
St Joan of Arc Elementary School, PA

Spring
Spring is near
Almost here
Spring is when the flowers bloom
Spring is when the trees go bright
Spring is when everything is nice
Spring is when butterflies come...
To have some more summer fun
Spring is when birds come back
Spring into spring

Alex Poluha, Grade 3
St Mary's Elementary School, MA

Snow
When it will snow,
Santa will say "Ho, ho, ho!"
I will sled,
With my friend Fred.
The snow
Will blow.

When the snow will flow,
I won't feel low.
If you ski,
It's free.
I will play hockey
With Jeremy Shockey.
The snow
Will glow.

Calvin Zimmerman, Grade 3
St Catherine Laboure School, PA

Monarch Butterfly
Butterfly
Pretty, colorful
Fly, eat, land
They are beautiful insects
Lay, flap, open
Orange, black
Monarch

Isabella Bastiani, Grade 3
St Joseph School, NY

My Sister Melanie
My sister is so pretty.
She likes the city.
She wants a kitty.
My sister is so tall.
She likes to call.
She is like a doll.
That why I call her
My sister.

Lindsay Scott, Grade 2
Pomperaug School, CT

Rain/Water
Rain
Wet precipitation
Helps plants grow
Makes homes for fish
Water

Connor Crowley, Grade 1
Mount Jewett Elementary School, PA

Baseball
Baseball
Fun, exciting
Throw, hit, run
What a terrific game
Dive, slide, bunt
Tough, rough
Leather

John Malandro, Grade 3
St Joseph School, NY

Animals

Thomp, stomp, thomp, stomp
What could that be?
Animals glide across valleys,
Deer stand proudly.
Rabbits hop around
Birds chirp, chirp, chirp, chirp
Why are they gliding?
Because spring is here
And the animals are happy again

Norman Cameron, Grade 2
Public School 397 Foster Laurie Elementary School, NY

Cats

They are
furry

They get chased by
dogs

They do not like
rain

I cannot have a
cat

I will
sneeze

Cats

Joseph Leone, Kindergarten
Plainview-Old Bethpage Kindergarten Center, NY

Life's a Short Time

Life's a short time,
you'll never know when you will die.
You'll probably make it up to ninety
who knows if you'll go past.

Some people make it up to a hundred.
They must be lucky.

Shamar Gittens, Grade 3
Public School 23 Carter G Woodson School, NY

Green

Green sounds like bullfrogs croaking on a summer evening.
Green tastes like a sour apple being dipped in nice caramel.
Green is a jumping bass in swirling water.
Green looks like a forest full of animals who are hiding.
Green is the smell of fresh picked peppermint.
Green reminds me of the smell of freshly cut grass.

Seth Beaver, Grade 3
Watsontown Elementary School, PA

Today Is the Day

Today
is the day
where there is snow up in the sky
falling slowly…

Today
is the day
when the snow is
as white as a puffy cloud.

Today
is the day
when I play
in the cold, white, freezing snow, brrrrrrrrrrrrrr.

Today
is the day
when I smell hot chocolate
steaming on the stove.
Mmmmmmm.

Today
is the first day of
WINTER!

Alexander Bilodeau, Grade 3
Ridge Park Elementary School, PA

Spring

Flowers are growing.
The boats are floating.
Billy loves to smell lillies.
I am so silly.

Lenique Huggins, Grade 1
Urban League of Pittsburgh Charter School, PA

Soccer Ball
Soccer ball is white.
Soccer ball is circle.
Soccer ball is black.
Rayhan Salam, Grade 2
Public School 148 Ruby Allen, NY

The Grizzly Bear
The Grizzly bear is big and hairy
and can be very, very scary.
Brown is the color
they are not like any other.
Big paws, big nose
Stubby tail and growl as he goes.
Calvin Tucker Jr., Grade 3
Hartford SDA Area School, CT

Cat
Cat
Cute, soft
Jumping, purring, eating
Likes to chase mice
My pet
Jenea Patterson, Grade 1
Daniel J Flood Elementary School, PA

Colors
Blue reminds me of a fun pool.
Yellow is like the color of the hot sun.
Orange is the color of a fruit.
Black is the color of my dog Shorty.
Isaiah Fuentes, Grade 1
Northeast Elementary School, NY

Frog
Frogs are green.
Toads are brown.
Lily pads are green.
Land is brown.
Frogs can go on land.
Toads can too.
Toni Arsenault, Grade 1
Glover Elementary School, MA

Halloween
I see people trick-or-treating.
I smell treats from my bag.
I hear the trees swaying in the wind.
I taste sweet candy.
I touch the grass with my feet.
Halloween
Stephen McCray, Grade 2
St Christopher's School, VA

The Storm
Storms can be a nasty pain
I always say "Go away rain!!"
Rains keep on, they never stop.
They make a mess. GO GET A MOP!
Kavita Rana, Grade 2
JF Kennedy School, CT

Spring
S weet
P eanut
R ose
I guana
N arnia
G arfield
Gabriella Lee, Grade 1
Christ the King Elementary School, NY

A Girl from Japan
There once was a girl from Japan.
She thought she was an Englishman!
She slipped and fell down.
She broke her confused crown.
Now the girl thinks she's Superman!
Monica Smith, Grade 2
Oakdale Elementary School, MD

Pencils
Pencils
Yellow, pointy
Erasing, writing, waiting
Doing all your homework
Pretty
Zachary Reimund, Grade 1
Daniel J Flood Elementary School, PA

The Car

My car is so fast by itself
it would mow your grass
The color of it is red
Oh my gosh
he is sleeping in my
bed

Kalid James, Grade 3
Public School 152 School of Science & Technology, NY

The Squirrel

Mandy is a squirrel and
a weird one at that.

She goes to work as a
flipper who flies.

She does eat nuts but
only when she watches T.V.

But she loves pizza,
yes pizza.

Mandy puts on a party in
the garage.

Mandy, oh Mandy
what a weird squirrel.

Angelique Lucien, Grade 3
Public School 152 School of Science & Technology, NY

Red Hot!

Red is lava and fire,
And the feeling of power,
Red is the taste of salsa,
Chili peppers and cherry pie smell red.
Getting teased makes me feel red.
Red is the sound of babies crying and ambulance sirens.
A fire alarm, a volcano erupting,
Pain and anger are red.
Red is HOT!

Quentin Clarke-Wing, Grade 3
Lycée Rochambeau (French International School), MD

Falling in Love with a Boy at the Beach

There was a girl named Sandy
She was really, really dandy
She went to the store to buy some candy
Then she went to the sandy
Beach
And fell in love with a boy named Randy
He had a sister named Mandy
And she had a brother named Andy
And they all came in handy.

Kelsey Gring, Grade 2
Cornwall Terrace Elementary School, PA

Chocolate

Sweet and satisfying
Smooth and creamy
Dark and light
Rich and soothing
My favorite treat

Dylan Gerstley, Grade 2
Christ the Teacher Catholic School, DE

Someone Tiny Went By

When I woke, I broke a tiny yawn
Went outside to morning dawn
Saw a giant footprint ahead
About the size of a giant bed

My sister said someone tiny went by
But no one saw it, so we all left at sunset
Then two hours later it came by
I said to sister, Oh my Oh my!

Storm Dolfi, Grade 3
William Penn Elementary School, PA

Heroes vs Villains

Heroes
Bravery, noble
Charming, saving, greeting
Mom, dad, devil, robbers
Capturing, harming, stealing
Sinful, wicked
Villains

Juliana Gentile, Grade 3
Our Mother of Perpetual Help School, PA

Thunder

I'm not scared
Of thunder in the sky.
I think it's up super high.
It makes a loud noise
Like all my toys.
I'm still not scared of thunder!
When lightning comes...
"Be aware..."
You might get a scare.
I'm still not scared of thunder!
I go to sleep without a peep
And don't care
About thunder...

Vincent Gerwer, Grade 3
Public School 5, NY

Snakes

Snakes are
green,
curvy,
pink,
harmful,
but not
beautiful.

Maritza Marcia, Grade 1
Northeast Elementary School, NY

Tigers

Deep in the jungle
Searching for some meat to eat
While prey is sleeping.

Manolis Psyllos, Grade 1
Public School 122 Mamie Fay, NY

Basketball

basketball
fun, entertaining
shooting, dribbling, passing
throw a basket to get a point
scoring game

Dylan Casey, Grade 3
Houghton Elementary School, MA

Winter Is...

Winter is the smell of pine needles and my mom's cookies.
Winter looks like a fluffy white blanket.
Winter is the coldness of Jack Frost.
Winter is the sound of jingling bells and crunching snow.
Winter is the time for snowball fights and making snowmen.
Winter is cuddly.

Jakobi Cutler, Grade 1
St Teresa of Avila School, NY

Good Charlie

Charlie opened a Wonka wrapper
Where he found a golden ticket
He will go to the chocolate factory
Good Charlie, good Charlie, everyone should be like him!

Augustus Glupe fell in the chocolate river
Les Carver blasted into the TV
Violet Boleguard turned into a big blueberry
Good Charlie, good Charlie, everyone should be like him!

Charlie is the only kid to make it through the factory
They rode a magic flying elevator
Wonka gives Charlie the whole factory
Good Charlie, good Charlie, everyone should be like him!

Yamir Nelson, Grade 2
Urban League of Pittsburgh Charter School, PA

White Reminds Me Of

If white were a smell,
It would smell like marshmallows at a campfire.

White sounds like
Popcorn popping at the movies.

White tastes like
Vanilla ice cream on a hot summer day.

White looks like
Snowflakes falling on my dog's brown back.

White feels like ice from my freeze
That I put in my cup of tea.

Clint Schooley, Grade 3
Watsontown Elementary School, PA

Football Madness

Football practice is my favorite thing
Because I like getting touchdowns.
I like my jersey.
It is black and gold.
Rigdon Doran, Kindergarten
South Side Elementary School, PA

The Silly Bear

I have a little bear
That likes to sit on its chair
It likes to eat his little pear
He likes to sleep and likes to stare
And he sure is a millionaire
That wants to be a famous mayor
That has his own chauffeur
What silly little bear
Jinan Oubaid, Grade 3
Al-Rahmah School, MD

Books

You read them.
You look at them.
They're paper and wood.
You can get them at the library.
They're fun!
Hanna Knox, Kindergarten
South Side Elementary School, PA

Spring

S un shines
P lants pop up
R ainy weather
I like watching birds fly
N ew grass grows
G ardens grow
Trac Shaw, Grade 1
Mount Jewett Elementary School, PA

Fireworks

Pop! That's the huge sound
Shooting in different colors
Soaring through the dark
Bailie Almeida, Grade 3
Acushnet Elementary School, MA

Blooming Beauty

Blooming strokes of yellow sun
corner, orange, corner, yellow
bursting pockets of sun color
smelling peach petals
rocket ship flying to orange, color ball
separation from a beauty line
as orange as the sun
as bright as a blossom
my flower of blooming beauty
Julia Nelson, Grade 3
Thoreau Elementary School, MA

Mrs. Warfield

Mrs. Warfield is nice.
Mrs. Warfield is pretty.
Mrs. Warfield helps people.
I love Mrs. Warfield.
I will miss her so much.
But no matter where I am,
I will always, always stay in touch.
Kasandra Acosta, Grade 2
Ulysses Byas Elementary School, NY

Wind

Wind
fluttering, moving
swooshing, flying
The wind moves the leaves.
Vidal Moscoso, Grade 1
Northeast Elementary School, NY

Beautiful World

Give money to the poor
So they can have more
So they can have a house
Or have a pet mouse
So they can cook
Or have a book
Give money to the poor
So they can have more
Jeffrey Barboza Jr., Grade 3
Acushnet Elementary School, MA

I'm a Little Mouse

I'm a little mouse, can't you see.
I live in my house made of cheese.
I'm a little mouse, can't you see.
I climbed to the top of Mount Cheddar Swiss Cheese.
I'm a little mouse, can't you see.
I trained a stray dog to fetch my cheese for me.
I'm a little mouse, can't you see.
I survived a crab bite in the deep blue sea.
I'm a little mouse, can't you see.
Well, there's lots more things
about me to know.

Emily Krupa, Grade 3
Thoreau Elementary School, MA

I Like Yellow

Yellow is the sun shining on a field of daffodils,
It's the curb on the edge of the street and forsythia.
Yellow makes me think of gold under the waves
With a *rock beauty* guarding it like a king.
Yellow makes me feel delightful.

Aaron Feigenbaum, Grade 3
Lycée Rochambeau (French International School), MD

Spring

S is for a sunny day.
P is for a perfect weather.
R is for the rain.
I is for icy cold rain.
N is for nice weather.
G is for a great day.

Jamal Andre Hazlewood, Grade 2
Little Flower Day Care Center and Prep School, NY

Seasons Tree

In the spring leaves start to grow on the trees.
In the summer flowers bloom and the leaves on the trees are green.
In the fall the leaves change color and they fall off the trees
And all of the vegetable are ready to be picked.
In the winter it snows all through the winter season
And all the tree's leaves are gone and the flowers are gone too.

Jahniesha Lindo, Grade 3
Hartford SDA Area School, CT

Snow Day
Snow day is…

Beautiful
fields
of
pearly
white
delight!

When
you
look
at
the
snowflakes
they
look
like
stars and
diamonds!

They fall from the
silver black gray white sky!
Joshua Benjamin Lovins, Grade 2
Dr Samuel C Eveleth School, MA

Steelers
Black, gold
Winning, playing, intercepting
Steelers dominated the Jets.
Team
Austin Housler, Grade 3
Mount Jewett Elementary School, PA

Summer
Summer is as hot as the sun,
Sky as bright as flowers.
Lots of rainbows for me to see.
I feel the cool pool,
That is so blue.
Matthew Gerics, Grade 2
St Rose Elementary School, CT

During Springtime
Cool, warm springtime,
Bringing lots of sun and rain,
Small blooming flowers.
Jon Kleinfeld, Grade 3
Hereford Elementary School, PA

Dad
Almost every morning
my dad is always snoring.
I can't watch TV.
Oh why me!
Please can't I be someone else!
Dad!
Josh Allard, Grade 2
Hyman Fine Elementary School, MA

My Friends
My friends are awesome!
They all like possums!
My best friend is Angeline.
It rhymes with tangerine.
My other friend is Taylor.
It rhymes with sailor.
My name is Patrice
It rhymes with police.
I love juice.
And I have a moose.
Another one of my friends is Ari.
It rhymes with safari.
She has a bunny.
It is very funny.
But our favorite animal is very funky!
It is a monkey!
Patrice Lonardi, Grade 3
St Catherine Laboure School, PA

The Girl
Once a girl was outside.
She met a girl.
They played and played.
But when the day was over they waved
and said goodbye to each other.
Ruth Davydov, Grade 2
Shaloh House Hebrew Day School, MA

Water
Water is a good thing to drink
People like water
Water comes from a sink

Water is for sharks
Who swim in the ocean
Deep down in the ocean it is dark

Boats float on rivers
Fish swim in them too
When you jump in it makes you shiver

People use water to cook
Water can steam and boil
Water is everywhere you look!

Rudy McBride, Grade 1
Urban League of Pittsburgh Charter School, PA

Apples
Apples are
red

Apples are
round

Apples grow on
trees

You can
pick them

Apples

Jordan Berson, Kindergarten
Plainview-Old Bethpage Kindergarten Center, NY

Spring
S is for the sunny days
P is for the pretty flowers I see
R is for relaxing days
I is for the ice cream I eat
N is for nature walks I take
G is for green grass I see

Maalik Walker, Grade 1
Little Flower Day Care Center and Prep School, NY

Me

I used to love boys
but now I think they are immature!
I used to love my brothers
but now we get in fights!
I used to watch Tellie Tubbies
but now I watch Jurassic Park
I used to be in second grade
but now I'm finishing third grade
I used to think my teacher was weird
but now I think she's really cool!

Casey Ulrich, Grade 3
Bradford Township Elementary School, PA

Bumblebee

Its yellow sunny stripe and black dim stripe,
Reflect off the cool blue sky and snowy clouds,
As it dances in the whirling wind,
Whispering a tune that fills your ears with joy.
It's weary stinger scares predators away,
While it peacefully sucks nectar from a flower.
BUMBLEBEE

Julia Dearden, Grade 3
Mast Landing School, ME

My Heart

My heart has a lot of feelings
Sad, mad, surprised, and even scared
My heart gets broken into half
my feelings are hurt
I feel happy my heart is calm
I get mad, my heart goes fast
When I am scared it too is scared
I am surprised my heart tells me that
I should always love my family
And listen to it

Gloridy Leon, Grade 3
Public School 65 Mother Hale Academy, NY

Weather

The sun is glistening.
The rain won't fall all day long.
It won't snow — it won't.

Lukas Bull, Grade 2
Fonda-Fultonville Elementary School, NY

Cichlids and Snails

The cichlids swim
all around the tank
kissing each other
and the snails
sleep all day

Danny DeVelis, Grade 1
Harry Lee Cole School, MA

Rain

Rain glitters in the sun
like a diamond.
The rain
makes flowers grow
like you.
But when it hits
the ground it goes
splash!

Elyse Davis, Grade 3
Afton Elementary School, NY

Bragging

Brittany brilliant Bostic
bragged about bragging
so Bracey bragged
about Brittany brilliant Bostic
and called Brittany Bostic
bruiser bragger.

Reagan Welch, Grade 1
Seneca Academy, MD

Fall

The leaves blow in the wind.
The sun in the leaves.
Leaves change color.
The temperature cools.
Pine needles fall from trees.
Kids wearing coats.
The sun in your shadow
on Halloween.
I love fall.

Mairin Sone, Grade 3
Wolcott School, CT

Puppies

Puppies are big.
Puppies are small.
Puppies are huge.
Puppies are tall.
Puppies are wide.
Puppies are thin.
My puppy makes me grin.
Bear Tompkins is my little one.
He isn't little but, he's still a lot of fun.
He's a Labrador Retriever, not a Labrador beaver.
I asked him what his favorite candy bar was, and he said Baby Roof.
He scratches on the door and leaves a mark.
I like to take him to the park.
He buries his bones in the backyard.
When he comes back to get them, he finds it hard.
His hair is blond and he plays in our pond.
His nose is brown and he doesn't like to frown.
His fur is cozy and he makes my cheeks rosy.
He is loving and has a big heart.
He is very strong and also very smart.

Samantha Tompkins, Grade 3
Weston Intermediate School, CT

Spring!

S now melts and flowers bloom
P lanting gardens start
R ain showers from April bring May flowers
I maginative ideas run wild
N ature wakes up from a long sleep
G ets warmer outside.

Tori Schmidgall, Grade 3
Oakdale Elementary School, MD

The New Season

S pring, green grass, shining in your face!
P urple, red, pink, white, all colored flowers you can think of.
R un! Run! We only have so much time!
I need more time!
N ow we must sleep and wait.
G oodbye spring. See you next year!

Spring!!!

Maya Elliott, Grade 2
Hyman Fine Elementary School, MA

The Storm
Crash splash the storm is here.
Boom! The wild thunder appears.
The trees were blowing all around.
The leaves are mushy on the ground.
Madelyn Sweedler, Grade 2
JF Kennedy School, CT

Clover
C lover
L eprechaun
O h so green
V ery lucky
E nchanted
R egion of the Irish
Hailey Roy, Grade 3
Acushnet Elementary School, MA

Plants
There are so many plants.
Poison ivy and oak leaves too.
So many kinds.
Hannah Mack, Grade 3
Marlborough Elementary School, PA

My Dogs
Big wide ears
Cute little eyes
Strong muscles
Loud bark

They like to play
Jump on beds
Get attention

Licking me and my sisters
Barking when someone comes in

Safe
Comfortable
Loved

I love my dogs!
Megan Carney, Grade 3
Meeting House Hill School, CT

Roller Coaster
I'm seeing a lot
All from the sky
I get to see my house
From a hundred feet high.

My mom is so scared
That I might die
At the end of the ride
I almost cry.
AJ Kelley, Grade 3
Meeting House Hill School, CT

Grouchy Boy!
People say I am a grouch…
Because I sit on the couch…
When I wake I am in a bad mood…
I just want to eat my food…
When I'm not supposed to watch TV.
My parents yell at me…
Then I am…
In a GROUCHY MOOD!!!
Adem Redzovic, Grade 3
Public School 5, NY

Green
Green grass blowing
Green trees shaking
Green frog ribbiting
Green balloon popping.
Green ice cream smelling good!
Green apple juicy when you bite it.
Green M&M smooth.
Green bowling ball swinging.
Green chalkboard erasing.
Green leaves growing.
Green flip-flops moving!
Green alligator snapping its mouth!
Green frog jumping high!!
Green ball bouncing.
Green crayon melting in the sun!
Madison Cohen, Grade 1
Fulton Avenue School #8, NY

Green, Green

Green smells like a freshly mowed lawn
and a lime being squeezed,

Green taste like a pickle with lots of juice
and an apple with a stem on it,

Green looks like the mean grinch at Christmastime
and a jumpy frog catching flies,

Green feels like soft moss under my toes
and a breeze of wind in the spring,

Green sounds like the Black Eyed Peas rocking on
and leaves rustling in wind.

Alexis Brougham, Grade 3
Watsontown Elementary School, PA

Spring

I nsects
V alleys turn green in the spring
Y ellow Jacket

B looming flowers
R ain
O utside
O rchid
K ites
E aster

Ivy Brooke Christensen, Grade 3
Susquehanna Community Elementary School, PA

Dragons

Dragons soar the deep blue sky,
They hide in caves on rocky peaks.
They eat like raptors, and hunt like eagles.
Majestic dragons oh-so-fine,
Their lovely scales really shine.
The sharp talons are very smooth.
These reptilian creatures dine on rats in their caves,
Hiding their jewels and protecting their young.

Rowen Price, Grade 3
Cornerstone Academy, MA

Butterfly

B eautiful butterfly in the sky
U nlikely to see a butterfly black
T urns into a butterfly
T ry to get out of it's cocoon.
E xcited to get to fly
R eturns to its home before dark
F rightened to be eaten
L ittle ones like to fly around
Y oung butterflies eat nectar

Tiffany Cupp, Grade 3
Bradford Township Elementary School, PA

Stars

Stars are really pretty to me.
There are a lot of shiny stars to see.

God made all the stars in the sky.
Stars come out in the night time.

God made all the stars in a zoom.
Sometimes they even light up my room.

God made the sky and put in stars.
You can see them even from Mars.

Stars make me really glad.
They sometimes make people mad.

Falling stars might go caboom!
Sometimes they can land in your living room.

Vanessa Vetere, Grade 3
Growing Life Christian Academy, NY

Pizza

There's toppings on pizza
Like pepperoni, mushrooms, and olives.
There's lots of toppings.
There's cheese and crust…
Even some crust and cheese mixed together.
It's really hot in your mouth.
You might want to get some water or milk
To cool your mouth down.

Jacob Hilliard, Kindergarten
South Side Elementary School, PA

Titanic

Ship
Scary, sad
Sails, floats, sinks
A real, true story
Run, jump, splash
Exciting, dangerous
Titanic

Kristen Reynolds, Grade 3
St Joseph School, NY

Spring

spring
flowers come up
growing, raining, budding
sunny days to go out and play
season

Courteney Hill, Grade 2
Wells Central School, NY

Spring

S pring
P laying
R unning
I ce cream
N ice
G iggling

Cheyenne Grier, Grade 3
Afton Elementary School, NY

Snow

Snow feels like Santa's beard
It's fluffy
It's as soft as polar bears.

Donald Packard, Grade 1
John F Kennedy School, MA

Thanksgiving

Thanksgiving
Food, family
Eating, stuffing, loving
My aunt is eating the turkey
Holiday

Mia Folino, Grade 3
St Rosalia Academy, PA

Blue

When I think of the color blue
I think of the sky, blue paint,
a blue mailbox and Neptune.
Those things make me think of blue everywhere I go.
It will be my favorite color until I go to the Heavens.

John Sandoval, Grade 2
Ulysses Byas Elementary School, NY

Bubbles

Bubbles, bubbles, bubbles!
I love to play with bubbles.
They have a lot of colors when you look through them.
Some are big, some are small, some are medium, some are tall.
Bubbles, bubbles, bubbles!
They pop in your face sometimes.
We jump for joy when it's playtime.

Allison Eng, Grade 2
Public School 205 Alexander Bell, NY

Summer

On those hot days
When the sun shines bright.
We look to the sky
To see the bright light.

The birds fly high
No clouds in sight.
We fly our kites high
Until it turns into night.

Akanni Joseph, Grade 3
Little Flower Day Care Center and Prep School, NY

Larry the Lucky Leprechaun

Larry the lucky leprechaun
He leaps and leaves a lot of gold
Larry the lucky leprechaun lays on a lily
Laying on a lake

Larry the lucky leprechaun
He sings, "La, la, la"
He will leave the lucky rainbow leaving lucky jewels
Larry the lucky leprechaun, "La, la, la"

Quinn Carey, Grade 3
St Stephen's School, NY

Skunks

S kunks are cute.
K is for king of cuteness.
U is for unbelievably adorable.
N obody will not like skunks.
K is for cutest.
S kunks are so cute!

Vicky Xu, Grade 3
Cornerstone Academy, MA

Silly Snowmen

Seven silly snowmen singing silly songs
Some silly snowmen are skating
Same the snowman slipped
Some snowmen saw a snow house
Seven snowmen have a snowball fight
Sammy the snowman shovels a path
Cindy the snowwoman sings silly songs

Robert Nappo, Grade 3
St Stephen's School, NY

When War Came

Boom, boom the cannons cry
Bang, bang the guns sigh.
Over the hill swarm blue and gray
The bright red flashes in the fray
And the cries of the fallen men
Never to be seen again.
The Union and Confederacy
Fighting over slavery.

Jack Jiranek, Grade 3
St Christopher's School, VA

Spring

S un shines
P lants grow
R ain helps flowers grow
I t is much warmer
N o more snow
G rass is green

Mark Smith, Grade 1
Mount Jewett Elementary School, PA

My Hands

My hands can give to poor.
My hands can teach a student.
My hands can pat a baby.
My hands can learn with sign language.
My hands can write a special note.
My hands can hug my teacher.
That is what my hands can do.

Aimee Gutin-Nedo, Grade 2
Susan Odell Taylor School, NY

The Storm

Clouds covered the sky so soon
I couldn't even see the moon.
Everything in town is wet.
This much rain gets me upset.

Christina DeCola, Grade 2
JF Kennedy School, CT

My Flowers

I have a flower bed in my garden.
I love one of them.
It's called the rainbow flower.
Once I picked it.
I love the flower.
I smell the flower.

Shaina Rodkin, Grade 2
Shaloh House Hebrew Day School, MA

Purple

meadow of lilacs
purple as a witches hat
sweet like a piece of candy

Purple

Gabrielle Arena, Grade 2
Marvin Elementary School, CT

Wind

Wind
swirling, twirling
moving, floating
look at that March wind go!

Brianna Zimmermann, Grade 1
Northeast Elementary School, NY

Beware!

The teachers are back
They are going to attack
With education and homework
As the students work, the teachers smirk
They're coming with reading and writing,
Science and social studies don't look so inviting
Get out your pitchforks and search the town
We look hard but with nothing we frown
'cause the teachers are back
and they are ready to attack!
So beware, beware
they'll give you a scare!

Angela Lauren Hatter, Grade 3
Brecknock Elementary School, PA

Crazy Crawly Cat

"Crash" went the clock
as the cat knocked it down.

The crazy crawly cat was about to lurch
upon a tiny little caterpillar traveling on and on.

She tried to con the caterpillar
but the caterpillar got away.

It saw a crack in the wall
and scurried fast away.

Gabrielle Granatiero, Grade 3
Frenchtown School, RI

Friends

Nice
Fun
Caring
Honest
Respectful
Admiring
Encouraging
Loving

ALWAYS

Samantha Jablonsky, Grade 3
Public School 152 School of Science & Technology, NY

Snakes
Some snakes are dangerous.
Snakes have no legs.
snakes have weird eyes
And soft skin.
Emmanuel Dourthe, Grade 1
Northeast Elementary School, NY

Cheetah
soft, mean, furry, claws
scary, big and mean not nice
sharp teeth and big claws
Giselle Torres, Grade 2
Public School 148 Ruby Allen, NY

Snowdog
Snowflakes
white, little, cold
forming, sparkling, floating
snowflakes fall from the blue sky.
designs
Kaitlyn Powers, Grade 3
Houghton Elementary School, MA

Birds
Birds
Bluebirds, lovebirds,
Tweeting very softly
Flying in the sky
Spring
Theresa West, Kindergarten
St Stephen's School, NY

Rain
Tip tap Tip tap
Rain is falling on your window,
Rain is falling on your roof.
You can hear the rain tapping tip tap.
The rain goes
tip tap
tip tap.
Michael Lee, Grade 3
Public School 131, NY

Anne
A great swimmer.
N ot good at somersaults.
N ever been to another country.
E xcellent at hand stands.
Anne Slevin, Grade 1
Oakdale Elementary School, MD

The Lazy Rabbit
There once was a rabbit named Hare.
All he did was sit in his lair.
He liked to sing.
As if he were king.
So this Hare got plenty of fresh air.
Allan Hitchcock, Grade 2
Oakdale Elementary School, MD

Snowman
Snowman
Fluffy, plump
Still, waiting, stuck
Snowmen sure are fun!
BRRR!
Brayden Tetreault, Grade 3
Acushnet Elementary School, MA

Nature in Spring
Green grass is sprouting
Shades of flowers everywhere
Clear skies all day long
Alexander Abraham, Grade 2
Long Meadow Elementary School, CT

Burger King
I see games
I see French fries
I see hamburgers
I see tables
I see families
I see happy people
I DON'T see dogs!
Nelson Lopez, Grade 1
Northeast Elementary School, NY

Red

Red reminds me of
a big, ripe strawberry and a volcano blowing out lava,

Red reminds me of
watermelons growing in a field,

Red tastes like
spaghetti getting slurped into my mouth,

Red smells like
a crunchy apple being eaten,

Red sounds like
a speeding fire truck's siren,

Red looks like
Dale Earnhardt, Jr.'s car racing in a NASCAR race,

Red feels like
bright, juicy tomatoes getting squeezed.

William Michael, Grade 3
Watsontown Elementary School, PA

What Are You Doing?

What are you doing
digging your nose?
What are you doing
scratching your toes?
What are you doing?
No one knows.

Casthley Olivier, Grade 3
Public School 152 School of Science & Technology, NY

Colors

Pink are the roses on a warm summer day
Black is the sky on a very cold night
Orange is Saturn in space at night
Blue are the blueberries I pick on warm days
Yellow is the fire on a camping trip
Purple is the homework folder I take home every day

Olivia Libby, Grade 3
Enfield Station School, ME

Mrs. Dye Fills My Heart with Joy
I love Mrs. Dye.
I love Mrs. Dye.
She is cute.
She makes me laugh.
Funny, funny, very funny Mrs. Dye.
I wish I could marry her.
She is the best P.E. teacher pie.

Hunter Hull, Grade 1
Williamstown Elementary School, NY

Index

Index

Celebrating Poetry – East Spring 2006

Index

Index